Adventures

with a

Texas Humanist

ADVENTURES
with a
TEXAS
HUMANIST

James Ward Lee

TCU Press
Fort Worth, Texas

Library of Congress Cataloging-in-Publication Data

Lee, James Ward.
  Adventures with a Texas humanist / James Ward Lee.
      p. cm.
  Includes bibliographical references and index.
  ISBN 0-87565-288-3 (alk. paper)
  1. Lee, James Ward. 2. American literature--Texas--History and criticism. 3.
English teachers--United States--Biography. 4. Lee, James Ward--Homes and
haunts--Texas. 5. Texas--Intellectual life. 6. Texas--In literature. 7. Texas--
Biography. 8. Folklore--Texas. I. Title.
  PE64.L44A3 2004
  810.9'9764--dc22

                                                2004002608

Printed in Canada

book design and illustration by
Barbara Mathews Whitehead

To
Don Graham and Tom Pilkington,
my betters

Contents

Foreword

Some would say James Ward Lee cannot call himself a Texan, let alone a Texas humanist. He was, after all, born in Alabama. Raised in Leeds and Birmingham, he took himself at the age of fourteen to St. Andrew's School, a boys' prep school located a mile from the campus of the University of the South at Sewanee, Tennessee. School was followed by a stint in the U.S. Navy during Korean War days, then graduate school, marriage and children—he has two sons: Steve is a lawyer in Austin and John is a policeman in Highland Park. In 1958 he arrived in Denton, Texas, where he would spend forty-plus years teaching British and American lit at what was then North Texas State College and is now the University of North Texas. Now he's finishing his career as acquisitions editor for TCU Press, a volunteer position that gives him lots of freedom—does he really work here?—yet keeps him active in the world he knows and that knows him.

Along the way Jim Lee made himself a Texan of the first order. He knows Texas better than most native Texans, to whom he often explains the state and its customs. And he knows the people—from sophisticates to the folk, as he sometimes calls them. Perhaps the outsider's eye allows him to see more clearly, but Jim can point out something really ridiculous about Texas in one sentence and embrace the state in the next. He's not quite a good ol' boy, for there's too much "learning" in him to play that role. But he likes good ol' boys and good ol' girls, and his affection for all things Texan comes across clearly. The Alabama boy made himself into a Texan primarily through professional activities, most of them mentioned in his introduction, where he generously credits the people who have taught him Texanness (a word I think he invented) over the years. Jim's list of essays and book reviews published and papers presented is outrageously long, but his output of books has not been large—he wrote *Classics of Texas Fiction*, in the year of the Texas Sesquicentennial, making himself read a book a week so that he could include fifty-two authors and their major works. And then there's *Texas, My Texas*, which showcases his talents as a folklorist and humorist, with lines like, "I God, I love a pie" and declares the best way to eat a piece of pie is standing over the sink, holding it in your hand. He's tried his hand at fiction, writing and publishing a number of short stories about a 1930s rural mail carrier in the fictional town of Bodark Springs, Texas. He says he is still three or four stories short of a collection, though I despair of his ever finishing the volume. And there was a gangbuster opening chapter for a mystery. He didn't know where to go from there and abandoned the idea.

He says of himself, instead, that he is more a "project person." He thinks up projects—ways he can use other people's writing, things he can get other people to do. For years, he used to call me from Denton to announce, "I've had a million-dollar idea." That meant he had an idea involving a lot of work on my part. Nowadays, he announces that from an office next to mine, so that I am less able to dodge the bullet. But it turns out well—we've done *Literary Fort Worth* together and are beginning to think about *Literary West Texas*. They are among his "million-dollar ideas."

All of this makes *Adventures with a Texas Humanist* a truly important book. It is his first major book, the first to bring together, in one cover, his strengths as a literary and cultural critic, a folklorist, and a humorist. Jim's major contribution to Texas letters has been his essays, reviews, and papers. He knows Texas writers, major and minor; he has perceptive judgments about their strengths and weaknesses; and he has the ability to put writing in the context of the state's literature.

But Jim flings a wider net than the literary one—as a folk-lorist, he has a deep knowledge of early Texas life, Texas music, western movies, Texas patterns of speech, even Texas foods. In fact, he can—and does—discourse on almost anything Texan that comes up. Sometimes I think his mind is a sponge, for he can keep up with more obscure facts and quotes than anyone I know.

With the personal essays that conclude this volume, Jim again displays the tongue-in-cheek humor that makes him the kind of after-dinner speaker who reduces the audience to helpless tears. As with all good humor, Jim uses the unexpected to startle the reader—introducing John Ashcroft in an essay on H-bomb experiments in the Pacific in the 1950s or describing naval drills that taught him to march and march and march until he was put on a ship and never marched another step. Perhaps it's related to his tendency to take the opposite stance on an issue as a matter of principle, to be, at times, a bit of a curmudgeon.

A note on editing this volume: Nowhere is Jim's knowledge of literature, both British and American, more evident than in his widespread use of allusion and quote. I started out in true schol-arly fashion to insist on documentation of each and every quote. I soon realized Jim was right—we would fall into the pedantic. So I decided to settle for identifying the author of the quote in the text. Even that became cumbersome. If readers don't know who penned "little two hours traffic on the stage," I refer them to *Bartlett's Famous Quotations*. As Jim says in one of his essays, "If I mention Mr. Fitzwilliam Darcy and his ten thousand pounds a year, I expect all my colleagues to know that I am referring to *Pride and Prejudice*." Lesson learned: Jim Lee's instincts triumph every time over *The Chicago Manual of Style*. I did, however, hold firm on using the full name of an author on first mention, this over Jim's plaintive cries of "How many Kants are there?"

Nowadays, as all of us age, I think of Jim as one of three god-fathers of Texas literature—the other two being Tom Pilkington and Don Graham, to whom this book is dedicated. They are not exactly like the "old Three"—J. Frank Dobie, Roy Bedichek, and Walter Prescott Webb, about whom Jim writes in this book—but there are some similarities. They are bound by an interest in Texas letters and they share a deep friendship, which Jim gracefully acknowledges in his introduction. They probably do not visit as often as did Dobie, Bedichek, and Webb, nor do they have "hobby ranch" getaways. But once again, as in the past, three men dominate Texas literature—or at least the criticism and understanding of that body of work, both past and present. Don is the most prolific writer, and Tom is the pure scholar, but Jim is the Renaissance man—scholar, folklorist, humorist, author, speaker, and good friend, bon vivant, real person.

Judy Alter
Fort Worth, Texas

Adventures

with a

Texas Humanist

Introduction

If I am ever a castaway on a desert island, I'm going to be sure to have with me the brand new *Oxford English Dictionary* that I just bought myself. When he spoke at the inauguration of the *OED*, Prime Minister Stanley Baldwin of Great Britain said that was what he would do. The *OED* is a fascinating source for all kinds of information, but I went to it recently for a definition of "adventure." The earliest definition listed is, "That which comes to us or happens without design," not the "perilous or hazardous enterprise" that most people associate with the word. I think that earlier definition is what Roy Bedichek had in mind when he wrote *Adventures with a Texas Naturalist*, the book from which I stole my title. Bedichek, who began his book at seventy, had spent much of his life wandering the state of Texas and looking at the natural wonders and natural commonplaces, taking what came to him without design. The design came later, when he sat down at Walter Prescott Webb's Friday Mountain Ranch to order his notes and compose his adventures, but his adventures were not hazardous unless he happened to step on a rattlesnake or fall from a cliff.

Nor are my adventures hazardous. Many were conducted from an easy chair with a book in hand, some from wandering the state and observing human nature, some from research and study, and many from remembering the past and projecting the future in my mind. Most of my adventures were without design—at least at the start. As time passed, I became absorbed in the study of Texas literature, and some of the essays here are attempts to make sense of what I read and talked with others about. The original plan of this book was to dust off some old essays and put them in one volume, a common desire of college professors and newspaper columnists. Such compilations seldom work and should not be encouraged. But most of us who have written a number of essays on this and that hope someone will suggest that we gather them up for book publication. That is what happened here. TCU Press suggested that I dig around in my files and find gems of beauty and wisdom. It didn't work out. I dug around and found very little of either beauty or wisdom. What I found was "a rhapsody," a "literary work consisting of miscellaneous or disconnected pieces"—I just learned this definition of "rhapsody" from my new *OED* too.

My rhapsody, my miscellany, was not really ready for prime time. I knew that if I wanted to produce a book, I needed to make more sense out of my adventures. That realization wrecked the original plan of dusting off the old essays. I set about writing two new chapters to help me organize my thoughts and prejudices. The first two chapters, "The Age of Dobie" and "The Age of McMurtry," are the fruits of my frustration. I decided that in order to understand all I wanted to understand about Texas life and literature, I needed to make some order—in my own mind at least—of the changes and trends that have taken place in this state over almost a century. I decided that the main force in Texas literature and culture for almost the whole first half of the twentieth century was to be found in the influence of J. Frank Dobie. That was hardly a revelation, for the shadow of Dobie hangs over the state in many minds to this very day. So I wrote about what I thought Dobie's influence was and what forces shaped Dobie.

After Dobie's 1964 death, Texas literature saw rapid changes. I decided that the central figure of this new era is Larry McMurtry. There are flaws in this reasoning, for McMurtry was never to Texas what Dobie was. McMurtry never really claimed to speak for Texas or hold the honorary title of "Mr. Texas," but he had some definite ideas about Texas life and literature and he presented them in his novels and a few essays. What he did, essentially, is put paid to the old Dobie ethic of Lone Star chauvinism and longhorn worship. I try to show that in the chapter on McMurtry. I wish I had shown it more to my satisfaction. It was a hard chapter to write, for it is hard to tell how much McMurtry was the actor or the acted upon. But I tried, and others will have to decide whether what I wrote makes any sense.

The other essays in the first part of the book are more or less things I dusted off. Mostly they are essays I had published here and there, but I found in the dusting process that some of them needed serious revision, though a couple I didn't touch at all.

In Part II, the essays on folklore are hugely rewritten versions of things I had published earlier or had read before some organization but had not thought fit to publish—or, more likely, others had not thought fit to publish. "The Uses of Folklore" was written to be read as the banquet speech at the Texas Folklore Society, an organization I have belonged to since 1958. After a few serious papers delivered to the TFS, I began to write essays that I thought were funny. Not everyone in the organization agreed, but enough did that I was encouraged to keep on with stand-up comedy. When I was invited to speak at the banquet, I was so honored that I tried to write a serious speech. I had already established a reputation as the class clown, and the night of the banquet was introduced as such. My serious speech was met by gales of laughter, much to my consternation. I later gave the speech at Eastfield College in Dallas to much less laughter, and then finally wrote a revised version to deliver as the McDermott Lecture at Casper College in Wyoming. The people in Wyoming took it as a serious commentary, and I felt somewhat vindicated. Now, after another revision, I present it here. At least I won't be able to hear laughter or jeers. I hope.

The other essays in that section are indeed attempts on my part to make sense of some aspects of Texas life and culture.

"Texas Sidekicks" was published earlier in "a rhapsody" of mine called *Texas, My Texas*, another stolen title. The essays in *Texas, My Texas* are supposed to be funny, which may account for the large number of remaindered copies lying in my office. I read "Texas Sidekicks" to an audience of Germans interested in the American West, and I noticed that they took notes rather than erupting into laughter. But they were Germans, and Germans are reputed to be more serious-minded than I am. I included it here because Bill Crider, the prolific crime novelist who also happens to have a Ph.D. in English, wrote me that my piece was better than anything he had ever read in *PMLA*, the learned journal of the Modern Language Association. I am not sure exactly what to make of that comment, for I have never managed to make it through but one article in *PMLA*. But then maybe neither did Crider. I did love the compliment.

I can't really defend the inclusion of the last set of essays in this volume. The only thing I can say is that J. Frank Dobie once published a book called *Some Part of Myself*, so I stole his title and included some personal essays. These are what many creative writing schools are pleased to call creative nonfiction. The first one was written when my friend Donna Walker-Nixon wrote to say that her new journal, *Windhover: A Magazine of Christian Literature*, had no creative nonfiction; she wondered if I might supply some. I don't have any serious Christian credentials, but I did attend a church school from 1945 until 1948. Being a person easily flattered, I wrote the piece included here, and when it was published I sent a copy to my late friend and classmate Hartwell Hooper. Hart did two things with it: he made a tape recording to send to another classmate, Claude Martin, who has gone blind, and he sent a copy to St. Andrew's-Sewanee School, which reprinted it in the school magazine. As you can see, I am a serious proponent of recycling.

I wrote "Boot Camp Days" because Donna Walker-Nixon

asked me to write something for a section of *New Texas* called "lagniappe." And I wrote "The Rain in Korea Is Awful Cold and Wet" because Francis Edward Abernethy called me one day. Ab is the finest secretary-editor in the history of the society (better than his predecessors, J. Frank Dobie, Mody Boatright, or Wilson Hudson—all good men and true). This day he said, "James Ward, we don't have any articles on the Korean War for our Texas Folklore Society volume called *Family Sagas*. Weren't you in the Korean War?" I admitted it and agreed to write something about my heroic adventures. The same thing caused me to write "Hydrogen Bomb Days." Jerry Craven of West Texas A&M called and said, "We don't have any creative nonfiction for *AmarilloBay.Com*, our online magazine." Guess what? I sent the bomb story electronically to West Texas and couldn't possibly prevent myself from recycling it here.

Except for the chapter on the poetry of Betsy Colquitt, I have done little with poetry but mention a few names. I am not competent to write a history of Texas poetry. To do so would be to step into a minefield. Texas has thousands of poets, maybe millions, and almost all of them feel neglected. There are many reasons that they feel neglected and put upon, but the chief one is the difficulty of finding a publisher. Hardly anybody will publish a volume of verse. So poets are left to publish individual poems in little magazines, to gather a few into small, often self-published chapbooks, or to enter one of the contests that charges an entry fee and hope that the book is chosen for a run of five hundred or so copies. I hate to say this, but of the thousands or millions of Texas poets writing today, most are not good—some are incredibly bad. There are a great many good ones, and there must be hundreds who are good but who never get enough poems in one place for a critic to write an intelligent commentary. Over the years while I was editing and coediting *New Texas*, I had the good fortune to look at and publish many good poems. I sincerely believe that some of the people whose works I published have substantial bodies of work that I would admire and could comment upon. But since most of them are only partially published, I have no opportunity to know. I could make a list of poets whose individual poems I like, but once you start to mention some, you necessarily omit others. So I am leaving this field to Billy Bob Hill, whose two fine anthologies of Texas poems make him much more knowledgeable than I am.

I have also avoided drama. There are not thousands or hundreds or even scores of good playwrights in Texas. Horton Foote always comes to mind, and I admire the plays of his I have seen and read, as well as movies like *On Valentine's Day, 1941, The Trip to Bountiful,* and my all-time favorite Texas movie, *Tender Mercies.* I should have written a chapter on Foote, but I didn't, nor do I have much to say about films and filmmakers. I once hired Ken Harrison to teach screenwriting at the University of North Texas, and I got to know the films he wrote and produced, but I think it takes a talent I do not have to talk about filmmakers. Don Graham does that too well for me to try to compete.

Now I am to the part of this introduction where the sensible reader is advised to close the book or go to one of the main chapters. I am at the part where I tell things that are mostly of interest to me and to the people who influenced me or helped me or encouraged me or at least did nothing to hinder me, If one looks at the dedication page of this book, he or she will see that I dedicated it to Don Graham and Tom Pilkington, "my betters," I call them. They are. Each of them knows more and has done more reading and writing about Texas life and literature than I have. The three of us have worked together on more than one project, and I have never failed to learn from them. The three of us edited *The Texas Literary Tradition* as a project of the University of Texas Centennial in 1983, and then, from that book we produced a film, *Texas Literature: The Southern Experience,* for the Texas Committee for the Humanities. I have asked many things of my two friends, and I have never been turned down. I like and admire both of them and am sincere when I say they are my betters.

If I weren't dedicating this book to Tom and Don, I would dedicate it to Judy Alter. She has dragged this book kicking and screaming out of me, has read it with care, has found the small errors and the large, and has been of more support than I deserve. But then she has always done things for me beyond the call of duty. It is she who appointed me to the editorship of TCU Press's Texas Tradition Series and then to the post which I now hold, acquisitions editor of TCU Press. Actually, that is the position as it appears on my letters to prospective authors and on my business card. On the official TCU faculty and staff rolls, I fill the important post of "Visiting Editor without Compensation," and I have a letter from the provost so designating me. I like my TCU Press job because it allows me to have an office and a place to go on most days. I don't have to work too hard, and I get paid travel money when I go to a few select conferences to man the TCU Press booth and talk to all my friends. In the office I have the fellowship and advice of Judy and the press editor, Susan Petty, who thought up the idea of my doing this book. Judy and I edited a wonderful book, *Literary Fort Worth,* and are in the planning stages of *Literary West Texas.* Judy is the perfect person to work with because she does all the work I am not good at and don't like to do.

Several years ago, Judy developed a vibrant reading group called "Contemporary Classics" that was run through the TCU Division of Extended Education. She used to invite me to lead an occasional discussion, and then about four years ago, she passed the group along to me. It was a part of Extended Education as long as Diane Lovin was coordinator of non-credit courses, and on her leaving that job, I kept the group going and now run it out of the Southwest Regional Library. I thank Judy for giving the group to me, and I especially thank Diane Lovin, my special friend, for nurturing it when I took it over and for being a dedicated reader. She also reads what I write and listens to me when I am at the podium. She goes to events with me even when she would be happier staying at home. I also thank the thirty to fifty participants who meet once a month to talk about books and help me keep current on contemporary literature. My secretary/sergeant-at-arms in the now-named Jim Lee Book Group is Ruth Orren, who keeps all the records and helps in many ways.

I learned about Texas literature and folklore from many people. My parents were southern folk, and they taught me the idiom and the customs and the beliefs and the stories. I did not know that they were giving me an education in folklore until I took a course in folklore from Mary Celestia Parler at the University of Arkansas in the middle 1950s. About a week into the course, I suddenly realized that I already knew all that I was hearing about—the tales and songs and legends and myths and superstitions. But Mary C. Parler helped me put what I knew in some order and taught me how to collect songs in the Ozark Mountains. She let me work as her assistant for a year and introduced me to Vance Randolph, probably the greatest folksong collector America has produced. Long after I was away from Arkansas, Mary Parler, once safely past seventy, married Vance Randolph, by then in his eighties. Part of their story is told in Donald Harington's novel, *Butterfly Weed*. Randolph once dedicated a book to Agnes Mabel and Becky. I wish I had such nerve.

While I am wandering outside the confines of Texas, I have a few words to say about the greatest repository of folk culture I have ever known. In 1986, Joyce Lee and I bought an 1860 log house deep in the Ouachita National Forest thirteen miles from Mena, Arkansas. Our closest neighbor and most fervent teacher was Edna Lawrence, who, for eighty-odd years had lived within five miles of this hamlet called Shady. Edna's knowledge of the flora and fauna, remedies and beliefs, the wisdom and language of the folk was amazing. She wrapped leftovers in "serene" wrap so they wouldn't "swivel" up, she grew a flower called a "high geranium," and she lamented the people her age who had "old-timers" disease. But despite having heard many things imperfectly, she was an intelligent woman who told a story with clarity and succinctness. Witness the tale of Tootsie Leins, who danced all night one fall, went home and slept "with her head in the window, caught the sinus, and died." My six years of knowing the late "Queen of Shady" was worth a college degree in folklore. Few people have ever had such an impact on my life.

Once I was at North Texas State College, Martin Shockley arranged for me to read a paper at the Texas Folklore Society's 1959 meeting. He shepherded me through writing the paper and gave me some advice on how one should present a paper. Never deviate from the text with clever asides, or at least not until you are famous. I never deviate from the text I have written, but once I become famous I am sure I will. Or not. Shockley died in 2003 at the age of almost a hundred, and I don't think he ever delivered asides in papers he read. The Texas Folklore Society became my academic mainstay from my first year in Texas until today. Over the years I have read dozens of papers and published many of them in the TFS's annual. The people I have come to know in that organization have helped me in hundreds of ways. Sometime in the 1960s I persuaded the Austin publisher Steck-Vaughn to let me edit a series of pamphlets on southwest literature. I turned to all my folklore society friends to do the work and enlisted some great writers to produce these forty-eight-page pamphlets on writers of Texas and the Southwest. Francis Edward Abernethy wrote the first pamphlet, on J. Frank Dobie. In the early years of that series I called upon the late John Q. Anderson, Edwin W. Gaston, Stanley Alexander, Tom Pilkington, James W. Byrd, Jo Lyday, Eleanor James, John O. West, Wilson Hudson, Sam H. Henderson, and forty-odd others to produce some very useful small studies on Texas and southwestern writers. All these writers taught me about Texas, and I am still in their debt. I am especially indebted to R. H. Porter, who had once been president of the Steck Company, but who in his final years occupied a corner office at Steck-Vaughn and made all the decisions about The Southwest Writers Series. I never knew Mr. Porter well, never even knew what his initials stood for, but I held him in awe. He knew more about Texas than anyone I have ever met.

I have done this before, but once again I would like to dedicate some part of this book to Joyce Glover Lee, who heard some of these chapters as papers and speeches, criticized and edited others, and kept me from some of my excesses in the pursuit of humor. She was an excellent and devoted wife, and now, even though we are divorced and she has remarried, she remains my best friend. Her book on the novelist Rolando Hinojosa taught me much about Mexican American literature.

My debt to Billy Bob Hill is a large one. We worked together on Texas literature during the time I was a committee member for his dissertation, and since then we have done many projects together. He published my short stories in his several fine Texas short-fiction anthologies, and we have worked together on his two celebrated poetry anthologies, *Texas in Poetry: A 150-Year Anthology* and *Texas in Poetry 2*. Billy Bob Hill has devoted himself to Texas literature for all his working life and through his own Browder Springs Press has published works by such writers as A. C. Greene, William Barney, and Paul Ruffin. We always promise ourselves we will do a book together before I become even more senile than now, and I would like to renew that promise in these dedicatory pages.

Betsy Colquitt, professor emerita of English at TCU, has been generous in her help with this manuscript. I met Professor Colquitt, founding editor of the literary journal *Descant* and longtime teacher of creative writing at TCU, when I was assigned to edit and write the introduction to her collection *Eve—from the Autobiography and Other Poems*. I had published several of her poems in *New Texas* over the years, but only when I read her entire collection did I realize how great a poet she is—and how good a friend. She is generous with her time and eagerly volunteered to read this manuscript, which she has seen in parts before. We have been close friends since 1996, and I have come to see why she is revered by many generations of TCU students and admired by hundreds of people in her native Fort Worth.

A year or so ago I met Ruth McAdams, chair of English at Tarrant County College's South Campus. She invited me to talk to her class, and the following semester, she let me be her co-teacher in a class on Texas literature and culture. I was more teacher's aide than co-teacher. I didn't have to take roll or grade papers or discipline students, but I got myself back in the flow of teaching and talking about Texas after I was well into my retirement from the University of North Texas. Her amazing enthusiasm for Texas literature and culture energized me, and though she tells colleagues I am her teacher in matters Texan, I find I rely heavily on her for new ideas about the literature and culture of the Lone Star State. She has criticized several of the essays in this volume and made many useful suggestions.

I need to thank Donna Walker-Nixon and Carolyn Poulter of the University of Mary Hardin Baylor. They took *New Texas* after UNT closed the Center for Texas Studies and let me continue as a coeditor, even though they were doing most of the hard work. They, along with Marilyn Robitaille of Tarleton State University, who came on as a coeditor in the last year of Donna's tenure at UMHB and is now coeditor with Donna of a new journal, *The Langton Review*, and they have agreed to let me serve on the board and write some articles—my first one on the noble and frustrating game of bridge. Donna has been a true friend to me. She let me be a pallbearer at the funeral of her late husband, George Nixon, and I take that as a great honor.

Nobody has been a more loyal friend and supporter than Joyce Roach. We have read papers on the same programs, she has let me write introductions to some of her books, and we have put on two or three joint presentations. We have planned several books together, but my laziness always gets in the way. I value her friendship immensely.

Finally, I want to mention some names of people who have befriended me over the years in the worlds of Texas life, literature, and folklore: Sarah Green of Gilmer; Phillip Fry of Austin; John West of El Paso; Jim and Mary Harris of Hobbs, New Mexico; Fran Vick of Dallas; Tom Dodge of Midlothian; George and Ruth Fortenberry of Arlington; John Graves of Glen Rose; J. T. and Hattie Lee of Powderly, Alabama; John Henry Irsfeld of Las Vegas (who once dedicated a book to me); Shelby Hearon of Burlington, Vermont; Pat and Shay Bennett of Abilene; Jim Sanderson and Jerry Bradley of Beaumont; Paul Ruffin of Huntsville; Gyde C. Martin of Arlington; Jerry and Sherry Craven of Amarillo; Bonnie Lovell of Denton; Bettye Bailey of Birmingham, Alabama; Phyllis Allen of Fort Worth; Wynona Alexander of Harker Heights; Deborah Douglas of San Antonio; Robert and Jean Flynn of San Antonio; Sister Phyllis Bunnell of San Antonio; Terrell Dixon of Houston; Jim and Jane Tanner of Denton; Yvette Blair of Dallas; Rick and Teel Sale of Denton; Elmer Kelton of San Angelo; Lou and Charles Rodenberger of Baird; Jim and Kate Lehrer of Washington, D.C.; Bob Frye of Fort Worth; Jane Roberts Wood of Dallas; Liz and Pete Gunter of Denton; Bill Mercer of Dallas; Sherry McGuire of Lewisville; Margie West of Fort Worth; Carolyn Barnes of Denton; Tom Preston of Winona; David Kesterson of Denton; Jeff Guinn and Mike Cochran and Bud Kennedy of the *Fort Worth Star-Telegram*; Bob Compton and Kent Biffle and Cheryl Chapman of the *Dallas*

Morning News; Clay Reynolds of Dallas; Paul Patterson of Crane; Fred Erisman of Fort Worth; Mark Busby of San Marcos; Rolando Hinojosa of Austin; Terry Dalrymple and Charlie McMurtry of San Angelo; Laurie Champion of San Diego, California; Kent Bowman of Justin; Sylvia Grider of College Station; Sharon Morrow of Arlington; Bert Almon of Alberta in Canada; Stan Alexander of Austin; Ann Gibson of Keller; David Lindsey of Austin; Bill Crider of Alvin; Margie and Art Hendrix of Commerce; Wayne Ray, cribbage player from Borger; Betsy Berry of Austin; Chris Willerton of Abilene; Jas. Mardis of Dallas; Walt McDonald of Lubbock; and some of my friends "hid in death's dateless night"—Benjamin Franklin Capps, Lawrence Clayton, William A. Owens, A. C. Greene, Martha Emmons, John Q. Anderson, James W. Byrd, Ernestine Sewell, Mody Boatright, Wilson Hudson, Martin Shockley, George Nixon, J. Mason Brewer, and Hermes Nye.

PART I

Texas

Literature

The Age of Dobie

Literature in twentieth-century Texas is dominated by two figures: J. Frank Dobie and Larry McMurtry. Both grew up on ranches, but life among cows and cowboys dominated Dobie's life and works in a way quite different from the way that world shaped McMurtry. Dobie found it romantic, McMurtry saw it as ironic. Dobie, who grew up on a ranch south of San Antonio, loved the West filled with men who carried side arms and herded cattle. The old stories about lost mines and famous cowmen informed his writing, his teaching, and his career as a folklorist. His many books on the region, the course in the Life and Literature of the Southwest he taught at the University of Texas, his radio programs, his newspaper columns, and the many speeches he made in a career that ran from the twenties until his death in 1964 made him a celebrated Texan. Lon Tinkle, a Dallas writer and professor, called James Frank Dobie "Mr. Texas." McMurtry, born when Dobie was already a famous figure, saw a different Texas and wrote in a vein far different from that of Dobie and his followers. McMurtry saw a world dominated by irony; in effect, he ushered in a new species of Texas writing that had been current in the world for a long time but was alien to Dobie.

In looking at the changes in Texas literature in the twentieth and twenty-first centuries, it is useful to consider what had been going on in world literature for centuries. All literatures, whether national, international, or regional, follow similar patterns as they move from primitive to sophisticated. Northrop Frye in his classic *Anatomy of Criticism* (Princeton UP 1951) says that western literature for the past twenty-five-hundred years has moved from mythic to heroic to realistic to ironic. The heroes of those eras descend from gods to superheroes to men and women of high degree to people like us and, finally, to antiheroes who merit our pity. Texas literature has followed a similar course in a much shorter span of time. We have moved from the gods and heroes of the Alamo and San Jacinto (Sam Houston, Jim Bowie, Davy Crockett, William B. Travis) to bold frontiersmen (Charlie Goodnight) to characters who are more confused or weaker than we are (Lonnie Bannon of *Horseman, Pass By*) to despicable anti-heroes (Hud of the same McMurtry novel).

Following or paralleling these changes in modes, there are also changes in style. The steps Wylie Sypher describes in his *Four Stages of Renaissance Style: Transformations in Art and Culture, 1400–1700* may not be the perfect expression of what has happened in Texas literature as the state's writing moved from the primitive to the decadent, but there are some similarities. New literary periods begin with the primitive and unsophisticated. Early works of a period are almost always simple and direct. Then time passes and rough edges are smoothed out as we approach the golden age. Finally, a stylistically decadent period follows.

Texas has moved from the primitive toward something like decadence in less than two hundred years. Writers like John C. Duval, A. J. Sowell, Andy Adams, Charlie Siringo, Alexander Sweet and John Armoy Knox, the early O. Henry of *Rolling Stone* days, and Mollie Moore Davis seem to me to be Texas primitive. Most commentators on Texas literature dismiss the early works and argue that Texas literature begins with the days

of J. Frank Dobie in about 1920, though neither Dobie nor anyone who has studied the whole history of Texas literature agrees
that it all began with him. It is true that Dobie became nationally
famous with his magazine articles, his books, and his anthologies
after 1920, but many of the early writers enjoyed some small
national attention.

Sweet and Knox turned *Texas Siftings* from a regional to a
national publication and moved it to New York. It was reprinted
in England and even translated into German. O. Henry's 1907
publication *Hearts of the West* included some of his Texas stories
and was nationally popular, and Mollie Moore Davis's novels and
poems were published and read nationally.

But for most readers, it all began with Dobie. He was devoted
to the simple and straightforward, but he is less primitive than
Sowell or Sweet and Knox or Duval. His master's degree from
Columbia and his professorship at the University of Texas, just as
the university was attempting national prominence, took the
edge off his natural lack of sophistication, or perhaps, as many
have suggested, his pose as an unsophisticated cowman was delib-
erate.

But sophisticated or not, from the 1920s until the 1960s J.
Frank Dobie spoke for Texas and dominated Texas letters as well
as Texas intellectual life. In the sixties, Dobie's influence waned
except among the Texana collectors, the folklorists, the historians, and the old grads from Dobie's classes at the University of
Texas—not to mention all the boys who grew up on his tales of
lost treasure and cowboy life. Starting in the late sixties, novelist
Larry McMurtry's reputation as the state's signature writer began
to grow. Even after the turn of the twenty-first century, the Texas
literary establishment looks toward Archer City and McMurtry
the way it used to give obeisance to the sages of Austin—Dobie,
Roy Bedichek, and Walter Prescott Webb—though McMurtry,
except for occasional essays on literature and culture, has never
sought to be the ultimate spokesman for Texas the way Dobie did.

Scores of writers sent Dobie their works to be approved of—
or at least in the hope of some favorable notice from him. And
since he was the spokesman for intellectual Texas for almost half
a century, what he determined to be the themes of Texas writing
and Texas thought were important to intellectual Texas. Scores of
commentators spoke lovingly of Dobie and his two intellectual
companions, Webb and Bedichek, as the "Old Three" or "The
Texas Triumvirate" or "the Holy Trinity." Ronnie Dugger edited a
book of tributes to Dobie, Bedicheck, and Webb under the title
Three Men in Texas, and William A. Owens edited their selected
letters under the title *Three Friends: Bedichek, Dobie, and Webb*,
with the subtitle *A Personal History*. In addition, critical and biographical studies and tributes to the three men number in the hundreds. Austin radio personality Cactus Pryor, a true Dobieite,
even has a one-man play entitled simply *Dobie*.

Despite the praise heaped on Webb and Bedichek, it is clear
that Dobie is the central figure, the godfather. Webb and
Bedichek, like everyone else in intellectual Texas, followed in his
wake until the emergence of McMurtry. And then the reactions
set in, the first of which Larry McMurtry announced himself in
his 1967 essay "Southwestern Literature?" Though Dobie,
Bedicheck, and Webb still have their hagiographers and fervent
admirers and though most of their works are still in print, their
age has passed and sometimes one wonders what it was all about.

But maybe not in Austin where the three men lived and
worked and are remembered in many ways. A bronze statue at
Barton Creek shows the three old men sitting around
"Philosophers' Rock," a shrine to be approached if not for healing
at least for succor and sustenance. It was from this rock that they
apparently engaged in the conversations that informed many of
the books they wrote. It may be from this rock that Dobie encouraged Bedichek to begin his own literary career late in life.

In addition to the famous bronze in Austin, there is Dobie
Mall at the University of Texas, and the university has named a

professorship for Dobie and a chair for Walter Prescott Webb. Dobie's Paisano, a hobby ranch on the outskirts of Austin, is home to the Dobie Paisano Fellowship and is administered by the university and the Texas Institute of Letters—of which Dobie was, reluctantly at first, a charter member. Webb's Friday Mountain Ranch—also a small hobby getaway—some sixteen miles outside Austin proper, is still a shrine to be visited by the old grads and historians who remember Webb. Bedichek repaired to Friday Mountain Ranch at the age of almost seventy to begin his literary career with the writing of *Adventures with a Texas Naturalist*.

To understand the meaning of Dobie, Bedichek, and Webb, it is necessary to understand how Texas was in the 1920s and afterward. The world saw Texas as a raw frontier, an intellectual wasteland peopled by cowboys and cactus. And Texans themselves didn't always have a different view of their homeland. In other words, they bought into the myth that dime westerns and powder burners and B-movies taught them. It was not as much of a cultural wasteland as it was pictured, but it must be admitted that Texas was in a state of raw growth and change from shortly after the Civil War until the latter part of the nineteenth century. It seemed to the world and to many Texans that there was no time for thought, there was only time for action. After the Civil War, Texas was the great beef supplier to the nation and the escape hatch for southerners fleeing the defeated South. What had been a state of slightly more than half a million in 1860 grew to three million by 1900. And, with the discovery of oil at Spindletop down on the Texas coast, suddenly the state was consumed in a boom even bigger than the boom of the cattle kingdom. It was just not as romantic, for you couldn't do it a-horseback. After Spindletop, oil derricks sprang up all over Texas. The names of the strikes have entered Texas mythology: Kilgore, Burkburnett, Corsicana, Ranger, the Permian Basin. The prevailing view was that Texas was on the move and had little time for reflection. By the 1920s, Hollywood was turning Texas into the land of the cowboy, the rustler, the stagecoach bandit, and the steely-eyed lawman. Don Graham, the J. Frank Dobie Professor of English at the University of Texas, in his study of westerns, *Cowboys and Cadillacs*, shows how Hollywood taught Texas and the world to see the Lone Star State. Never mind that most Texans had no cattle and most of them lived on dirt farms; even the farmers began to see themselves the way such Hollywood stars as John Wayne, Hoot Gibson, Tom Mix, Roy Rogers, Gene Autry, and Tex Ritter taught them. Interestingly, only two of these famous movie cowboys were from Texas: Gene Autry from the little cotton town of Tioga in North Texas and Tex Ritter from Panola County in Deep East Texas. Of course as everyone knows John Wayne should have been a Texan.

The Dobie era was a time of expansion and expansiveness in Texas. It was also a time for romance. Things looked rosy—there was a glow over the past, the present was booming, and the future was unlimited. As Wordsworth wrote of the French Revolution, "Bliss it was in those times to be alive, but to be young was very heaven." If Dobie, Bedichek, Webb were no longer young, at least the rising intellectual class was young. And all hands were participants in the romance of Texas. Dobie was not alone in promoting romantic Texas. The whole state was involved in heroes and hero worship, and everybody thought, as the centennial of the Texas Revolution approached, that the sky was the limit both literally and figuratively. The days of great deeds were not over.

In the past, Sam Houston and a ragtag army had defeated "the Napoleon of the West" as Santa Anna called himself. The heroes of San Jacinto established a republic, the only state ever to proclaim itself a nation. (For two months in 1846, a small group of Americans in California raised the Bear Flag at Sonoma and proclaimed a republic, but no one took that as more than a chauvinistic joke.) True, Texas's republic was a stepping stone to annexation, but for the years between 1836 and 1845, Texas had a series of presidents and legislators and ran its business as a nation. The idea that Texas was once a nation gave Texans a kind of pride—some say chauvinism—that lingered all through the nineteenth century and well into the twentieth. Those facts of Texas history coupled with the immensity of the state helped to give Texans a sense of empire. D. W. Meining's book, *Imperial Texas,* is worth study to see some of the reasons that Texans felt and feel the way they do about the state and about its history, culture, and literature. Over the years, Imperial Texas developed a culture that it not only reveled in but exported to the world. Some of this can be seen in the dime novels about Texas that flowed from Beadle & Adams in the nineteenth century, the powder burner westerns that still fill supermarket shelves today, and the movies that imprinted Texas history—real and imagined—on the nation's consciousness. It was this imperial attitude that made it possible for J. Frank Dobie to become such a presence in Texas life and literature during the period of Romantic Texas.

Texas grew in myth and in population in the years that Dobie was the chief spokesman for the state. The population of Texas was 4,500,000 in 1920 when Dobie began to make his move as a folklorist/writer. By 1930, when he began the course in Life and Literature of the Southwest at the University of Texas, the state had grown to almost six million people and to 6,500,000 by 1940. Huge fortunes were being made in the twenties and even in the Great Depression years of the thirties. Even though the nation was in the depths of the Depression in 1936, the Texas Centennial created a building boom and an infusion of money into the state—and generated another great burst of enthusiasm for all things Texan. Then World War II brought Texas rapidly out of the Depression; the federal government built air bases, military training camps, huge defense plants, and even some prisoner-of-war camps. Thousands of Americans who had only seen Texas on the silver screen made their way into the state as part of the war effort. Many stayed—even a number of German prisoners of war interned in Texas came back to live here. Thousands more took the Texas message back to the world—"The stars at night are big and bright . . . Deep in the Heart of Texas," as the popular 1942 song told the world. All these changes made the Dobie era ripe for the boom in Texas history studies and a resurrection of all the old-time Texas heroes. Sam Houston, of course, was the *great* Texas hero, and names like Bowie and Crockett and Deaf Smith and Sul Ross were again on everyone's lips. The 1936 Centennial Commission of Control named Dobie and two other non-professional historians, Texaco executive Louis Kemp and Catholic priest Paul J. Foik, to the Advisory Board of Texas Historians. Dobie lobbied hard for the inclusion of Texans who did not die at the Alamo or serve in the republic. He advocated the inclusion of writers, Texas Rangers, cowboys, cattlemen, and other less prominent citizens. In his book on the Centennial with the revealing title *The Year America Discovered Texas: Centennial '36*, Kenneth B. Ragsdale tells how Dobie pushed for the inclusion of Larry Chittenden, the cowboy who authored the famous doggerel verse so beloved of Texans, "The Cowboy's Christmas Ball" (99–101, passim).

During the Centennial year, Texas spent a great deal of money setting up the state fairgrounds in Dallas for the main exposition and building monuments and establishing museums all over the state. (Texas author Donald Barthelme's father was one of the architects.) The center of Centennial events was Dallas, but the flamboyant newspaper publisher and Texas booster Amon Carter staged a counter celebration, the Centennial Frontier Fair in Fort Worth, that included Paul Whiteman and his orchestra, a dazzling array of showgirls, rodeos, fan dancer Sally Rand, and Billy Rose's Casa Mañana show. Carter erected signboards saying, "For Education Go to Dallas, for Entertainment, Come to Fort Worth." The celebration was not limited to Dallas and Fort Worth. Ragsdale estimates that there were over 240 local celebrations ranging from the Raymondville Onion Show to the

Henderson East Texas Oil Jubilee to the Tyler Rose Festival to the Crystal City Spinach Festival that named the cartoon character Popeye as honorary mayor of Crystal City (160, 167).

As part of the centennial celebration, the federal and state governments allocated more than half a million dollars to San Antonio for refurbishing the Alamo, restoring Mission San José, and building the $100,000 cenotaph honoring the heroes of the Alamo. Over seven hundred memorials and monuments were created across the state, including the $250 million San Jacinto Battle Monument. The famous cenotaph just in front of the Alamo was not at all to Dobie's liking. He found the memorial and its creator, Pompeo Coppini, objectionable. Dobie called the sixty-foot-tall monument a "grain elevator" and said that the heroes pictured on it "looked as though they came to the Alamo to have their picture taken" (Stephen Harrigan, 142). Dobie also heaped scorn on the horse fountain that longtime San Antonio resident Coppini designed for the south entrance to the University of Texas campus. Dobie never limited himself to commentary on literature, history, and folklore. He was not backward about making his views on art and architecture known. His comment that the twenty-six-story tower on the UT campus should be laid on its side and a porch put around it is well known, as is his statement that the edifice was the university president's "last erection." These were heady times for Dobie, for everything he loved and wrote about was celebrated in the years around 1936. He was a favorite speaker at events, and his books, which had enjoyed a good audience since publication of A Vaquero of the Brush Country in 1929, became staples of the Centennial. In the early thirties he attracted a national audience with his articles in the magazine Country Gentleman, and throughout the decade published some of his best-known books: Coronado's Children (1931), Tales of the Mustang (1936), The Flavor of Texas (1936), Tongues of the Monte (1939), and Apache Gold and Yaqui Silver (1939). In 1941, he published The Longhorns and the next year his

Guide to Life and Literature of the Southwest. The Guide established
Dobie as the arbiter of Texas literature—that volume and its revision in 1952 became a bible for readers of old-time Texas, for
Texana collectors, and for students who were taking his course
and the courses that his ex-students and adherents were establishing all over the state.

In the *Guide*, J. Frank Dobie taught Texans what they ought
to like and read. This best-known of all bibliographies on Texas
writing has little to say about literature but a great deal to say
about Texas life. It points us to books about the heroes and legends of Texas, certainly that part of Texas that was most western.
There are lists of books on flora and fauna, nature and naturalists,
stagecoaches, pioneers of all sorts, cattle and cowboys, and folktales and songs. Only two of the chapters are devoted to literature. Dobie has about four pages in his chapter called "Fiction,
Mostly Modern" and two pages on poetry and drama. Novels and
stories that followed the cattle up the trails are listed in other sections. The fact of the matter seems to be that Dobie's reading was
largely limited to books about cowboys, treasure, and cattle. He
talked a great deal about his love for the likes of Wordsworth and
other great English poets, but little in his writing demonstrates
much real knowledge of the subject—or even much reading done
in the classics after finishing at Southwestern University in
Georgetown before World War I.

But Dobie is more than sound on the heroes and westerners
who helped shape Texas life in the early days. If the movie cowboys presented a Texas that never actually existed, the state had
a few cattlemen who achieved the mythic proportions of some of
the movie heroes. The iconic Texas cowboy, cattleman, and ranch
owner was Charles Goodnight, who came to Texas from Illinois at
the age of ten, fought the Comanches as a member of Cureton's
regiment of the Texas Rangers during the Civil War, and then, in
1866, joined Oliver Loving in blazing the trail from Fort Belknap
in North Texas to Fort Sumner, New Mexico, to carry beef to the

Indians. Goodnight, who lived until 1929, became the ultimate Texas cowman and was as famous in the Dobie era as Sam Houston had been for other generations of Texans. In fact, I suspect many Texans saw Goodnight as the reincarnation of Houston. To Dobie and men of his era, notably J. Evetts Haley, Goodnight's biographer, Goodnight became the symbol for old-time Texas. And Dobie, who grew up on a ranch in Live Oak County, became the chief spokesman for old-time Texas for the rest of his life. He wrote about cattle, lost mines, and cowmen like Goodnight—men who, Dobie said, came out of "the old rock." Dobie kept alive the reputations of Duval, whom Dobie called, "the first Texas man of letters," Andy Adams, who wrote *Log of a Cowboy,* which Dobie called "the best book that has been written and can be written about the cattle trails." In the *Guide* Dobie says of *Log of a Cowboy,* "if all other books on trail-driving were destroyed, a reader could still get a just and authentic conception of trail men, trail work, range cattle, cow horses, and the cow country in general. . . " (94). Of the dictated memoirs of the famous cowboy E. C. "Teddy Blue" Abbot, Dobie wrote, "Helena Huntington Smith, who actually wrote and arranged his reminiscences, instead of currying him down and putting a checkrein on him, spurred him in the flanks and told him to swaller his head" (94). This kind of folksy western writing endeared Dobie to the old cowhands—or Old West wannabes. He celebrated Bigfoot Wallace, Ben Lilly, Shanghai Pierce, and scores of other Old West heroes of Texas. For the most part, though, he had little to say about those Texans who weren't western but were southern.

His focus on Texas as a western state is understandable considering Dobie's own life, for he lived it in such a way as to try to live both in the rarified world of the intellectual and the practical world of the ranchman. He was born in 1888 and grew up on a ranch. His mother was the more intellectual of his parents and had him reading the standard works of British fiction and poetry before sending him off to live with relatives in Alice to go to high school. After high school, he attended Southwestern University at Georgetown, graduating in 1910. He worked on newspapers and taught school before going to New York to take an M.A. in English at Columbia. In 1914, he joined the faculty of the University of Texas, where he was a faculty member off and on until 1947. He served in the army from 1917 until 1919 and then spent a year managing his uncle's ranch in South Texas. He returned to UT Austin in 1921, but, since he did not have a Ph.D. and despaired of ever being promoted, he left to take a job as head of the English department at Oklahoma State University (then Oklahoma A&M). That interlude lasted only two years, and he was back at Austin where he was finally promoted—in 1933—to full professor despite the lack of a doctorate. He was the first faculty member in English to achieve that rank without the Ph.D.

Between 1930 and 1947, Dobie taught hundreds of students in the UT English department's Life and Literature of the Southwest course. It was that course that allowed Dobie to populate English and history departments throughout the state with his adherents, with students who became teachers and who taught the Dobie line—that Texas was the real West, that Texas was a world of cattle and cowmen, that the life in the brush country and the deserts of West Texas represented the true and authentic Texas. Old students of Dobie still remember his course and praise him as the most influential teacher they ever had at Austin. When he decided to offer the course, some of the more traditional English faculty members asked the question that McMurtry was later to ask: "Southwestern literature?" Dobie replied that even if the literature was scant, the region was bursting with life. It was, if you consider that the Texas and Southwest that Dobie loved and taught was the world of cattle drives and javelinas and outlaws.

But it was only partly from this academic platform that Dobie began the career that ushered in the Age of Dobie. In 1914, he joined the Texas Folklore Society, which was barely five years old, and by the early twenties, Dobie was secretary-editor of the organization and had imprinted his particular stamp on it, a stamp that is still part of the mythology of the Texas Folklore Society.

When Dobie joined the Texas Folklore Society in 1914, Dorothy Scarborough was president. Had she not left the state in 1919 to take a job at Columbia University, Dobie's place in the society might not have been so prominent. Scarborough was not only one of America's finest folklorists but also a successful novelist in the 1920s, the years of Dobie's ascendancy. Scarborough's *On the Trail of Negro Folklore* and *A Song-Catcher in the Southern Mountains* (published posthumously) made her national reputation before Dobie was well known across the country. Her works as a novelist are discussed elsewhere in this book.

Dobie is still the king when the TFS holds its annual meeting. He did a number of things to make the society important during his era. First, he began editing a series of annual volumes that continues to this day. For those annuals, he found, encouraged, and recruited many folklorists and storytellers, who not only added to the corpus of folklore and popular Texas culture but also became new members of the informal "Dobie Society." Among the early contributors was J. Mason Brewer, who went on to become one of the leading African American folklorists in the country. In the 1932 volume, when everything in Texas was still segregated, Dobie published Brewer's tales from the bottomlands of the Brazos. Brewer was the first black writer to achieve any recognition in the state, and it was through Dobie's advocacy that Brewer and many other black writers slowly came to be accepted in Texas.

Another Dobie folklorist/storyteller was John Henry Faulk, who went from being one of Dobie's star pupils at the University of Texas to conducting a national storytelling program on CBS radio from New York. Faulk, like Dobie, was a liberal Democrat, and after six years at CBS, he ran afoul of Senator Joe McCarthy

and his right-wing minions. AWARE, a McCarthy front, branded
Faulk a Communist, and he was blacklisted. He sued, and, after
some five years of wandering in the wilderness, Faulk was
awarded a judgment of $3.5 million . On appeal, the award was
reduced to $500,000, of which Faulk saw at best a fifth. John
Henry Faulk was never reinstated by CBS, but his book *Fear on
Trial* was turned into a movie that told his story to a large audience. Faulk ended his media career telling stories on the hillbilly
TV show "Hee-Haw." Faulk, like Dobie, was a supporter of civil
rights and was always in the forefront of movements for racial tolerance and equal justice. In 1983—at the age of seventy—Faulk
ran against turncoat Democrat Phil Gramm for the U.S. Senate.
He lost, as Texas drifted from being a state of conservative
Democrats to being a state of conservative Republicans. Sensing
the shifting winds, Gramm became a Republican. Faulk was such
an adherent of Dobie's that he named one of his sons Frank
Dobie Faulk.

The strong storytelling factor in the Age of Dobie is evident
in much of the fiction and nonfiction of the period from 1920 to
the publication of *Horseman, Pass By* in 1958. The kind of writing
that Dobie approved of was un-ironic, romantic in its portrayal of
Texas men and horses, or realistic when it came to telling of life
on ranch or farm. The year after Dobie won the first Texas
Institute of Letters Award for *Apache Gold and Yaqui Silver*, the
organization gave the award to George Sessions Perry for *Hold
Autumn in Your Hand*. The novel is strong and lacking the kind of
irony we find later in McMurtry or Edwin Shrake or Billie Lee
Brammer or Robert Flynn. Perry's book deviated from the Dobie
prescription in that it deals with farm life in Central Texas and
not life on the prairies and plains of Texas. Moreover, the heroes
are dirt farmers who could as easily be found in Alabama or
Georgia. This novel, which takes place in and around Perry's
hometown of Rockdale, is often compared to John Steinbeck's

classic masterpiece about the same era, *The Grapes of Wrath*. Perry's novel was filmed in 1945 as *The Southerner* by the French director Jean Renoir. Perry began his career as a reporter and as author of a series of stories published in *Saturday Evening Post* in the thirties. These stories, collected as *Hackberry Cavalier*, are typical of American humor of the times and of the storytelling that Dobie favored. Perry was an acolyte of Dobie's, and his 1942 book *Texas: A World in Itself*, pays homage to the great man in producing much folklore and popular history about the state.

The Dobie storytelling tradition exists today in scores of writers and storytellers who either studied with Dobie or one of his successors at UT Austin or fully absorbed the Dobie myth. Most of the state's Texana newspaper columnists are still writing in the Dobie manner. One of the popular storyteller columnists of Dobie's day was the Fort Worth columnist, brag writer, poet, and tale collector Boyce House. House's "Cowtown Columns" were devoted to oil and cattle and cowboys and western vistas. House, a native of Arkansas, became immensely popular with his columns (which ran in 130 newspapers), his radio show, and his several books—the best known of which is probably *Were You in Ranger?*—a series of stories about the oil boom. House became well known as a writer on oil matters and was hired as a consultant to the filmmakers of *Boom Town*, the popular Clark Gable/ Spencer Tracy movie based on a *Cosmopolitan* short story by Edward Stewart entitled "A Lady Comes to Burkburnett." *Boom Town* (1940) did a great deal to show the rest of the world what wheeler-dealers the Texas oil barons were and fitted perfectly into the romantic image of Texas that Dobie was so carefully fostering. Like Faulk, Boyce House sought a political career. He ran twice for lieutenant governor of Texas on the Democratic ticket. He never won public office and had almost been forgotten as a writer when he died in 1961. Dobie said of House, "he was a poet as well as a historian and wordwielder" (*New Handbook of Texas*, 710).

House's history is not taken seriously, but he wrote the kind of secondary-source history that Dobie approved of. Today, popular columnists like Leon Hale of Houston keep the Dobie Texana tradition alive in newspapers. And the late A. C. Greene for many years wrote popular history in the Dobie manner for the *Dallas Morning News*. Greene, who authored some twenty books, was very much in the Dobie tradition as both a journalist and popularizer of Texas. His *A Personal Country* depicts life in Abilene and the West Texas Greene grew up in. Also in the Dobie manner, Greene published his own guide to Texas writing. His *The Fifty Best Books About Texas* and its sequel *The 50+ Best Books On Texas* do not list as many books about Texas as Dobie's two bibliographies, but the two books have become influential among Texana collectors and book dealers. Greene's two bibliographies are, like most of his writing, anecdotal in the Dobie manner. Often the book Greene is discussing is given short shrift as he tells what he was doing or feeling when he first encountered the book. Greene, an excellent writer, did almost as much to popularize Texas history in his columns in the *Dallas Morning News* as Dobie did in his various writings. Such columns are popular all across the nation, and it stretches the argument to give Dobie full credit for the kind of newspaper piece that appears everywhere. But the strong focus on Texas and Texas history in such columns owes a great debt to the Dobie era.

Dobie was above all else a storyteller, and he drew to the Texas Folklore Society many others who were devoted to the myths, legends, and tales of Texas. His interest in folk music was limited, and that part of the Texas legacy during the Age of Dobie was left to John Avery Lomax (1867–1948), whose career in Texas folklore parallels and complements Dobie's. Lomax, more than two decades older than Dobie, ran into some of the same roadblocks at the University of Texas that Dobie did when Dobie was trying to establish his Life and Literature of the Southwest as a respectable course in English at the University of Texas. In his autobiography, *Adventures of a Ballad Hunter,* Lomax tells how his English professor made light of the cowboy ballads he had been collecting since childhood and how that caused him to go behind his dormitory and burn the manuscripts. Following graduation, he became the registrar of the university and manager of one of the dorms. Later, Lomax took a job teaching at Texas A&M, but by 1907, he was off to Harvard where he was encouraged by George Lyman Kittredge and Barrett Wendell to work with his ballad collection. He did so and was awarded an M.A. degree. His thesis led to the publication of *Cowboy Songs and Other Frontier Ballads* (1910), which made his name in Texas folklore. In 1909, at the urging of Kittredge, he joined Leonidas Payne of the University of Texas' in founding the Texas Folklore Society. Lomax served as secretary, a post that, a few years later, Dobie was to put his stamp on for all time.

Though Lomax was connected to the University of Texas for several years, his name is not attached to the university the way Dobie's is. However, like Dobie, he ran into political trouble and was fired in 1917—somewhat similar to Dobie's technical dismissal in 1947—and though he was reinstated upon the impeachment of Governor Jim Ferguson, he never returned there as a faculty member or administrator. He divided his time for several years between banking and working in alumni affairs for the university. By the mid-thirties, John Lomax was a fulltime lecturer and folksong collector and editor. His discovery of Huddie Ledbetter on a Louisiana prison farm led him and his son Alan to manage the career of the African-American singer called "Leadbelly" as well as to undertake folklore research and collecting for the Archive of American Folksong. The Lomaxes, using old aluminum discs and a cumbersome recording machine, captured some of the famous black singers of the era as well as Cajun songs and other southern music. Lomax and his son, who died in

2002, became the best-known folk music collectors and historians in the country.

Lomax has no place (except for an autobiography) on the literary side of the Age of Dobie, but he is an important figure in the cultural history of that period. And, as a pure folklorist, he is more important than Dobie, for Dobie was much less a folklorist than a popular storyteller. Dobie was not interested in the kind of folklore practiced by the members of the American Folklore Society and other trained, professional folklorists. He was not careful in recording the tales he heard, and he was willing to adapt what he learned from informants to his own ends as a storyteller. Dobie's main influence in his "age" was as a popular historian of Texas and the West, as a writer of tales, and as a scholar —at least in his books *The Mustangs* and *The Longhorns*. But most important, perhaps, is his role as a teacher and an arbiter and promoter of literary taste.

The era that I have called the "Age of Dobie" is very much in the un-ironic mode. Texas fiction and poetry were largely untouched by the modernist movement with its experimentation and irony and convolutions. The exception is Katherine Anne Porter, who, as she says, "got the hell out of Texas" as fast as she could. Her writing is definitely in the modernist mode, but by the time she became famous, she was hardly thought of as a Texas writer. Her renaissance as a Texas writer is very much a late-twentieth-century phenomenon. Aside from Porter, Texas had no Faulkner or Woolf, nor were there poets likely to be influenced by T. S. Eliot or E. E. Cummings. It is not true that all fiction had cowboys and Indians and schoolmarms as some have portrayed it, but it did tend to be linear in narrative and straightforward in theme and character. Those were the qualities of which Dobie approved. His affinity for the simple narrative of the folktales led many writers who lived in his era to practice a simple style and give a leading place to storytelling. The poetry, which I am not sure Dobie ever had much interest in, was as pre-modernist as the fiction. Writers who founded the Texas Poetry Society and who published the majority of the work before the age of McMurtry were as simple and clear as the fiction writers. Karle Wilson Baker, Arthur Sampley, Vaida and Whitney Montgomery, William E. Bard, Faye Carr Adams, Fay Yauger, Margaret Bell Houston (granddaughter of the hero of San Jacinto), Gene Shuford, and Berta Harte Nance were the poets of the age, and they all paid proper obeisance to Dobie in their writings. Dobie was the master. He was the man to please, for he had the outlets—a newspaper column, a radio show, and a pulpit in his classes, the Texas Folklore Society, and the Texas Institute of Letters. It did not do to neglect the great man. Not that he was mean or vindictive. It was just that he was "the bull of the woods" in Texas life and literature, and he required everyone's attention. In his role as Mr. Texas, he was the person New York called when it wanted information about Texas culture or literature. It is also worth noting that Dobie was invited to teach at Cambridge University in England in 1943–1944 and later lectured to American troops in England and—after the war—in Germany. Dobie's friend Webb also taught in England—first at the University of London in 1938 and then as Harmsworth Professor of History at Oxford in 1942–1943. But whether at home or abroad, Dobie and Webb valued the old ways of the West and the old tales from frontier times. And those writers who lived in the twentieth century and followed the Texana line. I am sure Dobie did not invent the term "Texana," but he certainly used it.

If there is one area where Dobie, Bedichek, and Webb are most a unit it is in the area of nature writing. All three wrote extensively about the flora and fauna of Texas, though Webb's main interest was in the effect that history had on the nature of the West—or the effect that nature had on the history of the West. His two great books, *The Great Plains* and *The Great*

Frontier, explain the West in terms of its natural resources, its climate, and the abuses man brought to the land. Published in 1931, *The Great Plains* explains many things about the area west of the 98th meridian that had puzzled historians and geographers for much of the nation's history. Webb pointed out that the region from the 98th to the California border was a great desert broken by oases—some of the oases created by mountains and some by rivers—but generally the area was arid and barely livable. Webb discusses the natural aspects of the region and the ways man has sought to outsmart nature. Though the population of the area has grown tremendously since 1931, journalist Joel Garreau in *The Nine Nations of North America* calls the Great Plains region "the empty quarter." In *The Great Frontier* (1952) Webb discusses Euro-American civilization for the past five hundred years in terms of the discovery of the western hemisphere and the resultant rise of capitalism and democracy. With the frontier now closed, Webb says, the world will find resources limited, and the world will come more and more dependent on state socialism and corporate monopoly.

The Age of Dobie lives today in many forms—in writers who subscribe to the naturalism of Bedichek, the history of Webb, and the realistic, romantic, and un-ironic doctrine of J. Frank Dobie. The best-known post-Dobie-era naturalist is John Graves, author of the celebrated *Goodbye to a River.* Graves acknowledges his debt to the Old Three in an essay he wrote in 1983 for the University of Texas Centennial, saying he read them "when I was a youth and young adult"; he came to maturity under the influence of Dobie, Bedichek, and Webb and still finds "magic in them." Rick Bass, now living in and writing about Montana, is another in the naturalist tradition, as are many lesser-known writers and ecologists. Writers like William A. Owens, philosophers like Pete Gunter, activists like Arch Fulgum, folklorists like Francis Abernethy, and politicians like Ralph Yarborough all had a hand in saving the Big Thicket from the timber industry and all readily admit a debt to Dobie, Bedichek, and Webb.

One of Webb's most popular books is *The Texas Rangers* (1935), the earliest serious study of the statewide police that began with a series of frontier Indian- and Mexican-fighting companies. The book's reputation among Anglos is much higher than it is among Mexican Americans, who argue that Webb is openly racist and fails to mention the racism inherent in the organization as it operated in South Texas—and in the early days deep into Mexico. One of the roles the Rangers played that rankles modern Mexican Americans was as protectors of white landowners and growers from the Mexicans and Mexican Americans who worked in the fields. Webb's well-researched and documented history of the Rangers does not go beyond the iconography of the Texas Ranger. If one thinks about the statue in the lobby of Love Field in Dallas that bears the famous inscription "One Riot, One Ranger," one can get a notion of Webb's view of the lawmen. (A ranger getting off a train in a riotous town was met by the local law who inquired why Austin had sent only one ranger. His reply, "You only got one riot, ain't you?") Stories like this are the stuff of stardom, and the movie industry has not failed to take advantage of the Ranger mystique. Hollywood began making movies about the Texas Rangers as early as 1910. The list of films about Rangers runs to hundreds, with such actors as John Wayne, Ward Bond, Willie Nelson, Nick Nolte, Clayton Moore, Clint Eastwood, Glenn Campbell, Gene Autry, Roy Rogers, Tom Mix, and George O'Brien playing Texas Rangers. In 1936, Webb received money and movie credit for a movie based on his book, but the film used the title and little else. The Texas Rangers are not merely movie figures, for real-life Rangers make up a large part of the folklore and history of Texas—men like Rip Ford, Bigfoot Wallace, Leander McNelly, the Spaniard Lone Wolf Gonzaullas, Frank Hamer (who set up the ambush of Bonnie and Clyde), Ben

McCulloch, James B. Gillette, and Sul Ross. And thousands of television watchers today probably think that the actor Chuck Norris of *Walker: Texas Ranger* is a real crime fighter. Not long ago *Texas Monthly* Magazine devoted its cover to a photograph of six-foot-five retired ranger, Joaquin Jackson, who appears as a sheriff in the Elmer Kelton film, *The Good Old Boys*. Jackson is the latest in a long line of Texas Rangers to be canonized by the media. He's at work on his autobiography, to be written with David Marion Wilkinson and called *Only One Ranger*. The digression above is not quite the sidetracked tale it seems, for by talking so much about the Rangers, I hope to show just how romantic and nostalgic the Age of Dobie was. Despite the sound scholarship and interesting projections of Webb's books on the Great Plains and the Great Frontier, he is still best known among ordinary Texans as the author of *The Texas Rangers*, which has an introduction by Lyndon B. Johnson.

The entire history project of the University of Texas is much in debt to Webb. His work in the Texas State Historical Association, his editing of *The Handbook of Texas* in 1952—later supplemented and even later completely rewritten in six huge volumes in the 1990s and now available on the Internet, his influence on the history collections in the Center for American History in Austin and collections in other universities, and his work with young historians remain notable.

Roy Bedichek's career is different from Dobie's and Webb's, but it bears some comment. Bedichek ran the University of Texas Extension Service's Interscholastic League. His job necessitated that he travel all over the state to visit the schools and supervise the various competitions—from athletic to academic. Bedichek drove his car with his tent in the trunk and camped out when he could. An especially keen observer of nature anyway, Bedichek's travels gave him the opportunity to observe the flora and fauna of the state and to study the land. When he was finally cajoled into writing about his travels and observations, he was able to "recollect in tranquility" all the things he had seen. Roy Bedichek was a good writer, and his *Adventures with a Texas Naturalist* is probably the best-written piece to come from the Triumvirate. *Adventures*, later followed by a series of essays on the Gulf Coast entitled *Karankaway Country*, continues Bedichek's ruminations on plants and animals and the geography of the Texas Gulf Coast. Bedichek, like Dobie and Webb, was not only an observer of nature but a man wedded to old ways of doing things. He favored free-range chickens and eggs that had not been laid by cooped hens. Not only were the Old Three naturalists and storytellers, they were sentimentalists and romantics. All three of them looked backward to a time when life was better and simpler. To read Dobie or Bedichek or Webb is to revisit a Golden Age when cattle and chickens ranged freely, when men were not hampered by excessive government regulation, and when bureaucrats did not run the world. There is the famous story of Dobie's jail time because he wouldn't pay a parking ticket. It was his God-given right to park his car at any hitching post without government interference. The jail scene (and it should be noted that Dobie was assigned a couple of days of clerical work) was also pure Dobie in that it put him again in the spotlight. If he had lived in a time of ubiquitous television news programs, Dobie would have been a danger to anyone who got between him and a camera.

Another little sidelight that may explain something about the Age of Dobie is the straight-laced nature of Dobie and his two close friends. Reading their works will not violate Trollope's dictum that the written word should not "bring a blush to a young girl's cheek." All three lived and wrote and acted in a world of strict conventions. One never cursed in front of the womenfolk. One never wrote the salacious or even the mildly off-color. A man always removed his hat in the presence of women and called them "Ma'am." As both Paul Patterson, the folklorist, and Elmer Kelton, the novelist who has over forty novels set in the West and all celebrating the same un-ironic values that Dobie espoused, have said in more than one place, the old-time cowboy was deathly afraid of a good woman. It seems to be the case with Dobie, Bedichek, and Webb. But Don Graham, in his collection *Giant Country*, has written that all three of them were in love with the scatological and salacious. The Old Three had notes for a book based on bathroom-wall graffiti, and the talk around the fire at Friday Mountain Ranch or Paisano was likely to be the kind heard in a smoker—or on present-day late-night television. The letters of the three men reveal much of this other side of the Holy Trinity. Graham's essay, "Pen Pals: Dobie, Bedichek, and Webb" will not please the worshipers at the shrine of the Old Three, for Graham has mined the letters and uncollected papers for every scrap of smut. He calls Bedichek "a master of the dirty joke" and says the naturalist "took a philosophical interest in excretory and sexual functions" (112–13). According to Graham, "Dobie was every bit as interested in sexual folklore as he was in cowboys and gold seekers" (113). The three of them envisioned a book—that never saw print—to be called *Piss & Vinegar* and another to have the odd title of *Privy Papers of Sitting Bull*. The latter was to be made up of dirty jokes going all the way back to Sam Houston, who, they claimed, "would ride across Texas with an erection and camp at a spot where the erection became limp" (114). Dobie, the folklorist, made his off-color collection a part of the profession. The great Ozark folklorist Vance Randolph made a collection similar to *Privy Papers*. It couldn't be published in his day, but four copies were made. One went into the library at the University of Arkansas, one was sold to Audie Murphy, and the other two can't be accounted for—at least by me.

To say that the Age of Dobie came to an end with his death in 1964 is to miss an important point about literary eras. And while the Age of McMurtry has been operative since the late fifties, it is easy to find many Texas writers today still living and practicing the kind of writing that Dobie taught the state to

value. Novelists like Elmer Kelton and the late Benjamin Capps
are clearly in the Dobie Age. The same is true of the late Tom
Lea, Jane Gilmore Rushing, and many others who have not paid
obeisance to the ironic mode.

The most significant heir to the world of Dobie, Bedichek,
and Webb is John Graves, called by someone in recent years
"Texas's most beloved writer." Graves embodies all the best qualities of the Old Three and is a much more elegant writer than his
predecessors. Graves is most like Bedichek in that he has devoted much of his life to the study of nature, but he has as clear a
grasp of the history of the region he has chosen to write about as
Webb, and he is as adept in telling stories about the old days in
his region as Dobie. Graves's career was quite different from the
careers of Dobie, Bedichek, and Webb. He has never had a permanent academic base the way they did, though he taught briefly
at the University of Texas just after World War II and spent a couple of years on the faculty at TCU during the time he was writing
Goodbye to a River, which came out in 1960 and made a great
nationwide splash. For most of the years since his first book came
out, he has lived on four hundred acres near Glen Rose that he
gave the name Hardscrabble. In addition to his first book, he has
published *Hardscrabble* and *From a Limestone Ledge*, both made up
of essays he has written about the life in and around his "place,"
as he calls it. He opens *Hardscrabble* this way:

> In Southwestern terms, it is not a big enough piece of
> land to be called a ranch without pretension, though that
> title is more loosely awarded these days than it used to be.
> Nor is enough of its surface arable to qualify it as a seri-
> ous farm. It is something less than four hundred acres of
> rough limestone hill country, partly covered with cedar
> and hardwood brush and partly open pasture. . . . (3)

This patch of ground has become, for Graves, the place he has chosen to look at nature and to live a life devoted to observation and reflection.

"Reflective" is the word that best describes John Graves. Most of his writing life has been spent observing and reflecting in the best tradition of the great American nature writers—Henry David Thoreau, Aldo Leopold, Edward Abbey, Barry Lopez, and, yes, Roy Bedichek. Graves is not a propagandist the way Thoreau and Abbey were but is more at home simply explaining what he sees and where he lives. One does not get the sense that Graves has, like Thoreau, felt the need to trumpet the fact that he has decided to back life into a corner and strip away all that is not life, though it can be argued that he has done exactly that. He is not a sermonizer; he is not at war with what Abbey calls "industrial tourism," though I suspect that he is not an advocate of it. Even in *Goodbye to a River*, his account of a canoe trip down a part of the Brazos River before the stream was dammed up, there is no strident attack on progress. He simply wants to take a last look at the river that was so much a part of the history and folklore of the region he refers to as, variously, "the Palo Pinto country" and "Tonk country."

After a degree in English at Rice University in 1942, service in the U.S. Marine Corps in World War II, and a master's degree at Columbia University, he spent several years in Europe—mainly Spain and Mallorca—working at fiction. He published a few stories, but never published "A Speckled Horse" or the other long fiction he wrote during these years. He says in *A John Graves Reader* that the novel is "a form for which I seem to be definitely unsuited" (291). After his sojourn in Europe, his father's illness brought him back to his native Fort Worth where he taught at TCU, spent weekends in "the Tonk country," and discovered the kind of writing that he has proven to be a master at. After a few years of visiting Hardscrabble on weekends, he decided to make it his permanent place of residence. And it is from there that he works his place, reads widely, studies the natural world, and writes essays. He is primarily an essayist, and his concerns are the "simple awareness of natural rhythms and ways while living on the land and through the seasons' cycle, year by year" (*Reader* 27). Like Verlyn Klinkenborg, the nature writer whose essays appear in *The New York Times*, Graves is aware of "wild creatures and plants and the way they function with dirt and terrain and climate to shape a whole pattern of livingness, even in tired and diminished places. Even here" (27).

Since he is mainly an essayist, his ruminations come in small but important studies of birds or plants or people who inhabit the land. Even his longest sustained work, *Goodbye to a River*, is essentially a series of essays as he moves from Possum Kingdom Dam in "the Palo Pinto country" down to where Highway 67 crosses the Brazos not far from Glen Rose in Somervell County. Along the way, he describes the lie of the land, the creatures and humans he sees, and remembers the days of the early settlers who drove out the Comanches and Tonkawas and Lipan Apaches. The book's glory is that John Graves does, in such short space, what Dobie, Webb, and Bedichek spent their lives attempting. He captures the history, the folklore, and the nature of a patch of Texas in a work that is as excellent as any writings of the "Holy Trinity."

Over the years, Graves has written a number of essays and introductions to the books of others, and all of these works have the same serious stamp found in what one might call his major works. A number of them appear in *A John Graves Reader* and some of the pieces have come out as small volumes—*Blue and Some Other Dogs* and *The Last Running*. He has contributed significant essays to several books of photographs with artists Jim Bones and Wyman Minzer and an introduction to the Gentling Brothers' great portfolio of paintings, *The Birds of Texas*. Even the essays in collaboration with photographers and painters turn out to be works or art, for John Graves is dedicated to excellence in every word he writes. And well past the Age of Dobie—and perhaps even past the Age of McMurtry—Graves continues the sometimes romantic, never ironic, traditions of the Old Guard.

I think Texas replicated the twenty-five-hundred-year cycle that Northrop Frye talks about in the short period from 1920 or so until the present. Our gods and heroes were the men and women who came from the old states to settle in Austin's colony and other colonies between 1821 and 1836 when Texas fought for independence. The heroes were Houston and Crockett and Bowie and Travis and lesser figures like Bigfoot Wallace and Deaf Smith and Noah Smithwick, an early chronicler of the state. These heroes have over the years passed into myth and have achieved near godlike status—at least in the minds of the Daughters of the Republic of Texas and descendants of the Old Three Hundred. Early books about Texas made Bigfoot Wallace a figure of legend like Paul Bunyan. And Josiah Wilbarger, the man who was scalped and lived to tell about it, has moved into legend so that people who don't even remember the story know that some famous Texan of eons ago lost his scalp to the Indians and survived to have a county named after him. The legendary figures of Texas include the kidnapped Cynthia Ann Parker, who was discovered among the Comanches many years after her capture and returned to "civilization" where she sickened and died. Her son, Quanah Parker, attained legendary status himself in the late nineteenth and early twentieth centuries—he died in 1911—when he made a successful conversion to Anglo life. He became a wealthy cattleman and was part owner of the Quanah, Acme, and Pacific Railroad. He never completely took on white ways, even though he was a friend of President Theodore Roosevelt, for he refused to convert to Christianity and insisted on keeping his seven wives. A Texas town near the Red River is named for him.

But if anybody represents the true hero of the Age of Dobie it is Charlie Goodnight. Dobie of course wrote about him, and the

ultraconservative historian and rancher J. Evetts Haley wrote the
definitive biography of him in 1936. Goodnight, who was present
at the recapture of Cynthia Ann Parker, blazed trails, fought
Indians, and established ranches. His most famous ranching project may have been to use the Palo Duro Canyon in the Llano
Estacado as a ranch. Goodnight lived until the end of 1929, and
the novelist Benjamin Capps once told me that when he went, as
a child, to Archer City one day, he heard talk among the grown-
ups that Charlie Goodnight had just died. Young Ben Capps was
amazed, for like most Texans, he assumed that the legendary cattleman had been dead for decades. Goodnight's fame as an independent cowman and Texan "out of the old rock" was such that
he is the prototype for all the big ranchmen of Texas fiction and
folklore. It is easy to see Goodnight in such characters as Kelton's
Frank Claymore in *Stand Proud* and Benjamin Capps's *Sam
Chance*. In fact, Capps once told me that he based *Sam Chance* on
Goodnight. Nobody writing about a Texas cowman is free from
the shadow of Charlie Goodnight. Even Larry McMurtry gives us
a version of Goodnight and Oliver Loving in *Lonesome Dove*,
using the story that Haley tells about how Charlie Goodnight
packed Oliver Loving's body in a charcoal-filled metal casket and
returned his body from New Mexico, where he was killed by
Comanches, to Weatherford for burial. Loving is buried in the
Greenwood Cemetery near the grave of the first famous black
Texan, Bose Ikard, a cowboy who rode with Goodnight and
Loving and who himself is a character made famous in Texas fiction. When Ikard died in 1929, Goodnight had a gravestone
erected over the African American cowboy that read, "Bose Ikard
served with me four years on the Goodnight-Loving Trail, never
shirked a duty or disobeyed an order, rode with me in many stam-
pedes, participated in three engagements with Comanches, splen-
did behavior." Goodnight said of Bose Ikard, born a slave in
Mississippi, that he trusted him "farther than any living man."
These men, and many like them, are men who peopled the West

that Dobie loved and sold to Texans and other Americans. There is no doubt that among these men there were "giants in the earth" and that their story is worth telling again and again.

The Age of McMurtry

2

Toward the end of J. Frank Dobie's life, things took a sharp left turn in Texas politics, literature, and culture. Politically, Dobie and many of his allies were old-line liberals of the Roosevelt-Truman stripe, minority liberals in a conservative, one-party Democratic state led by such notables as Pa Ferguson, Coke Stevenson, John Nance Garner, William P. Hobby, Sr., Sam Rayburn, and Lyndon B. Johnson. There had always been a number of Dobie liberals in Texas, but the new liberals of the sixties were of a kind that Dobie and his ilk were not prepared for. These new men and women were more obstreperous, more inclined to march for what they believed in, more racially and ethnically liberal, more radical in all ways. The new trends in politics started slowly: a genuine liberal, Ralph Yarborough, was elected to the U.S. Senate. What had been a relative handful of Bohemians seen on campuses and at Scholz Beer Garten in Austin morphed into Beats and then hippies and Yippies and Peaceniks. They fought against segregation; they marched with farm workers; they formed a new brand of Democrats and began publishing *The Texas Observer*; they exulted in the election of John Kennedy and mourned over his death

in Texas; they radicalized the campuses and fought the establishment; and, once Vietnam bogged the country down, they demon-
strated against Lyndon Johnson and "his" war. In many ways, the
rise of the new liberalism made the conservative Democrats see a
new light and shift to the Republican Party, the natural home of
many of the conservative Democrats. Democrats like Phil Gramm
and John Connally and Rick Perry shifted allegiance to the party
of Richard Nixon and Ronald Reagan. The political revolution in
Texas took place during the sixties and seventies, about the same
time Larry McMurtry and a new wave of writers burst upon the
scene.

The changes from conservative to liberal lasted much longer
in literature than in the political culture of Texas. For a while
there it seemed that Texas was abandoning the old ways of con-
servatism and reactionary politics. In the sixties, it seemed that a
real revolution might be taking place. It turns out, of course, that
the political winds did not blow strongly, for by the end of the
century, the reaction had set in and the state was firmly in right-
wing hands; those Democrats who became Republicans were just
the beginning of the trend away from liberalism.

The changing of parties fitted a pattern that should have
been predictable. After all, Oveta Culp Hobby, whose husband
had been a Democratic governor and whose son was to serve for
more than a decade as lieutenant governor, had come out for
Eisenhower in 1952 and was made the first secretary of Health,
Education and Welfare. Governor Alan Shivers, elected as a
Democrat, led the "Shivercrats" into the Eisenhower camp
against Adlai Stevenson. Most people were pretty clear that the
Democrats in Texas were not heavily committed to the national
party. During the fifties, the liberals saw as their enemies Sam
Rayburn and Lyndon Johnson. It was only later that Lyndon B.
Johnson began his crusades for voting rights and "the Great
Society." Even when Johnson was pushing for the Voting Rights

Act and the establishment of reforms like Medicare, the state was only mildly liberal, though it looked for a time as if the conservative state of Texas was joining the mainstream Democratic Party.

What seemed to be taking place in politics in the middle of the century was also taking place in literature and music and the general culture of Texas. The mid-to-latter part of the twentieth century in both Texas and the rest of the nation reminds one of many reactions to ages of progress and exuberance. The Victorian Age in Britain and America gave way to revolution and reform in both literature and politics. In Europe at the end of the nineteenth century, during what some have called the "Yellow Nineties," writers like Oscar Wilde, Aubrey Beardsley, Stephane Mallarme, Joris Karl Huysmans, Charles Baudelaire, and Algernon Swinburne broke away from what many saw as the certainties of a Victorian world. It was the beginning of a new round of literary decadence, and what took place in Texas in the 1960s was the beginning of a similar literary decadence.

Literary decadence is not a pejorative term: it simply means that the literature turns from robust and energetic to ironic and satiric, and in many case to experimentalism of form. Alfred Lord Tennyson gives way to T. S. Eliot, Charles Dickens to Virginia Woolf. One good description of literary decadence in general and in America is by critic Thomas Beers in his book called *The Mauve Decade*. Beers discusses the literary reaction against American Victorianism at the end of the century. He demonstrates that all across the land there was a strong reaction to what Mark Twain and Charles Dudley Warner called, in a co-written novel, *The Gilded Age*. Twain and Warner described a period when big business ran rampant, when railroads crossed the continent, and government giveaways to the railroads made men like C. P. Huntington, Charles Crocker, Leland Stanford, and Mark Hopkins rich at the peoples' expense. This was an era when John D. Rockefeller and his peers created huge monopolies and when politicians truly believed that the business of government was business. (That phrase belongs to Calvin Coolidge, who came along a generation or more after "the Gilded Age," but who still admired the robber barons and the rapacious corporations.) Writers like Frank Norris attacked the giant corporations; Upton Sinclair raked unscrupulous businessmen over the sharp edges of his pen; politicians like Eugene V. Debs began serious leftist movements. The labor unions were in their infancy. Journalistic muckrakers like Lincoln Steffens and Ida Tarbell Baker began pointing out the crookedness of city and state governments and the sickness of business society. In American literature the imagists flourished and T. S. Eliot and Ezra Pound stirred up both poetry and criticism. The late nineteenth century saw the beginnings of existentialism, a philosophical movement most people associate with the French intellectuals of the immediate post-World War II era. But existentialism is clearly the defining factor in the novels and poems of Thomas Hardy, the poems of A. E. Housman, the stories and novels of Ernest Hemingway. The German philosopher Friederich Nietzsche laid down many of the principles of the movement: God is dead, life is absurd, man is free either to become a superman or live in chaotic misery. Nietzsche's effects were not much felt in the Texas of the early and mid-twentieth century and certainly not in the works of Dobie and his followers. Life has meaning for them, nature has meaning, progress is possible, and there are some eternal verities. But there are no eternal, essential verities in Hardy, Hemingway, Housman. Man is "a stranger and afraid in a world he never made," Housman says, and his line is echoed in French existentialist Albert Camus's novel title, *The Stranger*, one of the chief documents of the age, and a work clearly influential in the Age of McMurtry.

In Texas about the time of the death of Dobie, movements mirrored those of fin de siècle America and Britain and France and much of Europe. Certainties faded, and there were strong reactions against entrenched political bosses like Lyndon Johnson and Sam Rayburn and John Connally. There was a stirring of union sentiment in a so-called "right-to-work" state. We saw the Old West of Dobie satirized, and the sacred cow of the oil industry, the 27.5% depletion allowance, come under fire. The sixties found us facing campus unrest like the rest of the nation, and writers like Larry McMurtry, Billie Lee Brammer, Edwin "Bud" Shrake, and a small host of others began looking beyond the cult of Longhorn and Aggie football, the adoration of the old trail drivers and cowpunchers, and the sanctity of the Alamo. Three years before Dobie died in 1964, both Billie Lee Brammer and Larry McMurtry published their first novels. Both were departures from what one had come to expect from Texas writers. Brammer's *The Gay Place* pictured a Texas in a state of serious change. Liberals were making a stir in Austin, and the governor of the state, Arthur "Goddam" Fenstermaker, was making liberal noises under his supposed conservative banner, much as Lyndon B. Johnson was to do later in his career. Fenstermaker was clearly a take-off on Johnson, soon to be president of the United States. The crudity that Johnson's intimates had always seen in private was unveiled for the public—and LBJ was not amused. Nor were the more solid of Texas citizens. Partly because there was "language" and the sexual activities were not merely hinted at, Johnson is supposed to have told Billie Lee that he could not get far into *The Gay Place* because it was too dirty for him. This from a man whose language was as crude as some of his actions.

While Brammer wrote harshly about Texas politics, Larry McMurtry took a dimmer view of the ranchman's world than Dobie ever did. In McMurtry's novel, which Tom Pilkington said "dragged the western kicking and screaming into the twentieth century" (*Literary History of the American West*, 511), we see a

West in a sharp moral decline. Hud, the character who lent his name to the movie made from McMurtry's novel, was not interested in the virtues that Dobie had long espoused for the western hero. Homer Bannon, Hud's stepfather, is out of what Dobie called "the old rock," but Hud kills him and will sell off the land that Bannon has nurtured for so long. Hud is only interested in the money to be made off the ranch, and he does not care how the money comes in. He will drill for oil on land that Homer held sacred for cattle, and Hud is not above selling the diseased cattle that Old Wild Horse Homer Bannon had to kill in the novel.

What Pilkington is really telling us by saying that McMurtry dragged the western into the twentieth century is that he turned the western from romantic/realistic fiction toward the ironic, that he helped to institute a revolution in literature in the state. Since irony is the mark of a decadent literary period and since there is always a movement in a literary and cultural period from myth and romance toward realism and irony, this mauve period in Texas literature and culture was to be expected. McMurtry, Shrake, Brammer, Dan Jenkins, and a dozen other writers of the period are ironists and satirists. Irony shows the reality behind the sham. Satire has been defined as poking fun at people and institutions in order to reform them, but another definition of satire is that it simply makes fun of people and institutions. Period. All the writers who might be called mauve were practitioners of irony and satire. McMurtry's first three novels satirize the ranching West and the small towns in ranch country. Jenkins takes on sports and sportsmen. Shrake satirizes the whole culture of Texas from cities to industrialists to politicians. Brammer largely confines his satire to the political and social scene. Even a straight-line West Texas writer like Jane Gilmore Rushing wrote a 1961 short story entitled "Against the Moon," which painted an ironic picture of ranch women. (The story was turned into a novel in 1968 and elaborated on the theme of the young wife whose husband and the other menfolk are interested in hunting and cowboying and expect " the little woman" to stay home contentedly.)

The cities had already come under some fire before the Age of McMurtry was underway. Two Fort Worth novels of an earlier period give unflattering pictures of city life. In 1926, a journalist named Frank Elser wrote a novel entitled *The Keen Desire,* which showed the underside of Fort Worth's Tenderloin area and the rackety world of newspaper life. Then in 1941, James Atlee Phillips wrote a scathing novel about Fort Worth and its country club set. *The Inheritors* pictured Fort Worth as a place of Philistines and trust-fund trash. The novel did not have a terrific impact across the state and nation, but it rubbed some Fort Worthians raw. In 1952, Madison Cooper's novel of Waco life, *Sironia, Texas,* created a similar stir in Waco. Cooper's incredibly long and detailed depiction of upscale and downscale Waco lambasted this old cotton city on the Brazos. These city novels ran counter to the old romantic Texas of Dobie and company, for they came before a time when irony had become endemic. Shortly before McMurtry's first novel, Hermes Nye wrote *Fortune Is a Woman* (1958), a small paperback original about Dallas in the 1930s that was a mild slap at the eastern-leaning and upwardly striving city on the Trinity. It never got the audience it deserved because it was a hundred-thousand-copy paperback and passed largely unnoticed except among Nye's friends. Nye, a lawyer, writer, folklorist, and coffeehouse singer, had his autograph party at a cut-rate drugstore in Dallas, which lays another layer of irony on Texas life and culture.

Beginning in the mid-fifties, even outsiders began taking an ironic and satiric look at Texas. Edna Ferber's *Giant* and the movie that followed it laid bare a number of flaws found in Texas life. She exposes matters of bigotry, vulgarity, and political malfeasance. It was one thing for an outsider like Ferber to take on the Texas myth, but when natives began what turned out to be a relentless assault on the shibboleths of Texas, the day of Dobie's certainties was almost over. Elser and Phillips and Cooper and Hermes Nye constituted a small and barely burbling spring, but with McMurtry and those of his generation, the spring became a river of discontent.

Another Texan, Terry Southern, may exemplify the ironic even more strongly than McMurtry and Brammer. Southern (1924–1995) made such a splash outside Texas that he is often overlooked as a native writer. Born in Alvarado, a small town twenty-five miles south of Fort Worth, Southern attended Southern Methodist University before he saw service in World War II. After the war he took a degree in philosophy from Northwestern University and went to Paris to study at the Sorbonne on what remained of his G. I. Bill. In France, he wrote a story for George Plimpton's inaugural issue of *The Paris Review,* and in 1958, three years before McMurtry and Brammer saw their first novels in print, Southern published *Flash and Filigree* and the next year, *The Magic Christian.* His novel *Candy* (cowritten with Mason Hoffenberg) was published in the United States but later had the distinction of being banned in France. It was made into an unsuccessful film in 1968. Needless to say, *Candy* was not the sort of thing that Dobie or the establishment figures of the Texas Institute of Letters of the fifties would have approved. Several of Southern's Texas stories came out as early as 1955 and are reprinted in his 1967 collection, *Red Dirt Marijuana and Other Tastes.* A few of stories in *Red Dirt Marijuana* reappear in his 1991 novel, *Texas Summer,* one of his few works set in Texas. For a number of years following his early novels, he devoted himself to screenwriting, authoring or coauthoring some of the great cult films of the sixties. He cowrote *Dr. Strangelove* with director Stanley Kubrick in 1964, the year Dobie died. *Strangelove* became the signature movie of the antiwar period, and it is always listed among the greatest films ever made. Peter Sellers, who played several roles, most notably the Kissinger-like Strangelove, is stamped on the sixties as almost no other actor unless it is Peter Fonda, who starred with Dennis Hopper and Jack Nicholson in Southern's *Easy Rider* (cowritten with Fonda and Hopper). Southern also adapted Evelyn Waugh's novel *The Loved One* for the movies, and he wrote the Jane Fonda film *Barbarella* and adapted John Fowles' novel *The Collector* for the movies. Terry Southern spent a couple of years in the early 1980s as a writer on the television show *Saturday Night Live*. He ended his career teaching screenwriting at Columbia University. It may help to place Southern firmly in this era of Beats and hippies by remembering that he is the only writer to appear on the cover of the Beatles' famous album *Sgt. Pepper's Lonely Hearts Club Band*.

During these years other writers began presenting a picture of Texas that would have been out of kilter with the works of the Old Three. Edwin Shrake's *But Not for Love* came out the same year as *Horseman, Pass By* and *The Gay Place*. In that novel, Shrake not only gives us pictures of Bohemian life in Fort Worth, but he excoriates the new millionaires who were making Texas a center for industries like electronics. And, like the others, Shrake is not careful of his language—or perhaps he is careful to shock by being the first writer to use the "m-f" word in Texas fiction. This new and irreverent brand of writing took place at a time when teachers were being fired for teaching J. D. Salinger's *The Catcher in the Rye* because of its use of the "f" word.

If you discount Terry Southern, who is the most un-Texan of Texas writers, Brammer and McMurtry and Shrake made up the vanguard of Texas writing and are the chief figures who taught us to see a new Texas. Things in Texas literature were never the same after these writers led the way. I am not sure that either Brammer or McMurtry meant to usher in a new age, but they did. Brammer, who only wrote the one novel, is, in certain quarters, a revered figure, but he is remembered as much for the waste of his life as for the novel. A talented journalist, Brammer succumbed to the drug culture and died early of an overdose. He is still remembered fondly by people who knew him and who have celebrated him in books and articles, but it is McMurtry who became the representative of his age, the leader in the anti-Dobie movement. His leadership is made clear by his early essay "Southwestern Literature?" in his 1968 book of essays, *In a Narrow Grave*, and his later "Ever a Bridegroom" in the *Texas Observer* in 1981. McMurtry has remained the writer most often referred to as the star of Texas fiction. But it can be argued that he just happened to come along at a time when a new Texas was being born. But there is no doubt that he did much to make the Texas of the second half of the twentieth century markedly different from the Age of Dobie.

McMurtry created a Texas that looked different from the Texas of Dobie. Even in his novels about ranch life, McMurtry is aware that the acids of modernity were eating away at the Texas of Charlie Goodnight and Shanghai Pierce and Teddy Blue Abbott. From *Horseman, Pass By* to his recent works, life on the plains and prairies and ranches lacks the solidity of the world Dobie lived in and wrote about. The exuberance of the Texas mystique is gone, ranches are being broken up, cattlemen are losing their independence, and small towns are dying off. The few McMurtry characters who resemble Dobie heroes are clearly pictured as a few years away from extinction. Homer Bannon of *Horseman, Pass By*, Gideon Fry of *Leaving Cheyenne*, and Roger Waggoner of *Moving On* may have the traits that Dobie so admired in his old-timers, but they are dinosaurs in a world of oil wells and private planes.

One serious departure McMurtry makes from the realism/romanticism of Dobie is that the younger writer fills his world with grotesques and caricatures who reflect the absurd state of the world and the existentialism that was creeping into modern Texas. As time passed and McMurtry became a success, the number of characters who are outright grotesques increases. In his first three novels, *Horseman, Pass By*, *Leaving Cheyenne*, and *The Last Picture Show*, we have our fill of satiric portraits, but few of them are the unbelievables and grotesques seen in his later novels. His novels of the seventies and beyond introduce us to characters as absurd as Danny Deck in *Some Can Whistle* or Vernon Dalhart in *Terms of Endearment* or Uncle El and his workers in *All My Friends Are Going to Be Strangers*. But even when McMurtry's characters are not as outlandish as Godwin Lloyd-Jons of *All My Friends Are Going to Be Strangers* and *Some Can Whistle* or the seven-foot-tall African, Mesty-Woolah, of *Anything for Billy*, McMurtry's characters tend to be caricatures of one kind or another. Even the old Texas Rangers Woodrow Call and Gus McCray are eccentric caricatures. Neither is a round character who makes us see the human side of people. They are types out of the western movies. Call is the stiff-upper-lip cowboy hero seen so often in Gary Cooper or John Wayne movies. Gus is the garrulous sidekick who is part Gabby Hayes and part James Stewart. It is instructive to note that McMurtry conceived these characters as movie heroes and hoped that he could sell a script that would attract John Wayne to play Call, James Stewart as Gus, and Henry Fonda as Jake. But none wanted to play a character declining into old age, so McMurtry turned his film project into a novel. In the television miniseries, Tommy Lee Jones and Robert Duvall are better as Woodrow Call and Gus McRae than the Duke and James Stewart would have been, and Jake, who is hanged in mid-series, could have been played by almost anyone. In *Lonesome Dove* we see not only cowboy stereotypes but cartoon characters like the girl who can run faster than the wind and the dastardly and unbelievable Indian Blue Duck, the murderous Indian.

Part of the reason for the proliferation of McMurtry's eccentrics is that after the film success of *Hud* and *The Last Picture Show*, he has tended to see his work in terms of film scripts.

And films about modern Texas almost demand a cast of eccentrics the way earlier films about the Lone Star State required steely-eyed cowmen like John Wayne in *Red River*. It may be that one of the things that distinguished the Age of McMurtry from the Age of Dobie is the pervasive effect of the movies on American life. There were movies during Dobie's period of ascendancy, of course, but the movies about Texas were most often horse operas or celebrations of the Alamo, the Republic, and the early days of the Lone Star State. But from *Giant* (1956) forward, the picture of Texas that emerged in the movies tended to show the greed of the oil barons, the rapacious nature of the cattle kings, and the vulgarity of Texans. James Dean's Jett Rink in *Giant* is emblematic of the kind of vulgarity Texans indulged in when they struck it rich. Even if the emerging picture of Texas was overdone and satiric, it became the way America saw Texas, and writers from McMurtry onward were likely to show us a Texas of absurdity.

Absurdity reigns in the novels of others in this period of revolution, decadence, and existentialism in Texas writing. Edwin Shrake, more at home in the wild and whirling world of Brammer and other overt radicals, may have been quite sure that he was involved in a revolution. A sports journalist, Shrake was a member of the group that Jay Milner writes about in his *Confessions of a Mad Dog*. The group that some called "Mad Dog Inc." included Milner, Brammer, Larry L. King, Gary Cartwright, Willie Morris, Pete Gent, Ann and David Richards, and—to a lesser degree—Dan Jenkins. The Mad Dogs, except for Jenkins, were far to the left of McMurtry.

It hardly needs to be said that Texas had been content with itself from the days of San Jacinto until the late 1950s. For most of its history it had been the largest of "the forty-eight." It had cattle and oil and land. And the land that was not in private ownership had been left to Texas by the annexation agreement in

1845. No other state controlled its public lands, and Texas's ownership of those lands paid off handsomely when oil was struck on
state land and a great amount of money was set aside for the
Permanent University Fund devoted to the University of Texas
and Texas A&M University. Texas was, to quote George Sessions
Perry, "a world in itself." But the aftermath of World War II
changed all that—or began the change. The fifties and sixties
began the shattering changes in old Texas. The Lone Star joined
the Union and began to savor all the angst, disillusionment, existentialism, bohemianism, and literary Modernism of the rest of
the country. Television and film helped defeat Texan insularity.
The eternal verities had long since been called into question in
much of the world, but French intellectuals like Albert Camus
and John Paul Sartre made existentialism a byword in the colleges
of the East and finally in small pockets in Texas by the late fifties.
Young Texans, urged on by the French and by Jack Kerouac and
Alan Ginsburg and the Beats of San Francisco, began to be
ashamed of the state in a way that would not have occurred to J.
Frank Dobie.

And then the election of John F. Kennedy did much to high-
light Texas as the land of the misbegotten. Despite the fact that
Kennedy chose Lyndon Johnson as his running mate, rabid right-
wing Texans went after the Irish Catholic Kennedy in full cry. The
Reverend Wally Amos Criswell, pastor of the largest Baptist
church in Christendom (that absurd billing was often promoted
by the First Baptist Church of Dallas in Criswell's day), wrote a
tract against Kennedy before the Massachusetts senator had
secured the nomination. Dallas oil millionaire H. L. Hunt had the
screed printed and personally slipped copies under the doors of
the delegates to the Democratic nominating convention. Even
worse, the bumbling Hunt was caught doing it. After Kennedy
was elected, the right wing in Texas became even more virulent.
A crowd in Dallas spat on Lyndon Johnson and Lady Bird, and

someone hit United Nations Ambassador Adlai Stevenson with a placard on a visit to Dallas.

Before Kennedy could serve out his term, he was killed in Dallas, the home of Neiman Marcus, H. L. Hunt, Lee Harvey Oswald, W. A. Criswell, and Jack Ruby. The aftermath of the murder of Kennedy cast a blight on Texas that lasted for a long time in the nation's consciousness and for an even longer time in Texas. Someone said, after the assassination, "It could have happened anywhere." Some disaffected Texan replied, "But it didn't." That retort was played up for years as a comment on Texas lawlessness. Kennedy's election had given the political left in Texas a life. Until the late fifties, Texas had been far to the right of most of the country. The Democrats who controlled Texas politics had been much more conservative than even northeastern Republicans. John Kennedy was in Texas on November 22, 1963, to help patch up differences between the old-right Democrats like John Connally and the new liberals represented by Senator Ralph W. Yarborough, Maury Maverick, Jr., and Henry B. Gonzalez. (Nelly Connally, in a 2003 memoir, denies that Kennedy was in Texas to patch up a rift, but her arguments are not fully believable.) John Connally, the sitting governor, had long been a sworn enemy of Ralph Yarborough and the "Democrats of Texas," an organization founded, and funded, by Ms. Frankie Randolph of Houston.

McMurtry was never the kind of outspoken liberal that Willie Morris was. Mississippian Morris was a crusading editor of *The Daily Texan* at the University of Texas, a Rhodes Scholar, and Ronnie Dugger's successor as editor of *The Texas Observer*, the state's only liberal publication at the time. Morris later went on to become editor of *Harper's*. Under his hand, the staid old magazine published Norman Mailer and other radicals in its pages. Morris at *Harper's* was helpful to the career of Larry L. King, as irreverent and anarchistic a writer as any to come from the Lone Star State.

Though not much is made of politics in McMurtry's essays or public pronouncements, it may be that the millionaire entrepreneur of Archer City has not outgrown his liberal ways. In March of 2002 he wrote a tongue-in-cheek article for the *Los Angeles Times* in which he takes some shots at the Bush administration and the Iraq war. In his essay, he casts the war as a movie with Tom Cruise playing George Bush and Jack Nicholson playing Vice President Dick Cheney. Of Cheney he says, "cooped up as he is, lurching only rarely out of his grotto to deliver his grumpy, power-to-the-powerful utterances, he almost achieves malevolence. And nobody beats Jack at malevolence" (11 Mar. 2002, B13). Other actors cast in McMurtry's projected movie are Clint Eastwood as General Tommy Franks, Meryl Streep as Laura Bush, and Adam Schindler as press spokesman Ari Fleischer. So apparently the enfant terrible of early days still rides the journalistic range.

The "better dead than red" ethic of the Joseph McCarthy's rabid anti-communism and right-wing ideology was challenged by more and more citizens. Larry McMurtry, Grover Lewis, and John Lewis, then students at North Texas State College, published a little mimeographed sheet called *CoExistence Review* that was a precursor of many of the underground papers that began to be published in Texas and the United States as the fifties and sixties saw a heightened awareness of liberal values. McMurtry and his colleagues were early in the era of change, for McMurtry was graduated from North Texas State in 1957.

The late fifties began the age of the underground newspaper of protest and cynicism. *The Village Voice*, the most famous of the alternative papers was begun in New York in 1955, and it was not until the sixties that the country was awash with underground papers of all sorts promoting radicalism, drugs, sex, rock 'n' roll, and civil rights. *The L.A. Free Press* was started in 1964, *The Berkeley Barb* in 1965, and *The San Francisco Oracle* in 1966. In 1968 Brent Stein, using the name Stoney Burns, began the radical Dallas paper *Notes from the Underground,* a paper quickly dismantled by the Dallas Police Department. But it was back in circulation within a few days.

By the sixties, rock music had progressed (or regressed in the minds of the mainstream Americans of the time) from the raucous lyrics of Elvis Presley and Little Richard and Texan Buddy Holly to the left-leaning, heavily antiestablishment works of Bob Dylan and a host of radical singers. In 1963, Bob Dylan's first album came out. It was titled *The Freewheelin' Bob Dylan* and included such songs as "Blowing in the Wind," "Masters of War," and "Talkin' World War III Blues." Dylan had begun life as Bob Zimmerman, a Jew from Minnesota, but he renamed himself in honor of Dylan Thomas, the antiestablishment Welshman who died of drink in New York City in 1953. Dylan Thomas's two successful reading tours of the United States made him a cult figure among the young of the emerging Bohemian revolution, and his remarkable readings helped give rise to the poetry readings in coffeehouses around the country.

Young Bob Dylan's songs played off many anti-establishment themes. He was influenced by the songs of the disaffected: Mississippi Delta blues, gospel songs of backwoods churches, protest songs from the Depression era, and mountain music before it became Grand Ole Opry fare. Dylan's songs have hints of Jimmie Rodgers and Leadbelly and Woody Guthrie and the Reverend Thomas A. Dorsey, gospel singer and author of "Precious Lord Take My Hand." Dylan signaled to the new generation that "The Times They Are A-changin'." The radical Weathermen, who espoused revolution in American, took their name from Dylan lyrics that ran, "You don't need a weatherman to tell which way the wind blows." Answers were indeed "blowin' in the wind."

Not only did we see the rise of underground papers in Dallas and Houston and Austin, but little towns like Denton had an antiestablishment paper called *The Denton Voice* in imitation of New York's *Village Voice*. Most of these papers were short-lived, but they had a serious impact on college students and left-leaning intellectuals. TCU's distinguished historian Paul Boller, who taught at SMU in the fifties and sixties, found himself in hot water with the Dallas establishment and was referred to by the *Dallas Morning News* as "an obscure professor" who was making trouble on the Hilltop, as SMU styled itself. Like many liberal professors, Boller was under an unofficial indictment by the conservative establishment. His book, *Memoirs of an Obscure Professor*, is an accurate portrayal of the way the leaders of Texas fought the changing times. *The Dallas Morning News* of that era presented the college professor in cartoons wearing tennis shoes, a beret, a ratty Van Dyke beard, and smoking through a cigarette holder. If the state of Texas had an official reactionary newspaper in the fifties and sixties, it was the *Dallas Morning News*, though there was no real liberal media outside the underground papers and *The Texas Observer*. The *News* was the standard bearer for the Hard Right, just as Dallas was home to some of the country's most reactionary citizens. Among the more flagrant was H. L. Hunt, who wrote a book called *Alpaca* (1960), which espoused the notion that people should be given votes in proportion to their wealth. In the 1950s Hunt met Dan Smoot, an SMU graduate and former FBI man who was an early member of the John Birch Society, and sponsored him on a radio show called "Facts Forum." Hunt also sponsored a radio show called "Life Line," a program of right-wing politics and fundamentalist Christianity. Dallas elected a Republican congressman named Bruce Alger who was one of the most reactionary politicians ever to serve in the U.S. House—at least before the days of Dick Armey and Tom DeLay. General Edwin A. Walker (whose flagpole flew the American flag upside down as a sign of distress) had been dismissed from the army for proselytizing for the right. He lived in a mansion on Turtle Creek

Boulevard and was probably the target of Lee Harvey Oswald's first assassination attempt.

Dallas was also home to Melvin E. Bradford of the University of Dallas, once the Wallace Party chairman for the county and later a Republican spokesman. During Ronald Reagan's first term, Mel Bradford was nominated for director of the National Endowment for the Humanities, but he was adjudged by Reagan conservatives as too right-wing and denied the post. Another Dallasite with far-right credentials was Bill Carruth, a John Bircher, whose fortune derived from early Dallas settlers. Carruth was a quieter voice who joined with Bradford and others to espouse right-wing causes. Long after the leftist fervor had died down, Carruth sought to become a behind-the-scenes mover for right-wing ideas in Dallas and at the University of North Texas, McMurtry's alma mater. But despite all the reactionary fervor in Dallas in the fifties and sixties, there was a strong coffeehouse/folk singing flavor that mimicked San Francisco and Greenwich Village. Hermes Nye, Michael Murphy, Lu Mitchell, B. W. Stevenson, Steve Fromholz, and many others of the left sang regularly at *The Rubiyat*, a coffeehouse named for the Persian poet Omar Khayyam, whose *carpe diem* philosophy seemed perfect for the sybaritic and disaffected. When a mini-Woodstock was held in Lewisville, a dozen miles outside Dallas, coffeehouse singer and songwriter Lu Mitchell wrote a folk-like protest song with the wonderful lines, "We were lewd and loose in Lewisville/ The Dallas *News* told us so." And the *News* told us so about many things: the perfidy of the left, the sanctity of American values, the dangers brought to us by rock 'n' roll, college professors, student protesters, and naked young people demonstrating at what were then called "happenings."

Hermes Nye, a cohort of Lu Mitchell's and author of *Fortune Is a Woman*, spoke out for liberal causes in Dallas at a time when such sentiments were unpopular. Nye came to Dallas from his native

Kansas, married the daughter of a successful businessman, and worked in the father-in-law's company for years. His novel about Dallas of the thirties owed a great deal to the Dallas of Nye's sixties. His self-published *Sweet Beast, I Have Gone Prowling* (1972) carries his iconoclastic views forward to the Age of McMurtry. Nye's Dallas was in the tradition of James Atlee Phillips's *The Inheritors* and Madison Cooper's *Sironia, Texas*, curious books that didn't attract the attention that McMurtry's did. *Sironia, Texas*'s size of over a million words makes it more or less unavailable to general readers (Larry McMurtry called it a doorstop), but it is a magnificent production and shows a southern city of moderate size in all its pettiness and in some of its magnificence.

In many ways Waco is a Texas eccentric itself. It was once a great cotton center and had as one of its great features the Cotton Palace Exposition, a kind of state fair of agriculture. It is home to the world's largest Baptist university, but, oddly enough, the city has been "wet" longer than many Texas towns and cities. It sits in the middle of German and Czech country and has a flavor of Old Europe mixed with a Deep South tinge. Back in the nineteenth century, Waco had a red-light district that was very much in the open, and it was home to William Cowper Brann, whose paper, *The Iconoclast*, was a precursor of many of the underground papers of the sixties and seventies. Brann, who called Baylor University a "great storm center of misinformation," was gunned down by a disgruntled Baylor supporter on the streets of Waco in 1897. Before he died, Brann pulled his own gun and killed his attacker.

So while there were bursts of outraged liberalism at the time of Brann and in Texas in the 1940s and 1950s, it took the Cold War/Vietnam period for the times to change significantly. All across America after World War II, the times were indeed a-changin', and the changes were soon evident in Texas. In Crystal City in South Texas, Hispanic groups like PASO (Political

Association of Spanish Speaking Organizations) and La Raza were helped by the Teamsters Union to elect a slate of Hispanics to run the city government. In Rio Grande City, a melon strike broke out, and the Texas Rangers were called in to break heads. In 1968, a Farm Workers March, begun in the Valley, aimed for the state capitol in Austin. Governor John Connally met the marchers in New Braunfels and urged them to stay away from Austin, but the group made it all the way to the steps of the capitol. Egged on by new Texas politicians like Senator Ralph Yarborough and a band of liberals that included Ann Richards, Henry B. Gonzalez (later to be a U. S. congressman), state senator A. R. "Babe" Schwartz, attorneys Oscar Mauzy, David Richards, Otto Mullinax, and Wayne Burnett, liberals seemed about to flourish. At the time Texas had a number of liberal federal judges, notably Sarah T. Hughes of Dallas, who swore in Lyndon Johnson as president aboard Air Force One while it was still parked on the runway in Dallas following the assassination of Kennedy, and William Wayne Justice, a man hated by conservatives and as beloved by liberals as Ralph Yarborough.

Texas's storied vulgarity, the radical rightward politics, and the assumed backwardness made many new Texans ashamed of the state in a way that J. Frank Dobie never was. The vulgarity that Texans had always gloried in became something to be explained away. It may be that Texas vulgar reached its apogee when the Shamrock Hotel was opened to great and embarrassing fanfare in 1949. *Life* magazine covered the opening of the hotel decorated with thirteen shades of green—the selfsame hotel parodied in the movie *Giant*, a film that caused new Texans a good deal of discomfort but a sense of "I told you so: see, we are that vulgar." Texas the rough and tumble and independent was suddenly reduced to Texas the embarrassing. Texas oilmen, long thought to be tough, resourceful roughnecks like Spencer Tracy and Clark Gable in *Boom Town*, are now shown to be beneficiar-

THE AGE OF MCMURTRY

ies of the 27.5% depletion allowance on oil, and by lobbying for and accepting that tax break marked themselves as feeders at the federal tough.

Neiman Marcus, which Texans had long thought of as the symbol of Texas good taste, was revealed as an emporium of Texas vulgarity with its Christmas presents costing a million or more dollars. Stanley Marcus, who came back to Texas from Harvard in 1927 with the mission to invent culture—and teach Dallasites to eat dark chocolate and ape French fashions—saw himself as the bearer of the best that has been thought and said on the East Coast. Neiman-Marcus was refinement itself, and southerners and southwesterners all came calling. One famous cartoon showed a farmwoman standing in front of a shack some-where in East Texas with an oil well gushing in the background. The cut line reads, "Wonder what time Neiman Marcus closes?" And William Humphrey, who had long since moved to New York, wrote a short story about a family like the Beverly Hillbillies who load up in an old pickup, drive their oil money to Dallas to stay at the Adolphus Hotel, and make straight away to Neiman Marcus.

Segregation remained in place longer in Texas than in many other parts of the South. The Southwest Conference was fully segregated until 1966 when Jerry Levias received a scholarship to SMU. North Texas State College had integrated much earlier. In 1956 Abner Haynes and Leon King became the first black ath-letes to play football for a non-black college in Texas. Haynes became an All-American at North Texas State and went on to be the most important player in the new American Football League when he signed with the Dallas Texans in 1960, fully six years before a black athlete was admitted to the Southwest Conference. Dallas schools fought integration, and well into the seventies Dallas was called "the most segregated city in America." In the spring of 2003, the thirty-year-old desegregation order was lifted, but by then white flight had made the Dallas schools a minority operation.

David Richards, once married to ex-governor Ann Richards, has told the liberal story in his *Once Upon a Time in Texas: A Liberal in the Lone Star State*. Richards, a labor lawyer, fought the fights associated with unions, underground papers, segregation, migrant workers, and the attempts to overturn the Johnson/Rayburn axis that controlled Democratic politics in Texas. In his book, Richards re-fights all the old fights involving John Connally, who was Johnson's Democrat and Nixon's Republican. He lays out the perfidy of the *Dallas Morning News* back in the days when it was the standard bearer for reactionary politics. Richards replays the struggles over the rights of underground papers, like Austin's *Rag*, over the movement to unionize Texas and the battles fought against Birchers and other rabble-rousers.

Not only was Texas literature and politics undergoing change, but even the music of the state moved from the traditional to the experimental. Texas and Tennessee had been the strongholds of traditional country and western music. Many of the stars of Nashville's Grand Ole Opry were Texans. Jimmie Rodgers, Bob Wills, Ernest Tubb, Lefty Frizzel, Milton Brown, and Hank Thompson had been the stars of the Dobie era, but by the seventies and eighties, Willie Nelson and Waylon Jennings and Jerry Jeff Walker were introducing a new kind of "outlaw" country music to Texas and the world. This "outlaw" or "progressive country" had its center in Austin, which began vying with Nashville to be the mother church of country music.

During these years, other musicians went against the mainstream. Latin-flavored Tejano and conjunto music were anti-establishment, as was much indigenous rock 'n' roll. The best-known Tejano musicians were Flaco Jimenez, "Little Joe y La Familia," Freddy Fender, and Joe Teusch of Dumas, who renamed himself Joe "King" Carrasco after Gomez Fred Carrasco, a famous

San Antonio gangster killed in a prison break in Huntsville. Joe
(King) Carrasco and the Crowns bill their music as Tex-Mex rock
'n' roll. Texas rock 'n' rollers included Roy Orbison, Doug Sahm
(of the" Sir Douglas Quintet" and later allied with Flaco Jimenez
and Augie Meyers as "The Texas Tornados"), Domingo "Sam"
Samudio (of "Sam the Sham and the Pharoahs"), the strange "?
and the Mysterians" (known only for the hit "96 Tears"), blues
singer Marcia Ball (formerly of "Freda and the Firedogs"), and, of
course, Janis Joplin, who got her start singing at Threadgills in
Austin in the sixties.

Another revolutionary musical icon was and is Kinky
Friedman, who added genre mystery fiction to his musical career.
Friedman, whose father was a professor at the University of Texas,
organized a band called "Kinky Friedman and the Texas Jew Boys,"
which featured "They Ain't Making Jews Like Jesus Anymore." As
of 2003, Friedman began writing a column for *Texas Monthly* and
announced his candidacy for governor of Texas.

The Austin music scene's most famous venue was Armadillo
World Headquarters, an old armory building in downtown Austin
that became the headquarters for rock/country/conjunto for most
of the late twentieth century. The early story of Texas iconoclastic music is best told in Jan Reid's *The Improbable Rise of Redneck
Rock*. (A side note: Heidelberg, the publisher, was a short-lived
publishing company started by David Lindsey, later to become the
finest crime novelist of the Age of McMurtry.)

In the process that took Texas from a ranching, oil-derrick
state to an urban, industrialized region, there is no question that
Larry Jeff McMurtry "broods like an aged eagle" over the state's
literary scene in a way that nobody else does. He is the main figure because he has had the most critical success and has made the
most money. There was a time when a non-Texan would invoke
the name of Dobie if Texas literature came up in conversation or
in print. Now one is likely to hear, "Is there anyone else writing in

Texas except Larry McMurtry?" This rankles Texans with a taste for literature, but even to Texans who don't keep up with the state's literary scene, the question seems reasonable. A recent cover profile in the *Los Angeles Times Magazine* is typical of the McMurtry legend. The cover photo shows him standing in the deserted street of Archer City looking dour. The article makes it seem as if McMurtry is the only story in Texas literature. But the McMurtry legend has some questioners: Scott Blackwood, in reviewing Don Graham's *Lone Star Literature* in the *Austin American-Statesman* on November 3, 2003, calls, "El Paso's own Cormac McCarthy . . . possibly Texas's greatest contemporary writer." Blackwood, himself a recently published fiction writer, is seconding a good many critics in lauding McCarthy. Blackwood laments the fact that McCarthy is absent from Graham's book, but notes that McCarthy does not allow his work to be reprinted. Some have questioned whether Cormac McCarthy is really a Texas writer at all. A relative newcomer to Texas, McCarthy began his career in Tennessee, where he wrote several novels in the Faulkner manner before moving to El Paso and choosing to remain aloof from the local literary establishment. His novel *Blood Meridian* (1985) caused a small stir in literary circles, and his Border Trilogy of *All the Pretty Horses, The Crossing,* and *Cities of the Plain* made his name here and in other parts of the country. Some younger Texas critics organized the Cormac McCarthy Society, a kind of literary fan club, and have praised his works immensely. Others have dismissed him as someone writing mostly of Mexico and remaining distant from the locals. McCarthy was given a MacArthur "genius award" and seems to have no need for fellowship among his peers. Some have even questioned whether McCarthy is as good as his partisans allege. The role that he plays in Texas literature is still unsettled. And to borrow (and twist) a line from Waylon Jennings's song about Bob Wills, "When you're down in Texas, McMurtry's still the king."

Since McMurtry is the central figure of his "age," more about his own career needs to be said. To go back a ways: McMurtry burst onto the scene in 1961 with the novel, *Horseman, Pass By.* The book won the Texas Institute of Letters award for the best fiction of the year and would have enjoyed the same fate, I suspect, as most TIL winners: it would have sold a few thousand copies and lain fallow awaiting McMurtry's next book. But in 1963, the novel was turned into the blockbuster movie *Hud* starring Paul Newman, Melvyn Douglas, and Patricia Neal. This was just the beginning for the young Texas writer; each of his first three novels was filmed. *The Last Picture Show* was an Academy Award winner that made the careers of Cybill Shepherd, Ben Johnson (a character actor in many John Ford westerns), and Cloris Leachman. Johnson and Leachman won Academy Awards, as did McMurtry and Peter Bogdanovich for adapting the novel for film. The third film from what is now called *The Thalia Trilogy* was *Loving Mollie,* a real dud made from one of McMurtry's best novels, *Leaving Cheyenne.* Had it not been for the movies made from the first three McMurtry novels, the young author might have gone through the next twenty-five years as "a minor regional novelist," as a T-shirt he once wore proclaimed him. But those three novels and the two excellent films established McMurtry as the new voice of Texas letters.

But Larry McMurtry was not through after his successful early novels and movies. Now, forty years later, he is author of more than thirty books and manages to produce a book a year. He went from novels about small towns to novels about the cities and then to a multiplicity of subjects. But no matter how far afield he wanders, his intellectual and literary base is Texas.

McMurtry has spoken out against Texas writing and writers, and he has argued in more than one place that the day of the bucolic novel was over and that Texas authors should confront the more complex life of the city. At first he practiced what he preached and followed the *Thalia Trilogy* with what Clay Reynolds, Mark Busby, and other critics have called the *Houston Trilogy—Moving On, All My Friends Are Going to Be Strangers,* and *Terms of Endearment.* They make an interesting contrast to his early works, which the author himself dismisses as juvenilia. The three Houston novels are the essence of the mauve period, though later novels like *Some Can Whistle, Texasville, Buffalo Girls, Anything for Billy,* and *Duane's Depressed* focus heavily on absurdism and the grotesqueries of life. But it is in the Houston novels that we see most strongly McMurtry's break with what at one point he calls "country and western" fiction. The characters in all three novels, like so many of McMurtry's characters, are feckless or disappointed or grotesquely eccentric. I don't think any one of the novels is a success, though *Terms of Endearment* became a successful movie starring Shirley MacLaine and Jack Nicholson. Each of those novels bears a stamp that has marred many of Larry McMurtry's novels. The trouble is that he can't contain himself. He has a book moving along smoothly, and then suddenly the novel is off down some trail that is only tangentially connected to the plot he is developing. The result of these meanderings is that McMurtry produces books filled with interesting plots entangled by subplots that distract. At least two hundred pages of the July Johnson subplot and a few other extraneous matters could be cut from *Lonesome Dove.* The July Johnson material takes us away from what we most want to follow, that is, the movement of Gus and Woodrow and their crew up the trail. I could point to dozens of places in that novel and most of the later ones where the story gets away from McMurtry. It is possible to argue that the McMurtry subplots are in keeping with postmodern fictional tendencies, but they are probably the result of his inability to edit and delete.

I mentioned earlier the eccentric grotesques like Blue Duck and Danny Deck in *Some Can Whistle* and noted that McMurtry's tendency toward the absurd and unbelievable marked his later novels, but even Danny Deck in the 1972 *All My Friends Are Going to Be Strangers* is on the far edge of ordinary. Deck publishes a novel, drops out of school, marries an unbelievable girl/woman who hates him, and begins wandering the country from Texas to San Francisco and back. He falls in with some Ken Kesey types, visits a mad uncle who employs a worker who has sex with a posthole, and drifts drunkenly about the West and Southwest. In Deck's later appearance in *Some Can Whistle*, he is found wearing a caftan and living in a town like Archer City in an adobe mansion. Danny has made his money by writing a television show, and now he is living with the madcap bisexual Dr. Godwin Lloyd-Jons and some equally grotesque hangers-on. Out of nowhere, Danny receives a phone call from the daughter he never knew he had and has to rejoin the world briefly to get her and her absurdist entourage back to his home, which is not far from Wichita Falls. One hopes that Deck is not autobiographical, though there are some scary parallels between him and his author. McMurtry married briefly, went west and fell in with Ken Kesey's Merry Pranksters, and wound up living in a remote town on the South Plains of Texas. Readers of Tom Wolfe's *The Electric Kool-Aid Acid Test* remember that Kesey and his pranksters loaded up in a psychedelic bus and headed for Houston to visit McMurtry, who was teaching at Rice at the time. McMurtry has none of Danny Deck's fecklessness, for he has always worked hard. In addition to more than thirty books of fiction and nonfiction, he has written for newspapers and review journals and runs one of the largest bookstores in the country in his native Archer City. His bookstore is scattered all over the small, dusty town that we are all so familiar with from *The Last Picture Show*. There is little else in Archer City now. McMurtry has filled many of the town stores with his books—probably half a million by now.

It is not clear why all of McMurtry's novels are botches, but they are. Even the good ones. I can think of no McMurtry novel

that does not have a serious flaw. The one thing he can't resist is
the prolonged riff that could be cut out to make the book better.
Some years ago, I heard McMurtry say he writes five pages a day,
day in and day out. At home or away. Such discipline may lure
him into these sidelights that detract from his fiction. Sometimes
they are funny and interesting, but even then they interrupt the
main point of the book. It is hard to think of a McMurtry novel
that is not in some way absurdist fiction. Think of some of his
characters: Blue Duck, Earl Dee, the killer in *Some Can Whistle*,
the General and Aurora and Vernon in *Terms of Endearment*,
Uncle El and his mad wife in *All My Friends*, all the characters in
Anything for Billy and *Buffalo Girls*. The list could fill many pages.
Even his normal characters often stretch credulity. Patsy
Carpenter of *Moving On* cries hard and soft and often throughout
the book. Gus and Call are a fine pair of eccentric Texas Rangers
living past their times. One is taciturn and stolid, the other garrulous and full of fun. At one point Gus says, "I always wanted to
shoot an educated man." Duane in *The Last Picture Show*,
Texasville, and *Duane's Depressed* moves from normal to odd over
the course of the sequence. McMurtry loves a funny scene, and
he will write them even when they don't fit the story. But he is
also deadly serious about many things, including his fiction and
his nonfiction and apparently his business interests.

It is really hard to know what to make of Larry McMurtry. He
is remote and unfriendly on most occasions. He is generous and
open on others. He is a true intellectual and a writer of madcap
scenes. His essays on film, on the West, and on literature are serious. He is a fine essayist, and in his essays he manages to avoid
the drifting asides that mar his fiction. His early essays—the ones
he is famous for as a critic—are pamphleteering in that he is at
pains to rid the Texas literary world of Dobie, Bedichek, and
Webb. Part of that is sound criticism, but part of it is to pave the
way for Larry McMurtry. He does what William Wordsworth did

in "The Preface to *The Lyrical Ballads*." Wordsworth wanted to rid the world of Alexander Pope and the poetry of the past in order to prepare the way for his kind of verse. McMurtry is doing some of the same things in "Southwestern Literature?" and "Ever a Bridegroom."

It is not fair of me or anyone else to focus full attention on the two famous or notorious essays that McMurtry wrote about Texas writing, for he has written many clear and intelligent essays on many subjects. The essays collected in *Film Flam* mark him as a serious film critic in the class with James Agee and Pauline Kael, two of America's best-known and most-trusted commentators on movies. Some of the essays from that volume are incisive essays on Hollywood in general, on television, and on McMurtry's life in the film world. Even some of the essays in *In a Narrow Grave* are memorable, though the tone often used in that volume is sarcastic and ironic. Witness the piece on the old fiddler's convention and the building of the Astrodome in Houston. But everyone admires "Take My Saddle from the Wall: A Valediction," which is an essay on an uncle as well as a paean to the spirit of the American West. In *Walter Benjamin at the Dairy Queen: Reflections at Sixty and Beyond*, McMurtry looks at the art of storytelling and his own role in the creation of fiction. He notes that the German critic Benjamin is careful not to confuse the novelist with the storyteller and then McMurtry says,

> The question I want to investigate is how someone like myself, growing up in a place that had just been settled, a place, moreover, in which nothing of consequence had ever happened, became a novelist instead of being content to worry over an old woman who had been traded for skunk hides, or a dairy farmer who had given way to despair. Does mere human memory, the soil that nourished storytelling, still have any use at all? (34)

The volume explores serious questions about novel writing and about how McMurtry himself developed from a failed cowhand on his family's ranch to a writer of fiction. In a book that has some of the same meandering qualities I have criticized in his fiction, McMurtry does a good job of showing how his life and his family and his place shaped him into the author of so many novels.

In *Paradise* McMurtry writes from a vacation in far-off Tahiti about the marriage of his parents and the late-learned fact that Hazel McMurtry had been married before she married Jeff, Larry's father. Part memoir and part recollection of a life with his parents, the book shifts back and forth between his vacation in Tahiti and the Marquesas and his memories of his parents' marriage and, after more than forty years, their separation. At the end of the book, he returns to visit his mother in the hospital in Wichita Falls. She is dying, and he says, "When I squeezed her hand, there was no response. I was there but she was far, far as the Marquesas, near the place where the light leaves. She had, perhaps, been waiting, though and perhaps knew I was home. She died the next afternoon" (159). This very short book is revealing and moving and shows a side of McMurtry not often seen.

Roads is a book about McMurtry's drives across America. He is a famous long-distance traveler like his main character in the novel *Cadillac Jack,* and in this volume he says he wants one last go at the highways of America. Along the way in this delightful book, he wanders far afield, telling tales about places on the way and people who have lived and are living in the byways of America. It captures something about McMurtry's interests and curiosity about a life he often seems aloof from.

Sacagawea's Nickname: Essays on the American West is a compilation of a dozen essays he published in *The New York Review of Books* over the years, ranging from the Lewis and Clark explorations to lives of the Zunis and the Five Civilized Tribes to writers like Angie Debo and Janet Lewis. McMurtry notes in the introduction that he had reviewed much fiction over his career but had avoided books about the West. The essays here are his return to the subject that has absorbed him, either consciously or unconsciously, for his entire life. The essays in this collection show McMurtry at his best: He is clear, intelligent, and constantly using his essays to learn about the world around him.

The two most famous of the McMurtry essays brought down a great deal of criticism on his head, for the Dobie legacy was alive when he wrote "Southwestern Literature?'" in 1968. There was a second outburst when "Ever a Bridegroom" appeared in 1981. The Dobie legacy continues in the works of people like Elmer Kelton and a host of Texas writers who write of a romantic/realistic Texas, but there are many more who have been freed to write existential or satirical material since McMurtry made the genres respectable. The list could include scores, among them John Henry Irsfeld's *Little Kingdoms,* a gritty and terrifying novel about a trio of killers terrorizing West Texas, or the mystery fiction of David Lindsey, who presents Houston as more of a wasteland than McMurtry ever imagined. And it is not surprising that Mexican American writers like Rolando Hinojosa, Tomás Rivera, Lionel Garcia, Max Martínez, Aristeo Brito, and Américo Paredes are not only violently anti-Dobie but much in the McMurtry world of satire and absurdism. Paredes has a buffoonish J. Frank Dobie take-off named H. Hank Harvey in his bitter Brownsville novel *George Washington Gomez.* (Don Graham thinks Paredes might have meant H. Hank to represent Walter P. Webb also, for he had little use for Webb, whose hagiographic book on the Texas Rangers showed them in a light far different from the view the Texas Mexicans had of the *rinches,* whom they saw as a blood-thirsty band of enforcers of white supremacy in a brown land.) Paredes wrote *George Washington Gomez* back in the thirties when he was a newspaperman in Brownsville and long before he earned his Ph.D. at the University of Texas with a dissertation on the corridos written about the Mexican border hero Gregorio Cortez. Paredes's study of Cortez was published as *With His Pistol in His Hand* and set him off on a distinguished career as a professor and folklorist at the University of Texas. Many Texas Mexican writers credit Américo Paredes with beginning the movement toward an authentic Mexican-American literature. If Paredes is not thought of as the begetter of Tex-Mex lit, then the honor is often accorded Tomás Rivera, whose 1970 book. *And the Earth Did Not Part* ("y no se lo trago la tierra"), is the first noteworthy narrative of Texas Mexican life. Rivera's book (later retranslated by Rolando Hinojosa as *This Migrant Earth*) tells the story of a family of migrant farm workers moving north with the crops during the hard days when bracero laborers followed the harvests from the Mexican border to the northern parts of the Midwest.

The most important of the Texas Mexican novelists is Rolando Hinojosa (he has been published variously as Rolando Hinojosa y Smith, Rolando Hinojosa-S, and Rolando Hinojosa-Smith, but his recent works are under the name Rolando Hinojosa). Hinojosa fits into this age of revolution and decadence because he presents a picture of the Rio Grande Valley with the gloves off and because his works are very much modernist and post-modernist in form. The books in Hinojosa's *Klail City Death Trip Series* are mostly sketches of life in "the Valley." His first books bear titles like *"Estampas del Valle y otras obras"* ("Sketches of the Valley and Other Works") or *"Notas, Generaciones, y Brechas"* ("Notes, Generations, and Trails"). These works are indeed sketches, and in order to read the books, it is necessary to interpolate a great deal. Characters appear, sometimes in half a page, only to appear later in connection with some other character or event. Characters who seem unimportant often appear later—or in another book—as major figures. All Hinojosa's books are short, and almost all are disjointed and disconnected. If all his works were published in one volume, the whole opus would not be more than four hundred pages, if that long. His themes are several: life among the mexicanos as lived under the noses of the Anglos, who own the land and the banks and the main businesses; the porous nature of the border between the United States and Mexico and the refusal of Border mejicanos to respect the nationalism of Mexico and the United States; the plight of the farm laborer; the attempts by educated Texas-Mexicans to make their way in the Anglo world by education and financial success. The main Anglo family in Klail City descends from Colonel Klail (read Captain Richard King of King Ranch fame). The Klails and the Belkens dominate the Valley in the same way the King-Kleberg family did for several generations. The city is Klail City and the county is Belken. The Mexican-American protagonists are Rafe Buenrostro and Jehu Malacara (Buenrostro can be roughly translated as "good face" and Malacara as "bad face"). The two young men are Hinojosa's age and represent the two sides of his and perhaps everybody's personality. In half a dozen very short volumes, the ironies of the Valley and the dire lives lived by the poor Mexicans are played out. Hinojosa attempted to write more connected and lengthier fiction in his mystery novels, *Partners in Crime* (1995) and *Ask a Policeman* (1998). In these novels, both imitations of standard mysteries, the lives of the Valley Mexicans are still central issues.

Women writers have also been freed by McMurtry. Shelby Hearon's series of Texas novels about marriage and divorce, women's issues, infidelity, and city life present a version of Texas that is modern and often disturbing. Sarah Bird's *Alamo House* (1986) and *The Boyfriend School* (1990) are blistering satires on Austin life in the same madcap way that her *Virgin of the Rodeo* (1993) satirizes the rodeo world and her *Yokota Officer's Club* (2000) takes aim at military life. Also strongly present in the McMurtry world are Mary Karr's dark memoirs of family dysfunction on the Gulf Coast, *The Liar's Club* (1995) and *Cherry* (2000), and Kim Wozencraft's *Rush* (1990) about the horrors of being a female undercover narc in Beaumont during "the war on drugs."

Two writers worth comment who landed in the middle of the Age of McMurtry and who represented a generation behind McMurtry and Brammer and Shrake are Pat Ellis Taylor and Kathryn Marshall. Taylor has two books of nonfiction, a number of poems and stories, and one novel of interest. Entitled *Afoot in a Field of Men and Other Stories from Dallas* [no apostrophe in original publication] *East Side,* the collection is a series of a dozen sketches about hippie life in Dallas in the seventies. An anonymous reviewer on an Alibris website said of the book, "Amidst low riders and Harley bikers, hard-shell Baptists and cut-rate marijuana, a strong woman holds her strange and decidedly nonnuclear family together. . . . " Another dust-jacket commentator, also anonymous, calls the book a collection about "rednecks, hippies, and small-time con men in the fraying slums of Dallas. . . . " The stories were published separately in various little magazines and were collected under the title listed above by Slough Press in Austin in 1983. And then in 1988, Atlantic Monthly Press republished the book and gave it nationwide circulation. The main character, whose husband is growing a giant marijuana plant in the closet, works as a secretary in Dallas by day and lives the hippie life after hours. The book does a good job capturing the whole era of drugs, sex, and rock 'n' roll. One of the memorable pieces is the visit Pat and some of her women friends make to the male strip club La Bare. Note: pat and leo and all the characters are set in small letters, carrying out the hippie, experimental phase, so popular in the sixties and seventies. Ms. Taylor, who now calls herself Pat Little Dog, won a Southwest Book Award for her *Border Healing Woman* about the Big Bend curandera Jewel Babb. She had earlier won an NEA writing fellowship and was a Dobie-Paisano fellow in 1986.

Ten years earlier, Kathryn Marshall, who is somewhat younger than Ms. Little Dog, was also named to the Dobie-Paisano Fellowship and spent a term at the J. Frank Dobie ranch outside Austin. She had already published one novel, *My Sister Gone* (1975) and was to write only one more, *Desert Places* (1977). Like Ms. Little Dog, Kathryn Marshall was firmly fixed in the hippie movement and her novels feature drugs, drink, and sex and reflect the ennui of the young of the era. Unlike McMurtry and some of the older writers who seem to be looking in from outside, Marshall and Little Dog know the territory firsthand. After her two novels and a few stories in a similar vein, Kathryn Marshall took a job first with *American Way*, the airlines magazine, and later with Alabama's Oxmoor Publishing (best known for cookbooks and *Southern Living*). Her last book was a series of interviews, *In the Combat Zone: An Oral History of American Women in Vietnam* (1987). She gave up writing altogether and became a nurse. While Marshall was at the Dobie ranch, her sister, Caroline, an artist, stayed with her and helped her paint out all the memorable sayings and cartoons of previous Dobie-Paisano fellows, all this to the consternation of Dobieites and Paisanos everywhere. Caroline Marshall later studied screenwriting with Terry Southern at Columbia and wrote a memory of the late Alvarado author for *The Paris Review*. She and Southern penned a screenplay about a Texas sheriff, but it has not been filmed.

Another writer who is on the far side of Texas romantic is James Crumley, whose novels are set mostly in Montana, where he teaches at the University of Montana. Crumley, who was born in South Texas and attended Texas A&I in Kingsville, wrote first about army life with his *One to Count Cadence* (1969), but his private-eye novels set in the Pacific Northwest go beyond the genre and capture the freewheeling times of hippies and dopers. His early work is best: *The Wrong Case* (1975), *The Last Good Kiss* (1978), and *Dancing Bear* (1983). His best work features private detectives living on the edge—one getting by on peppermint schnapps and cocaine and all running the roads from Montana to Washington to California.

James Lee Burke, a native of Houston, has more than twenty detective novels set in Louisiana and Montana, where he now teaches. Burke has a series set in and around New Orleans and New Iberia, another group set in the Texas Panhandle, and scattered novels set in Montana and environs. Burke is more serious than many genre writers and is often near the mainstream. Burke's world is, like Crumley's, one of legal and ethical borderlands where the heroes are often as ravaged as those found in McMurtry's city novels.

No listing is ever complete and no argument is ever fully rounded, but I hope I have shown some of the effects that McMurtry and his colleagues of the mauve decades of Texas fiction and nonfiction have wrought. With them, the romance of Old Texas is replaced by the irony and existentialism found in the post-World War II world in European and American literature.

Dobie and Porter:

A Marriage Made in Hell

3

In 1939, J. Frank Dobie was acknowledged all across Texas as the state's premiere writer. But on national and international levels, the best-known writer from Texas was Katherine Anne Porter. She published a number of well-regarded short stories in the 1920s and by 1939 had three major books in print: *Flowering Judas and Other Stories* (1930), *Noon Wine* (1937), and *Pale Horse, Pale Rider* (1939). Though both were Texans, it is hard to imagine two more dissimilar writers. But Porter and Dobie are united—even in their extreme dissimilarity. What binds them is geography and an insignificant literary prize awarded to Dobie in 1939. What separates them is also literary and geographical. Dobie was the archetypal westerner— at least in his version of the Old West. Porter was a modernist, an etherealist, and an inventor of an Old South that she had no more inhabited than Dobie had his West. Though they were born a couple of years and about two hundred miles apart, the two writers couldn't have lived in more opposite writing universes. Dobie wrote of cows and trail drives and was loved by people in his home state. Porter transformed herself from small-town Central Texas girl to "moonlight and magnolias" southern woman to internationalist. Dobie spent most of his life in Texas. Porter left Texas early in life and wandered the world for a large part of the twentieth century. Dobie died in Texas in 1964; Porter outlived him by sixteen years and died as far east of Texas as you can get and still be on the continent.

Despite all their differences, the two remain married in the minds of many Texas commentators—partly because of that obscure literary prize and partly because of a universal desire to proclaim somebody "best of show": as A. C. Greene, author of *The Fifty Best Books On Texas,* once said to me of lists, "Everybody loves a Hit Parade." Greene's comment is borne out by the recent lists of 100 Best Novels, 100 Best Movies, and Greene's updated *The 50+ Best Books On Texas.* In any case, as each year passes and things should settle down, Dobie-Porter arguments become more bitter, and theirs seems a literary marriage made in hell.

Critic Tom Pilkington, who calls J. Frank Dobie "the father of Texas literature," says, "If Dobie is the father, the matriarch of Texas letters is Katherine Anne Porter." Don Graham, who is, ironically, the J. Frank Dobie Regents Professor of American and English Literature at the University of Texas at Austin, was quoted in the *Dallas Morning News* saying that Porter "stood out among tall men." Graham's comment is quoted in an editorial, which goes on to say, "Translated, that means she fares well against such Texas legends as J. Frank Dobie and Walter Prescott Webb."

Despite Dobie's fading reputation today, among his old guard followers he is still the king. And the Dobie/Porter wars still heat up whenever the two camps gather. There is no quicker way to start a literary argument than to bring up the cause célèbre surrounding the 1939 Texas Institute of Letters literary prize. And it almost always comes up when Texans gather to talk about literature. It is never brought up by the Dobieites, for to them it is an embarrassment. But the Porterites never miss a chance to decry the blindness of the TIL fathers and mothers in awarding the prize to Dobie instead of to Porter. As Dobie's reputation has waned, Porter's has waxed. A passionate dean at the University of Texas at Arlington, in opening a Porter conference, once called Katherine Anne Porter "the only star in the Texas firmament." The distinguished Porter critic Janis Stout of Texas A&M University says in her *Katherine Anne Porter: A Sense of the Times* that "as a literary artist. . . her stature is indisputable" (248). But despite these laudatory comments, Old Guardsman/historian/belletrist/literary commentator A. C. Greene does not list Porter's famous *Pale Horse, Pale Rider* in his *The 50+ Best Books About Texas*. This omission incenses Don Graham, a Porter devotee despite his credentials as the Dobie professor. In a *Texas Observer* article titled "Outlaw Heart," Graham calls Greene's latest 50 "[a] puny pantheon" and "a new, weird update" of the original Greene list.

When it comes to Porter, passions run high, higher with each passing year, it seems. The nascent restoration of the KAP home place in Kyle, numerous conferences devoted to Porter, the glamorous photograph of Porter that graces the 1998 Texas Writers Month poster, and the ever-increasing stock of articles and books devoted to Porter's rather slender output all suggest that Porter is indeed the "only star in the Texas firmament." Or at least she was until the recent canonization of Cormac McCarthy by the Texas literary establishment. (In "Outlaw Heart" Graham takes a swipe at A. C. Greene for "booting out" KAP and calls for a "long moratorium on the subject of Texas writing." After Graham has had his say, one presumes.)

Passions indeed run high where KAP is concerned. And none higher than Joan Givner's in her 1982 Simon and Schuster biography *Katherine Anne Porter: A Life*. One of the things that she found most distressing about Porter's treatment by Texans was the fact that, in 1939, the barely fledged Texas Institute of Letters failed to give its first "best book" award to *Pale Horse, Pale Rider,* the very book that A. C. Greene "booted out." Instead the TIL gave its first award to J. Frank Dobie's *Apache Gold and Yaqui Silver.*

In 1983, at a celebration of the University of Texas's centennial—in the very heart of Dobie country and not six blocks from the spot where Dobie died—Givner said, in a much-quoted passage, that Dobie would have "won out over Jane Austen, Jean Rhys, Eudora Welty, Marianne Moore, Virginia Woolf, and the entire Brönte clan lumped together. And he would have done so even if these writers had been born in Waco." Not quite so often quoted is what comes just before Ms. Givner's catalog of non-winners. She says:

> One hardly needs to invoke complicated arguments to express the difference between J. Frank Dobie and Katherine Anne Porter. His cowboy image and style was as flauntingly and exaggeratedly masculine as hers was feminine. I would suggest that the "indigenous nature" of Dobie's subject matter was that its masculinity conformed more to the spirit of the West. There was none of that tremulous sensibility, that preoccupation with the inner world of the imagination, with relationships between men and women or with what George Eliot has called "the roar on the other side of silence." (58–60).

It is impossible to argue with Givner that Dobie's 1939 winner was "flauntingly and exaggeratedly masculine"; indeed, all of Dobie's work was. Dobie lacked "tremulous sensibility" or "the preoccupation with the inner world of the imagination," and, Lord knows, Dobie's roars were not "on the other side of silence." But I cannot agree that there is no need to offer complicated arguments that might help to explain the difference between J. Frank Dobie and Katherine Anne Porter—or rather the difference between the works of KAP and the works that were written and approved in Texas during the Porter-Dobie era. And I don't think the last word has been said about the controversial 1939 Best Book Award by the Texas Institute of Letters.

First, a few words about the beginning of the Texas Institute of Letters. Its early struggles are told by founder Billy Vann in *The Texas Institute of Letters, 1936–1966*. In 1939, TIL was in its third year, and its beginnings had been "tremulous." For one thing, Dobie, the reigning intellectual in the state at the time, had misgivings about joining the rather pompously titled organization. And he was not the only Texas writer to hesitate: folklore collector and college registrar John Lomax objected to a proposed list of charter members by saying that there were too many who "teach English rather than writing it effectively" (6); and the now-almost-forgotten novelist Donald Joseph wrote the founders to say that "not half a dozen people in Texas are doing nationally recognized creative writing" (5). Despite the reservations, the new organization got off the ground more or less during the Centennial year, but it was still struggling three years later when it was proposed that "the Institute undertake to make suitable recognition of the outstanding Texas book of each year" (15). Three members—Hilton Ross Greer, Stanley Babb, and Ann Pence Davis—were appointed to "make plans." I am not sure whether the three of them chose Dobie over Porter or whether there was a vote of the members, but Dobie was chosen, and the rest, as they say, was scandal.

But think for a second about the masculine versus feminine argument, which seems to be applied today every time the 1939 controversy arises. Here are a couple of facts. For one thing, a quarter of the charter members of the TIL were women. This does not prove conclusively that there was no gender bias among the members, but to think otherwise merits some consideration.

Another fact: the president of TIL that year was a woman. Poet and novelist Karle Wilson Baker was the second president and third fellow of the organization. In fact, between 1939 and 1946, Ms. Baker, Rebecca W. Smith, and Lexie Dean Robertson all served two-year terms as presidents of the organization. Again, not conclusive proof. Another fact: the book that won the award in 1940 was Dora Neil Raymond's *Captain Lee Hall of Texas*.

I am aware that there is no way to prove that the TIL was not masculine-dominated and male-centered and gender-biased, but I have a suspicion that it was not as much a men's club as it has been pictured. Nor am I sure that masculine versus feminine is what was going on in those early years of the institute. I do think J. Frank Dobie would have won against all comers in 1939— against Welty or Woolf or Jane Austen. Not because he was a male but because he was J. Frank Dobie. The organization, in its years of infancy, was eager to clutch the vain and cannily pompous Dobie to its collective bosom. And what better way was there to do that than to give him an award? This turned out to be one way to help turn Dobie into the literary dictator that he was determined to be. And I don't think anybody questions the fact that Dobie dominated Texas letters in the middle decades of this century. As I have said elsewhere, he did this by force of personality and self-promotion and industry but without literary taste. But because I plan neither to praise nor to bury Dobie here, I will not detail his shortcomings as a critic. But I do have some things to say about him as a determiner of taste and a master publicist of himself and of romantic Texas.

Because Texas literature during the Dobie years was in its last great burst of Lone Star romanticism, what amazes me most about the 1939 imbroglio was that Porter was considered at all for an award by TIL. Perhaps her nomination came from those English-teacher members that Lomax had decried earlier. After all, by 1939, the New Critics were beginning to make inroads into

English departments, and Robert Penn Warren and Cleanth Brooks had just published *Understanding Poetry*, the second most influential English textbook ever published in America up to that time. (The *McGuffey Readers* still hold first place.) *Understanding Poetry* became the Bible, or rather the first of several Bibles, for the New Criticism. And if any writer ever wrote works that fitted the prescriptions of the New Critics it was KAP. Her work was allusive, ironic, often open-ended, and as mystifying as critics and English teachers demanded. The most admired of the Porter stories, "Flowering Judas," is a perfect example. It cries out for deep explication. A common reader is left in the dark, and it remains for the critic to untangle the images, symbols, allusions, patterns of reflexivity, and what sophomore students are given to calling "hidden meanings." Teachers can spend several days with "Flowering Judas" or "The Grave" and still not exhaust the possibilities. Critics can spill words over hundreds of pages in attempts to "explicate the last verse" of either of those works.

Someone once remarked that for the New Critics to appreciate a poem, it had to be as close as possible to the works of the seventeenth-century metaphysicals. T. S. Eliot, in many ways the father of New Criticism and modernism, devoted a great deal of space to reviving the metaphysicals—John Donne, George Herbert, Andrew Marvell, Richard Crashaw, and others. As the British and American New Critics gained ascendancy in the literary world, Percy Bysshe Shelley and William Wordsworth and Alfred Lord Tennyson were consigned to dim poetic corners; John Keats was transformed into a demi-metaphysical; and new writers began writing to the fashion of the day. John Crowe Ransom's poetic reputation rests on his ability to write mock-metaphysical, which he did superbly. The tensions and ironies of the poets fed over into fiction, and writers like James Joyce, D. H. Lawrence, Virginia Woolf, William Faulkner, Katherine Mansfield, and Porter wrote novels and stories requiring the same deep analysis as John Donne had needed. Virginia Woolf once noted that a novel should be "at least as well written as a poem." I think that means that fiction should have the same density, the same impenetrability and some scrupulous attention to style, as the poems being admired at the time. As for writers like Anthony Trollope and Tennyson and Charles Dickens, there was hardly a place for them in the new pantheon. Someone once dismissed Tennyson by referring to "the glutinous syllables of the poet laureate." But with the modernists there were no more "glutinous syllables," no more focus on mere story.

Given the temper of the times and Porter's friendships with many of the Southern Agrarians/New Critics it is easy to see how her works became very models of metaphysical, ironic, decadent twentieth-century writing. And it seems to me that such works were not playing well in Texas in 1939 among any but the most advanced critics and belletrists. What obtained in Texas letters in 1939 was not tinged with Ms. Givner's "tremulous sensibility."

Maybe European and American letters had moved from romanticism to modernism, but Texas was still more than a generation behind. Everyone has a theory about the movement of artistic periods, but most agree that they move from primitive to decadent. Perhaps the simplest way to look at the progress of a movement from primitive to mature to decadent is to think of the three capitals that top Greek columns. In grammar school, we learned that the movement from Doric to Ionian to Corinthian was from simple to complex, from plain to ornate, from primitive to decadent. These progressions constantly repeat themselves. What, after all, is modernism but the decadence of romanticism? If we have William Blake and Wordsworth, we are almost certain to have Tennyson and Robert Browning and later Thomas Hardy and A. E. Housman and Oscar Wilde and Faulkner and Woolf and James Joyce and Katherine Anne Porter.

The modernist movement, which I argue is the decadence of romanticism, was in full flower when Porter shook the dust of

Tarrant County off her feet, denied she had ever worked for the *Fort Worth Star-Telegram* or had been married to a Texan, and set out for what many inferiority-complexed Texans at the time called the "civilized world." As she put it in a letter to William Humphrey, "I got out of Texas like a bat out of hell at the earliest possible moment and stayed away cheerfully half a lifetime" (Stout, 36). Unlike Huck Finn who lit out for the territories, KAP lit out from the territories.

While Katherine Anne Porter was establishing cosmopolitan credentials and writing stories that attracted the attention of the New Critics, James Frank Dobie was staying at home promoting the Texas of his imagination. His Texas was expansive, optimistic, filled with certainty; in short, it was romantic by almost any definition. Dobie represented Texas as it saw itself in the 1920s and 1930s. It was in full flower. It was the finest blossom of the American West. Never mind that Texas was a southern state where cotton was the principal export and that the majority of its inhabitants saw themselves as southerners, Dobie and Hollywood were projecting Texas as the gunslinger West, what Owen Wister once called a "playground for young men." This view of Texas as the Wild West was as old as the dime novels, but it was working toward a fever pitch in the 1930s. The Centennial was on the horizon, and it hardly needs to be said that Dobie was on the advisory panel on Texas history for the hundred-year celebration. He was ubiquitous in those days. By 1932, he had already begun on a weekly radio show called "Longhorn Luke and His Cowboys," from station WOAI in San Antonio. (He got paid $25 a program plus expenses to and from Austin.) In 1939, he began his syndicated newspaper column "My Texas." Lon Tinkle says that by the time Dobie won the first TIL award, he was already being called "Mr. Texas."

Not only was Dobie the main intellectual spokesman for Texas, he was both a shaper and a reflector of Texas writing. And the writing of that time had little that was decadent or ironic or modernist about it even when it was not written about Dobie's "West of the Imagination." Little in Texas literature was touched by irony and "tremulous sensibility." The Texas pictured by Lone Star writers was not always tinged with the romanticism of Owen Wister and J. Frank Dobie, but there was little irony in those pre-war days. Writers like Dorothy Scarborough, Ruth Cross, Barry Benefield, Clair Ogden Davis, and Karle Wilson Baker were producing fiction that was as unlike Virginia Woolf's experimentalism or KAP's interiority as Dickens was unlike Marcel Proust. The 1930s in Texas was the time of Berta Harte Nance's poem that begins "Other states were carved or born, / But Texas grew from hide and horn." These years produced Sallie Reynolds Matthews's *Interwoven,* a nostalgic and romantic family history, and George Sessions Perry's *Hackberry Cavalier, Walls Rise Up,* and the great *Hold Autumn in Your Hand.*

The main line of Texas literature remained straightforward, un-ironic, un-decadent throughout the war years and through most of the 1950s—and remains so in the works of writers like Elmer Kelton today. In *The Literary History of the American West,* Tom Pilkington wrote that in 1961 Larry McMurtry dragged "southwestern fiction kicking and screaming into the twentieth century" with *Horseman, Pass By* (511). Another way of stating Pilkington's thesis is to say that McMurtry's first novel lays to rest the romantic West as Dobie and his followers saw it. But before *Horseman, Pass By* appeared, Texas fiction was well on the way toward its ironic mode, its decadence. Madison Cooper's *Sironia, Texas* (1952) is hardly in the Texas mainstream as Dobie knew it; instead it bears the marks of decadent writing in its ironic and almost Faulknerian treatment of Waco society. William Humphrey's dark and Porter-influenced stories began appearing as early as 1949, and his important *Home from the Hill* came out in 1958. Another Porter devotee, William Goyen, began publishing parts of what would become *The House of Breath* as early as

1949. It was not long before a great many antiromantic works began to appear, writers we associate with the 1960s and early 1970s like Bud Shrake, Bill Brammer, R. G. Vliet, Bill Casey, and John Irsfeld portray a Texas that Dobie would have found unappealing if not unrealistic.

None of this is to say that Texas writing today is totally given over to "the roar that exists on the other side of silence," but when I look at a Texas tradition of existentialism and despair and decadence that begins with Porter and continues through Goyen and Humphrey to Cormac McCarthy, Edward Swift, and James Crumley, I feel called upon to echo William Butler Yeats on Ireland: "Romantic Texas is dead and gone, it's with Frank Dobie in the grave." But it was not in 1939. And I don't find it all that strange or even inappropriate that *Apache Gold and Yaqui Silver* won the first award given by the Texas Institute of Letters.

The Old South in
Texas Literature

4

I n myth and the popular imagination, Texas is a western
state. Its icons are longhorns,
oil wells, cowboys on horseback, and mavericks. Its landscape is
prairie and desert—often with Monument Valley, Utah, looming
in the background. The men wear Stetson hats, and the women
are barrel racers. Rodeos are held in every town and at the huge
stock shows in Houston and Fort Worth annually. The facts are
different. Texas is largely urban today, but for most of the state's
history, the state was southern. Most Texans live east of the 97th
meridian, east roughly of Interstate 35, which divides East Texas
from the west. There is more land in the western part of the state,
but most people have always lived east of this dividing line. When
literary festivals are held and programs are printed, the illustra-
tions all tend to be western; there is almost never a cotton boll or
a farmer tilling the land. In the popular imagination Texas literature is a branch of western literature, and over the years the representative writers have been J. Frank Dobie, Roy Bedichek,
Walter Prescott Webb, Larry McMurtry, Elmer Kelton, Benjamin
Capps, Fred Gipson, and John Graves. Even fairly serious students

of Texas writing think of William Owens, George Sessions Perry, and William Humphrey as being well outside the mainstream. They can be set aside the way J. Frank Dobie did John W. Thomason in his *Guide to Life and Literature of the Southwest.* Dobie dismissed Thomason when he said, "he followed the southern tradition and not the western" (183). That seemed to be Dobie's way of putting aside all that was not western in the literature, the folklore, and the culture of the state.

But there are a great many writers who followed the southern tradition and not the western. For most of the twentieth century, the mainstream of Texas literature was southern. Until well after World War II many Americans and most Texans saw the state as southern, not western. It is a fact that between World War I and the end of the Korean War there were scores of books written by Texans and published by major publishers that had nothing to do with cattle, six guns, barbed wire, rustling, or trail driving. The non-western books that appeared during these decades were apparently widely read. Some became best-sellers, some won national awards, and a surprising number were made into motion pictures.

During the years that J. Frank Dobie was, to use Lon Tinkle's phrase, "Mr. Texas," he did all he could to promote Texas as a far western state untainted by its Confederate background or its fields of cotton or its slaves. People who read Dobie's books got a picture of the state as it existed west of an imaginary line that passes between Dallas and Fort Worth, goes to the west of Waco and the east of San Antonio, and enters the Gulf at Matagorda Bay. It is true that Dobie's range country contained the largest amount of land, but the Texas of corn, cotton, and mules contained the largest number of people.

Texas east of the dividing line was founded by the people who followed Stephen F. Austin and who, Leon Hale says in *Turn South at the Second Bridge,* "fanned up the river bottoms and farmed Alabama and Georgia style, with slave labor." Hale goes on to say that "Many people, at the mention of Texas, never think of it as a state with moss-hung oaks, pine-covered hills, rice fields, and sandy beaches. . . . My part of Texas has always struck me as happily unrepresentative of the public notion of what the state is like" (13). The public notion is perhaps represented by the draw-ings on the brochure announcing the 1983 Texas Literary Tradition Symposium, a gathering to celebrate the centennial of the University of Texas. The brochure included a spur, a branding iron, a marshal's badge, a ten-gallon hat, a six-shooter, a rat-tlesnake, and a wagon wheel. There is no plow, no horse collar, no cotton in bloom, no slice of watermelon, and no hoe. The design-ers of the program were representing the Texas that everyone has come to accept. Few remember that Texas was saved from the poverty of the post-Civil War period by cotton, a crop that pro-duced most of the state's wealth in the last quarter of the nine-teenth century. John Spratt, in his book *The Road to Spindletop*, says that Texas cotton produced a million dollars a year during the closing years of the century. He comments that he grew up on the myth that cattle production insulated Texas against the poverty endured by other southerners. But Spratt says, "cattle ran a distant second to cotton. In dollar value of the product, in num-ber of persons employed, and in industrial activity generated, cot-ton stood alone—far, far in advance of all competitors" (83). It was only about 1950 that livestock began to surpass cotton, though Texas agriculture still far exceeds livestock in money pro-duced. Spratt does admit that the "Cattle Kingdom surpasses the Cotton Kingdom" in "romantic appeal," and he wonders why "the loneliest person on earth, the cowhand of the late nineteenth century [has] been clothed in heroic glamour, while the cotton farmer . . . has been dubbed an 'ignoramus'"? (85–86). George Sessions Perry helps explain the myth in *Texas: A World in Itself*:

To us Texans there is a quality of go and glamour about cowmen that farmers never attain. I don't know what makes it. Is it the fact that they ride horses? That probably has something to do with it. But I am led for some reason to believe that it is the cowman's mixture of pride and arrogance—plus his knowledge that he has casually put something over on the rest of us. For while the rancher goes through the violent motions of labor, he is actually having a wonderful time earning a living. . . . (73)

Perry ends his paragraph with the statement that ranchers are perhaps the "last free men in a swiftly industrializing America" and are "noble and enviable" symbols of what the rest of us have lost. The last part of Perry's comment is standard romantic propaganda of the Dobie school. It may be that Perry is right about the horseback activity, for the ennobling of the "chevalier/ caballero/ritter" predates even J. Frank Dobie. Perry is certainly right that the cowman and his apologists and propagandists put something over on us. They made us see Texas, not as all of it was, but as some of it might have been. They made us forget cotton and mules and blacks and tenant farmers and remember the West of Webb's Texas Rangers and Gene Autry's singing cowboy.

Today, it seems, the Dobie dream of Texas has come true. During the last thirty years or so the state has been steadily changing from southern to western. This is not to say that the Klan can't still assemble a good-sized klavern in Pasadena, and it is certainly a matter of record that Dallas fought to keep segregated schools well into the 1970s and only had the judicial bans lifted in 2003. But the days when the majority of Texans saw themselves as southerners are apparently over. The change in attitude was most evident to the expatriate William Humphrey when he returned to Clarksville after a thirty-two-year absence. He says in his autobiographical volume *Farther Off from Heaven,* "Red River County has ceased to be Old South and become Far West. I who for years had had to set my Northern friends straight by pointing out that I was a Southerner, not a Westerner . . . found myself now in the Texas of legend and the popular image" (239). It is the Texas "of legend and the popular image" that dime novels of the nineteenth century, dime movies of the twentieth, and J. Frank Dobie sold to the world.

But the region as most Texans knew it in the first half of the twentieth century can be seen best in the writings of William Owens, Humphrey, William Goyen, George Sessions Perry, J. Mason Brewer, and, making allowance for some distortion, in the works of Katherine Anne Porter. But there are many others "who followed the southern tradition": Dorothy Scarborough, Ruth Cross, Barry Benefield, Laura Krey, Dillon Anderson, John W. Thomason, Karle Wilson Baker, Jewel Gibson, John W. Wilson, Madison Cooper, Leon Hale, Sigman Byrd, Mary King O'Donnell, and Elizabeth Lee Wheaton. And the list, believe it or not, is selective. Many of their books are deservedly forgotten, but some of the books by authors on this list are among the best writing in Texas—past or present. Dorothy Scarborough is remembered for one novel, *The Wind,* her book about West Texas, and her distinguished career as a folklorist. This is as it should be, for her novels of the Brazos cotton country are badly dated and are interesting mainly for their bits of folklore and local color. Her "darkies" are picturesque, her planters mostly kind, her Baylor students diligent, and her rednecks merely mis-guided. A good number of these writers ought to be read by any serious student of Texas literature. Ruth Cross is forgotten and deserves to be. Or if Ruth Cross is remembered at all, it is for *The Big Road,* about farm life in East and North Texas and for a rather overheated novel set partly in Austin called *The Golden Cocoon.*

In that story, a girl from the poorest farm in Lamar County comes to the University of Texas, where, by the time she is nineteen, she is courted by two men who will later oppose each other for governor. At twenty-seven, while she is First Lady of the State of Texas, she runs away to New York, changes her name, becomes a successful Broadway playwright, and ends up back in the arms of her ex-governor husband, who is now Woodrow Wilson's most trusted advisor.

If all the writing produced by Texas writers in the southern tradition were of Ruth Cross's quality, there would be no need for a discussion of the Old South as it appears in Texas literature. But it is not. A number of books deserve to be kept in print and repay the reader for his time. Mary King O'Donnell's *Quincie Bolliver,* set in Beaumont during the oil boom, does a creditable job of seeing the time and place, of portraying a young girl's coming to awareness, and of capturing the idiom of the people. Winner of a Houghton Mifflin Fellowship, *Quincie Bolliver* was published in 1941, the same year that saw the publication of Elizabeth Lee Wheaton's *Mr. George's Joint,* a novel about blacks in the Texas City area that won the Thomas Jefferson Southern Award of the *Virginia Quarterly Review.* Wheaton's novel of life among Gulf Coast blacks is interesting and treats the characters in a sensitive and sympathetic way. The only flaw in the novel is in the handling of black dialect. The novel is tedious because Wheaton attempts to spell every word as it is spoken rather than using spelling to suggest and relying upon speech patterns to complete the illusion of the dialect. The same problem in reproducing the speech of Texas blacks occurs in J. Mason Brewer's folktales about Negroes along the Brazos. It is possible to solve the dialect problems in other ways. William Owens does it in *Walking on Borrowed Land,* a novel about blacks set in the Little Dixie section of Oklahoma, and John W. Wilson is successful representing

African-American life in his novel *High John the Conqueror* about life along the Brazos near Navasota.

Some of the writers in the southern tradition from the 1930s and 1940s who are still readable but not easy to find nowadays are Dillon Anderson, Barry Benefield, and Sigman Byrd. Anderson's *Collier's* and *Saturday Evening Post* stories collected as *I and Claudie* and *Claudie's Kinfolks* are humorous and folksy and often pleasant to read, but they lack substance. Jefferson native Barry Benefield was a writer who had serious intentions, but his work now seems dated and flat. The first section of his novel *Valiant Is the Word for Carrie* is excellent, but the rest of the novel is trivial. Nevertheless, *Carrie* was made into a motion picture, as was another of his novels, *The Chicken-wagon Family*. Sig Byrd's novel *The Redlander* captures the flavor of country life in East Texas but fades when the main character goes to the state capital. His *Tall Grew the Pines*, a loosely constructed novel about growing up in East Texas, is his best work. His only other book, *Sig Byrd's Houston*, is a newsman's look at his city that rates among the top of its genre.

In the years since World War II, fewer and fewer novels in the southern tradition have been written. Except for Owens, Humphrey, and Goyen, there is no writer who has produced a body of work, though there are a couple of notable southern books—Madison Cooper's *Sironia, Texas* and John W. Wilson's *High John the Conqueror*. Both are excellent and still deserve a place on every Texana shelf. Harder to find but worth the trouble are Jewel Gibson's *Joshua Beene and God* and *Black Gold*, and John Cherry Watson's *The Red Dress*. Leon Hale's *Bonney's Place*, a novel about honky-tonk life in the area north of Beaumont is eminently readable and is a favorite of college students who take courses in Texas life and literature. Hale's novel never develops characters with depth, but it is excellent in its presentation of beer-joint life in the Piney Woods of East Texas. Hale has a knack for recording the language spoken by the country people and for picturing accurately the way they live.

The writers in the southern tradition in Texas literature are not discernible from writers in any other part of the Deep South, for the Texas writers treat the same general subject matter and explore the same themes as writers in Alabama or Mississippi or Georgia. Southern writers of this century are concerned with racial problems and social distinctions and with the extent to which time, place, and family help to identify self. Southern styles are marked by reliance on oral narrative techniques, the King James Bible, and the speech of common people. And in southern writing, no matter what the level of sophistication, the culture of the folk and the spirit of fundamentalist Protestantism are always present. The most important aspect of southern writing is the way that history—including the history of family and of place—has "dominated the imagination." C. Hugh Holman, one of the leading critics of life in the American South, calls the southern imagination historical. It is unlike the imagination of the New England Puritan or the New England romantic, for the Puritan's imagination was

> typological, catching fire as it saw men and events as types of Christian principles. The imagination of the New England romantics was fundamentally symbolic, translating material objects into forms and ideas. The southerner has always had his imaginative faculties excited by events in time and has found the most profound truths of the present and the future in the interpretation of the past. (1)

This southern preoccupation with history, place, and family is evident in most of the Texas writers who are in the southern tradition. It is an obsession with Humphrey and a major consideration with Owens, Goyen, Perry, Madison Cooper, and John Wilson. None of this is to say that the theme never comes up among western writers, for it does. But it never occupies them as completely; in fact, the settlers who left the other sections to settle the West often went in the hope of living in the present and putting aside the past as an issue never to be raised again. Sam Chance, the title character in Benjamin Capps's novel of the settling of Northwest Texas, says, "Damn the North and damn the South too" (13). Chance is not only damning the sections, he is damning their histories and, like Huck Finn, is expressing his view of history as a nightmare as he "lights out for the territories." In the novels of our best western writers, the land has a meaning, but it is not an extension of one's soul. Charlie Flagg, in Elmer Kelton's *The Time It Never Rained*, is committed to his land as totally as is any character in a novel by Humphrey, but the land does not define him, nor does the past bind him. Nor does he fit into an unalterable family lineage. It is unlikely that Charlie Flagg's son Tom, who gives up during the drought and leaves, will ever return to Rio Seco the way William Owens did to Pin Hook. Owens ends the introduction to *This Stubborn Soil* by saying, "So I am from Pin Hook and Pin Hook is a part of me. All my life has been a flight from it, but now, after many returnings, I see that it has overtaken me at last" (4).

William Humphrey, the Texas writer most given to comment on history, family, and place, says in *The Ordways* that the past lives in the southerner in his "book of books," that "collection transmitted from father to son of proverbs and prophecies, legends, laws, traditions of the origins and tales of the wandering of his own tribe. For it is this . . . feeling of identity with the dead which characterizes and explains the Southerner." Also in *The Ordways* Humphrey says that the southerner must be conscious of his family lineage, for "in his time he is priest of the tribal scripture, to forget any part would be sacrilege. He treasures the sayings of his kin. . . . If he forgets them, he will be forgotten. If he remembers, he will be remembered, will take the place reserved and predestined for him in the company of his kin, in the realm of myth, outside of time" (38).

In a similar vein, William Goyen in a 1982 speech reprinted in *The Texas Observer* of October 29, 1982, tells how his past became

> a lost time that came to rest in me like the stone founda-
> tion for whatever structure I could build upon it. It was
> the wanting to accept the present, to grasp what was hap-
> pening to me now, in this world and the reality it presents
> to me, to make bearable what passes away. Not a "reliv-
> ing of the past," not "nostalgia" . . . . but a sense of an
> urgent raw presence in the very livid now. . . .(11)

All the concerns with family, with the past as part of "the very livid now," and with place as an extension of self appear and reap-pear in the writings of those Texans who followed the southern tradition. Not only are the typical southern themes found in Texas writing, but the structuring and stylistic devices common to Deep South writers are also evident in seven books that afford a good picture of the Old South tradition in Texas literature. They are William Owens's *Walking on Borrowed Land,* John W. Wilson's *High John the Conqueror,* George Sessions Perry's *Hold Autumn in Your Hand,* Madison Cooper's *Sironia, Texas,* J. Mason Brewer's *Dog Ghosts* and *The Word on the Brazos,* and C. C. White's *No Quittin' Sense.*

Walking on Borrowed Land may seem an eccentric choice since the book is not set in Texas at all but takes place across the Red River in Oklahoma and since Owens's first two volumes of auto-biography are probably his best-known books. But *Walking on Borrowed Land* is the best of Owens's three novels and the most southern of all his books. Published in 1954, it is Owens's first novel, preceding *Fever in the Earth* by four years and the novelette *Look to the River* by nine. All three of the novels are set in Owens's Deep South Texas, but *Fever in the Earth,* set in the oil fields around Beaumont at the turn of the century, is less focused upon time, place, and family than upon the greed that oil causes and the destruction that follows the discovery of it. *Look to the River* is a forty-thousand-word novelette greatly admired by critics but kept by its brevity from developing but one effect—the fear that proffered friendship causes in a boy who is distrustful of human relationships. The motif of the wanderer, without ties to a place and a family is suggested, but, because of the story's length, it is not fully explored.

Any commentator on Owens's work is always tempted to devote much discussion to *This Stubborn Soil* (1961) and *A Season of Weathering* (1973). Those two autobiographical volumes are, by everybody's assessment, among the very best books to come out of Texas. They give painful pictures of life lived on the edge of rural poverty, show in minute detail what small-town life was like in Texas in the first quarter of the century, and make the reader suffer the young person's embarrassment at being countrified. His later volumes of autobiography, *Tell Me a Story, Sing Me a Song* (1983) and *Eye Deep in Hell* (1989), lack the grittiness of Owens's growing-up years and, being written late in his life, lose much of the punch of his earlier writings.

Another reason for considering *Walking on Borrowed Land* is that it gives the best and most complete fictional picture of life among southwestern blacks in the days before desegregation. The novel opens when Mose Ingram arrives in Columbus, Oklahoma, during the Depression to be principal of the town's black school. It is the "colored school," separate and unequal, dominated by unreconstructed whites, dedicated to a curriculum centered on training maids and porters. When Mose sees his new home in the Little Dixie section of Oklahoma he knows it is "just like all the Columbuses in the Deep South. The sidewalks were not marked 'For Whites Only,' but Mose read the signs there in the eyes of the whites he met"(38). Mose knows that he will have to practice the "good nigger manners" that he had learned in his native Mississippi and that his Chicago education has not freed him from his past. Mose Ingram has nothing but his integrity, his intelligence, and his dignity to see him through. They do, and at the end of the novel, despite being hampered by his wife's plantation-slave mentality and her devotion to Sister Brackett's Holy Roller church, despite the death of one son at the hands of a sadistic redneck lawman and the defection of another to Chicago to play jazz, and despite the system that effectively keeps blacks in their place, Mose prevails. At the end of the novel he has not triumphed, but in the few years he has been in the town he has helped his school and his people make some advances. As one of his teachers tells him, "And you done it without being no handkerchief head" (303). The thing that makes *Walking on Borrowed Land* a success is its authenticity. Not only is Mose real to the reader, but so is his wife Josie, and so are the whites of Columbus and the blacks of Happy Hollow who have to be out of Columbus by nightfall. Owens, who made his early reputation as a folklorist, has captured the customs of the blacks, their superstitions, their family structure, and their language. His thorough knowledge of the folk culture of the South informs every page of the novel. Owens's awareness of the unwritten laws of behavior that existed between southern whites and blacks is evident throughout the novel, as is his knowledge of the informal social structuring inside the black community. Mose Ingram is a fully realized character who grows and changes throughout the novel. He does not appear to the reader as a character who is already fully formed. He develops as the novel progresses, and his insistent search for meaning in his pilgrimage across "borrowed land" is dramatized and not merely posited by the author. Mose "surprises us with his human complexity," which E. M. Forster says is what separates caricatures from round characters. *Walking on Borrowed Land* is one of those books that fulfills what Joseph Conrad says is the

objective of the true artist: "to make you hear, to make you feel—
it is, before all, to make you see."

One of the themes in *Walking on Borrowed Land* is the importance of family in realizing self, and another is the disorientation
that occurs when one is uprooted and lives on borrowed land,
away from his spiritual home. The same themes dominate John
W. Wilson's novel *High John the Conqueror*, which, like Owens's
novel, focuses on life among southern blacks. The novel, published in 1948, is about farm life in the area near Navasota where
the Brazos joins the Navasota River. The crop is cotton, mules
pull the plows, and the blacks are mostly sharecroppers on white-
owned land. *High John* is set in the late 1930s or early 1940s and
follows a family of blacks through a disastrous crop year which
forces them to sell their small farm to John Chaney, the white
man who owns most of the land in the area and who wears out a
new Studebaker pickup each year driving from one of his farms to
another to supervise his sharecroppers. The story of the novel is
not nearly as neat as my summary, for, despite the novel's successful elements, structurally it is a mess. There is a prologue in
second person spoken by a traveling hardware salesman who
reflects on the life in the area. He never appears in the novel
proper, and his reflections have little to do with the story line.
The novel begins with the story of young Cleveland and his new
wife, Ruby Lee. Cleveland is the son of the family who will later
be forced off their land by the failed crop. But the novel never
stays focused on anyone for very long. There are a number of sections that cut back and forth between the story's present and
events in Cleveland's family that took place before he married
and left home. Then for a while there is a steady focus upon
Cleveland and his fear that John Chaney is sleeping with his wife.
The book ends with Mr. John buying the farm owned by
Cleveland's family, who are giving up farming to move to town.
Every possibility that the novel opens is closed down before it gets

well started. Despite the flaws in the plot and despite the failure of the author to pursue one theme steadily, the novel's good points outweigh its bad ones. For one thing, when the author turns his attention to a scene, he captures all the possible effects: the unwritten codes between blacks and whites, the spirit of place, and the exact language of the people. The various sections of the book are carefully and precisely written, and *High John the Conqueror,* in its series of loosely connected parts, is one of the best accounts of life among Negro sharecroppers and small farmers that exists. I do not know a Texas book that deals adequately with the life of big city blacks, but Owens's *Walking on Borrowed Land,* Wilson's *High John the Conqueror,* Wheaton's *Mr. George's Joint,* and White's *No Quittin' Sense* manage to render life among blacks in small towns and on farms without sentimentality and without condescension.

The best novel of farm life among the poor whites of Texas is George Sessions Perry's *Hold Autumn in Your Hand.* Perry was one of Texas's most popular writers during the 1930s and 1940s, but most of his writing has not worn well. His journalistic tour of the state, *Texas: A World in Itself,* is, despite its title, not a bad book at all. Some of his sidelights on life in Texas at the end of the Depression are still interesting and readable. His short piece on turkey raising as the farm woman's province is just one of a number of cleverly written sections. But most of his nonfiction is overdone and depressingly cute, as journalism about life in Texas often is. His stories in *Hackberry Cavalier* are embarrassing and not nearly as good as Dillon Anderson's *I and Claudie* stories, which are not as good as A. C. Greene thinks and not as bad as Larry McMurtry says they are. But *Hold Autumn in Your Hand* is a good novel, despite what Larry McMurtry says in his "Ever a Bridegroom" essay.

Hold Autumn in Your Hand is, like *High John,* a novel about life in the cotton patch. In Perry's novel the characters are poor white sharecroppers who live at the bare subsistence level along the San Gabriel River. Sam Tucker wants to prove that he is a cut above the sandy-land sharecroppers by getting a place in the rich bottomlands that require much harder work but produce more cotton. He is successful in talking a large landowner into letting him "day-labor" a rundown farm. The rest of the novel follows Sam's year with all its predictable problems—floods, cows in his garden, sickness. The Tuckers survive the year, but they are not much better at the end of it than at the start. Sam is tempted to leave farming and move to Houston to take a factory job, but he will not because he is a man who lives in proportion to his ability to identify himself with the land and with his past and his kin. The novel's weakness is that Perry is never able to make his characters rise much above caricature. Sam Tucker is, when all is said, a type—the southern sharecropper, the man fulfilling his duty to his wife and children and to his grandmother, the man of nature drawing his spiritual sustenance from his closeness to the soil. Those comments must make the novel sound like sentimental, Rousseau-like drivel, but it is not. *Hold Autumn in Your Hand* is saved from sentimentality because it is so completely and flatly accurate and true to its surroundings. Larry McMurtry calls the novel "workaday," meaning dull, flat, and pedestrian; but "workaday" can only be applied to that part of the novel that is grounded in the ordinary drudgery of farm work and the necessity of making a living as best one can. It is one of the best novels, southern or otherwise, to come out of Texas. Its southernness, by the way, was apparent to Jean Renoir, for his film version of the novel is titled *The Southerner* and stars a badly miscast Zachary Scott as Sam Tucker.

Sironia, Texas by Madison Cooper is an amazing novel. There is no way to summarize this seventeen-hundred-page novel; it certainly fits Henry James's category of "loose, baggy monsters." *Sironia, Texas* is over a million words long, longer by two hundred thousand words than all of Virginia Woolf's novels, three times as long as *Bleak House*. And it is an involved story of a southern city as seen by five or six families. *Sironia, Texas* has everything a "big" southern book should have—generals in the family and skeletons in the closet; genteel undersexed women and blowsy wenches; an afflicted son cursed by tainted blood; men with Rhett Butler's temperament; and "faithful darkies" as far as the eye can see. The novel also has something not always found in the sprawling southern novel—hundreds and hundreds of carefully crafted scenes that capture every detail of the life of the times. Cooper's closely written descriptions and his care with his minor characters make the little scenes work, and in an ironic novel of manners it is the little scenes, the deft touches, that determine success or failure. The satire is not raucous the way it is in many novels about Texas; it is subtle and mocking. Cooper sets out to ridicule the Deep South snobbery of the first families of Waco. His Waco women are the sole guardians of culture, and they wage total war against social climbing, decaying morals, uncouth practices in society, and the general letting down of barriers following the War Between the Sections, to use a phrase often heard in the South. The men in Cooper's novel are what men are supposed to be—lusty—but they are kept in line by fear of offending the women's sensibilities. *Sironia, Texas* is unremitting in its attack upon what was once the most Confederate of Texas cities. Waco, the center of upper Brazos culture, supplied the largest number of Texas generals to the Army of the Confederacy; it was for many years the home of the Cotton Palace and the big cotton festival; it is still the home of our most southern university, Baylor, and the spiritual home of the Southern Baptist Church. Cooper's main concern is not so much with the effect of place upon his characters as with the entanglements of family and the way individuals are shaped by the generations before and after them. His themes are southern, and his handling of language and customs put him directly in the Old South tradition.

No survey of the Old Order in Texas literature is complete without some discussion of the folktales collected by J. Mason Brewer in the Brazos bottoms and some mention of the Reverend C. C. White's *No Quittin' Sense*. J. Mason Brewer was for years Texas's only black literary figure. He was also one of America's best-known folklorists, and much of his reputation rested on the black folktales he began collecting in the late 1920s and early 1930s. His "Juneteenth" tales appeared in the 1932 volume of the Texas Folklore Society, and he published regularly in TFS volumes during the rest of the 1930s. His books began to appear in the fifties—the best known are *The Word on The Brazos: Negro Preacher Tales from the Brazos Bottoms* (1953), *Aunt Dicy Tales* (1956), and *Dog Ghosts and Other Negro Folk Tales* (1958). In these volumes Brewer preserved a great deal of folklore that might have been lost during the period when blacks were attempting to escape their negritude and achieve cultural integration. Brewer's collections help to keep alive the language, customs, superstitions, and religious practices of the blacks who were only a generation removed from slavery.

Brewer's tales capture the tone and the cadences of black speech, though he goes almost too far in his attempts to spell all the words as the blacks of the bottoms pronounced them. He also goes near to caricature in his characterizations, and his shaping of the tales often seems designed to please his white audiences. Still, it is only in Brewer's early works that we get the exuberance that the blacks felt over their freedom and the joy that religion provided them during a hard period of their history. Despite the broad dialect of the Amos 'n' Andy variety, the tales that Brewer retells have a vitality often missing from fictional stories of southern blacks. When Brewer himself told the stories to an audience, all doubts about their accuracy of language and about its appropriateness were dispelled, and folklorists are fortunate that he was able to audio- and videotape many of them before his death in 1975. Brewer's work is being kept alive by the republication in a single volume of *Dog Ghosts* and *The Word on the Brazos* by the University of Texas Press and by the work done in black folklore by Brewer's white colleague, the late James W. Byrd. Byrd worked with Brewer for a number of years, wrote a critical study of his works, and replaced him as the state's leading collector and scholar in the area of black folklore.

Equally indispensable to anyone interested in the black experience in Texas, in Texas folklore and folk culture, and in the Old South as it once existed in Texas is *No Quittin' Sense* by the Reverend C. C. White and Ada M. Holland. In 1964, Ms. Holland learned of seventy-nine-year-old Charley White's reputation as a preacher and provider for the poor of the Jacksonville, Texas, area and went to write an article about his works among the local blacks. The article led to a series of tapings and final publication in a volume by the University of Texas Press in 1969. The book is one of the best autobiographies to come out of Texas and ranks alongside Owens's autobiographical volumes in presenting a picture of East Texas farm life in the early part of this century. White begins his life story with his earliest memories, and the first quarter of the book strikes a few sentimental notes and becomes slightly tedious. But when C. C. White begins to tell of his experiences from age fifteen onward, the book suddenly comes to life and the reader cannot but be engrossed at the brilliance, accuracy, and simplicity of the Reverend Mr. White's narrative. His observations are clear and real and unsentimental. He never seems to regard himself as a hero of his own tale but as an observer of life.

Here is a brief example of White's style of telling his story. He is walking the thirty-three miles from Nacogdoches to Center and goes through an area where blacks are not allowed:

"Man don't you know they don't allow no niggers here?"

I said, "I'm just passing."

He said, "They don't allow no niggers here at all."

I said, "I'm going through." And I kept on walking.

Out along the road on the other side of town I met a man on a horse and he told me the same thing. Said, "They just don't allow colored people in this part of the country. They'll sic dogs on you." He was trying to be nice to me. Said, "If somebody sics dogs on you, you go up a tree. Don't let them dogs catch you, they'll tear you up."

I kept walking toward Center, but I did stop and cut me a stick. It was a strong, green pole about the size of my arm. I carried it like a cane, and I meant to swing it hard at anything that tried to hurt me.

When I walked through Martinsville I saw some men up on a porch roof painting a house. They started laughing and hollering. They said, "Oh-oh, there goes a nigger. Let's go down and paint him."

I walked on, with my big stick, acting like I hadn't heard them and they didn't do nothing. (86)

The section ends without further comment. The event is allowed to speak for itself. White's whole narrative is handled that way, and the result is perfect. *No Quittin' Sense* captures place, time, history, and man's humanness, in all its manifestations.

The Old South of Owens, Humphrey, Goyen, Charley White, and Perry is going, supplanted by the Far West, or, worse, urban America. Texas no longer sees itself as related to Tennessee and Arkansas and Louisiana. It is now either related to New Mexico, Colorado, and Arizona, or it has become what the trendy like to call the Third Coast. The literary heart and soul of Texas used to be located east of the Brazos. Dobie sought to move it west to

Paisano Ranch. For a time it seemed that Larry McMurtry would like to move it still farther west, but perhaps the literary heart of Texas will not go west at all but will end up on the border, in Rolando Hinojosa's *Klail City and Its Surroundings*.

The Novels of

Shelby Hearon

5

Any middle-aged housewife hoping to become a novelist would kill for Shelby Hearon's initial success. Not to mention the career that came after. Consider a few facts. At the age of thirty-seven, Hearon, herself a middle-aged housewife and aspiring artist, had her first novel accepted—over the transom, no less—by Alfred A. Knopf, one of the country's most respected publishers. While Shelby Hearon has never had the kind of blockbuster success that landed Danielle Steele and Stephen King atop the *New York Times* Bestseller List week after week, her books have sold well and have been widely and appreciatively reviewed. She has never had to resort to second-rate publishers, her books coming from such distinguished houses as Knopf, Atheneum, and Doubleday. All her books have enjoyed good sales in hardback and in mass-market reprints. She has gathered in awards and grants and prizes. And she has had no end of invitations to speak and teach and lead workshops at major universities. More than thirty years after her first success, Shelby Hearon, now in her seventies, is still at the top of her form as a novelist. The fourteen novels that follow *Armadillo in the Grass* are as fresh and new as the one she mailed from the Austin, Texas, post office to Alfred A. Knopf back in the late 1960s. More than that, Hearon has grown in wisdom and stature as a writer over the past four decades, though the themes she explored at the start still inform her fiction at the turn of the century.

In an interview and in several introductions and commentaries, Shelby Hearon has insisted that her novels deal with the disguises we wear as we struggle to understand the world we find ourselves in. There is no doubt that disguises—and other deceptions—play large thematic roles in her works, but she also explores a number of other themes: appearance versus reality, free will versus determinism, the natural rivalry between mothers and daughters, and the struggle of women to free themselves from traditional roles. Hearon is also concerned with the role of the artist and the way women use art to realize their full potential. But no matter what the particular themes or plots, almost all of Hearon's novels focus on the lives that women lead in the modern world. One exception is *Five Hundred Scorpions,* the only novel that features a man as the protagonist. But even in that book, there is a great deal of emphasis on the women who surround Paul Sinclair. None of this is to say that Shelby Hearon wears blinders where male characters are concerned, nor is it true that she engages in male bashing. It is just that she knows the roles of women, has worked to understand them, and depicts them in her works with great sensitivity.

Shelby Reed Hearon was born in Marion, Kentucky, on January 18, 1931, to Charles Reed and Evelyn Roberts Reed. Her androgynous name, Shelby, comes from an ancestor who was a governor of Kentucky, but despite her Bluegrass State roots and her early years there, she spent much of her life in Texas, the setting of many of her novels. Charles Reed was a geologist, so the Reed family followed him as he prospected for gold in the mountains of North Georgia, oil in Texas, and fluorspar in Kentucky. In 1947, when Shelby was sixteen, the Reeds moved to Austin,

Texas, where Charles was doing seismic work for the oil industry and where Shelby was to remain for thirty-seven years. While the family was still in Kentucky, the Reeds took Shelby out of the public high school, which lacked a college preparatory curriculum, and sent her to the Sayre School in Lexington. There she studied Latin and Greek and learned to circumvent the strictures of the Presbyterian girls' school with its emphasis on ladylike behavior and the avoidance of "the appearance of evil."

In Austin, Shelby Hearon, an outstanding student, finished high in her class, bore up under her androgynous name, and won the state extemporaneous writing contest—the news headline read "Austin Boy Wins Ready-Writing." (Years later when she was turned down for a Guggenheim Fellowship, her letter of rejection said, "Mr. Hearon, your work was given every consideration.") At the University of Texas, Shelby was accepted into the Plan II honors program and graduated—with honors—in 1953. That same year she married Robert Hearon, her high school sweetheart. In a marriage that lasted until 1976, Shelby and Robert Hearon became the parents of Anne and Reed. Anne Hearon Rambo attended Sarah Lawrence, earned a Ph.D., and is now a psychiatric therapist in Florida. Reed studied mathematics at the University of Chicago and is now a well-known celebrity chef/owner of three restaurants in San Francisco. During her years with Bob, Shelby Hearon lived the typical life of an Austin attorney's wife of the time: she was active in her local PTA, volunteered for Planned Parenthood, and was a member of the Junior League. She became president of all three organizations and was one of Austin's outstanding young matrons. She told interviewer Elizabeth Bennett of the *Houston Post* in 1975 that she tried to be all things—Betty Crocker in the kitchen, Brigitte Bardot in the bedroom, and Dr. Spock with the children.

It was out of this mother/housewife/civic matron life that she began writing her first novel, *Armadillo in the Grass* (1968). The publication of *Armadillo* didn't immediately change her life, for she continued being wife and mother for another eight years; however, she knew that she would never be the same person once she had made her start as an artist. Fifteen years after the publication of *Armadillo* she wrote in the introduction to a second edition, "it is the one you broke your past for, the one you turned and went the other way to get to." Her turning began with *Armadillo* and continued with *The Second Dune* (1973), *Hannah's House* (1973), and *Now and Another Time* (1976), but it was not until 1976 that she sought a divorce from Robert Hearon, her husband of twenty-three years.

As she wrote in an introduction to her fifth novel, *A Prince of a Fellow* (1978), "When I began the novel . . . I was, for the first time, a woman living alone. I was in a rented apartment with rented furniture high in the treetops above Barton Creek (near Austin, Texas)." By the time the novel was finished, she was living in a farmhouse west of Austin and writing of a "world where nothing was what it seemed, where every face and voice masked a different identity, where even the past dissembled and deceived, and the very dead refused to stay put."

The fifteen novels and seventeen stories she has written since 1968 have brought her many awards and honors, as well as a steadily growing reputation as an artist of serious intent. Two of her novels, *The Second Dune* and *A Prince of a Fellow,* won awards from the Texas Institute of Letters; five of her stories won the NEA/PEN short story prize. In addition, she has received awards, grants, and fellowships from the John Simon Guggenheim Foundation, the National Endowment for the Arts, and the American Academy of Arts and Letters. She was the recipient of an Ingram Merrill grant, and, in 1993, was chosen as a distinguished alumna of the University of Texas at Austin, an honor given to only a handful of distinguished alumni. She has been visiting writer and workshop faculty at some sixteen universities, including Middlebury, the University of Massachusetts at Amherst, the University of Miami, Colgate, and the University of Illinois at Chicago.

Hearon is principally a novelist. Though she has written stories, she does not consider them the chief business of her writing. Many, she told me in a telephone interview, were written in connection with her workshops and her teaching in various universities. Though the stories are uniformly good, they are not what she wants to be known for and space doesn't allow for discussion of them, her reviews and essays—or of her collaboration with the late congresswoman Barbara Jordan on Jordan's memoirs.

Shelby Hearon's first novel, *Armadillo in the Grass*, is interesting because it mirrors the life that she—as wife, mother, and emerging artist—was living in the 1960s. PTA and Junior League only go so far in satisfying an intellectual person's thirst for identity and status. As Clara Blue's friend Sarah says in *Armadillo*, "Women must have devised their social life as a prevention for madness" (129). Like Clara Blue in *Armadillo*, the Shelby Hearon of teas and Planned Parenthood meetings needed an artistic outlet, so when her children were of school age, she spent five years writing and rewriting the book that "she broke her past for." The novel was accepted by Knopf and was condensed in *McCall's* in August 1968. Hearon was launched, and she embarked on a career of writing that has taken her through fifteen novels and a number of other works. With that novel, she began casting aside the life "of the ordinary housewife." As one of her characters says in *Armadillo*, "If your husband idealizes you at a moment in the past, and your children are too lost in themselves to know you are there, who is there to see you?" (113)

Since 1968, more and more people "see" Shelby Hearon as a writer of sensitive and provocative novels. The Shelby Hearon that we read at the beginning of the twenty-first century had her fictional beginnings almost forty years ago. But like Clara Blue,

Shelby had a long way to go before she found her true voice as a writer. In many ways, *Armadillo in the Grass* is an apprentice novel. There is a naïveté in the voice of Clara, the first-person narrator, and the plot lacks the sophistication evident in later Hearon novels. Things come too easily and quickly for Clara; it is almost as if the author is in a hurry to get her character launched.

Armadillo in the Grass takes a year of Clara Blue's life and follows her from mother and wife and amateur naturalist to budding artist. Clara's husband, Archer Anslow Blue, a professor of history, gives her a twenty-five pound block of clay and challenges her to reproduce the animals she sees in her yard when she is tending her children and observing nature in the hills around Austin. Clara persuades sculptor Locke Smith (Hearon may be going a little too far with the locksmith/unlocking pun) to take her on as a student, and in the course of her study, she falls in love with Locke the way patients fall in love with their analysts. Nothing, however, comes of her crush. Locke tells her, shortly after she professes love for him and after he has discerned her talent, that if he takes her into his arms, she "will wake up at 6 A.M. tomorrow a culturette" (92). We know, as Locke does, that there is more to Clara than the bored housewife who embarks on an affair and a life of dilettantism. Locke leaves Austin, and Clara is on her way to realizing herself as an artist.

Shelby Hearon has noted in several places that her novels seem to come in pairs. Although this is not always the case, it is true of *The Second Dune*, the novel that followed *Armadillo*. The themes are complementary in that the central figures are women struggling to find themselves in a world of men. In *Dune*, we see for the first time Hearon's handling of the mother-daughter motif. In the novel, the central character, Ellen Marshall, is a woman searching for meaning for herself and her four-year-old daughter, Eleanor—always called Ellen Nor by herself and her mother. Learning to be a woman is still a work-in-progress for Ellen. The traditional way of learning how to be a woman is outmoded in the modern era. In an earlier time, mothers taught daughters "to look across the gulf to men and count ourselves only as they counted us. We learned to take our hearts and wrap them in ribboned boxes to be raffled at socials to the dark one on the right. . . . Although we thus learned early to tune our ears to the language of men, it is from female to female that the Word is passed" (6). And while Ellen is trying to learn another language, the new language of women, she hopes to be able to pass it to her daughter—and maybe to her husband and son.

Before Ellen married John Marshall, they had a rather hole-and-corner affair while she was still married to Franklin Hawkins, the father of Frank, Jr., now twelve and resentful of John and Ellen—and Ellen Nor, his half-sister. And so she escapes to John and finds that while things are better with him, she still has to find her way to total womanhood on her own. "The trouble is that happily-ever-after is a country run by husbands. . . . My conviction is that girls who know the right spells to cast can get out of their own towers without waiting for some passing prince" (81). This is one of the themes that runs through every Shelby Hearon novel: everyone is pretty much on her own, old rules don't serve, "princes of fellows" rarely are what they seem, and the lives of women have to be reinvented by women. And women often have to disguise themselves as wives and mothers and daughters and tower-bound princesses.

The mother-daughter motif is the strongest element in Hearon's third novel, the outstanding *Hannah's House*, published by Doubleday in 1975. The dust jacket of the novel calls the book "a novel of mothers and daughters," but that is not a subtitle; nevertheless, the book is very much a mother-daughter story. *Hannah's House* is sharply focused on the lives of Beverly Foster and her daughter Hannah—and on the failure of each to take the full measure of the other. Beverly, a woman of great humor and irony, always signed her school papers "Bananas Foster" and has gone through life thinking of herself as "Bananas." Her daughter, on the other hand, has no sense of humor, no sense of fun, no feel for irony. The house of the title refers to the yellow stucco house in Austin that Beverly has to buy to launch Hannah on her life as a sorority girl, engaged debutante, and starry-eyed bride. Hannah is the perfect picture of the vapid University of Texas sorority girl of the 1970s. She does all the right things—pledge parties, teas, and football games with her fiancé, the stultifying Eugene. What Beverly "Bananas" Foster buys is a living room suitable for Hannah's launching. She goes about her role as the mother of a sorority girl in the most ironic way, for Bev is a hippie who works for HEXPOP (Halt Exponential Population Growth), has a college professor lover, and fits in with Hannah's life not at all. She is happily divorced from Hannah's father, the CPA ("Certified Public Asshole") and is very much in sync with the Bohemian life of Austin of the sixties and seventies.

Hannah's House is Hearon's first completely satisfactory novel. The plot works perfectly, both Hannah and Bev are fully realized characters, and the life in a world of do-gooders, professors, sorority girls, and hippies is perfectly captured. And what is most refreshing, the humor shines through even in the most serious parts. Hearon proved her ability to handle irony without savagery. The themes that inform all Hearon's novels are evident in *Hannah's House.* Bev's "Bananas" disguise as an ironic and sharp-tongued modern Bohemian protects her essential vulnerability; Hannah's disguise as an airhead is assumed to please her mother, her aunts, her grandmother, and the world of the perfect coed. Things are definitely not what they seem in Hearon's third novel.

The following year, 1976, the year of Shelby's divorce from Robert Hearon, saw the publication of Hearon's most confusing and in many ways least satisfactory novel, *Now and Another Time.* The novel traces two—sometimes three—generations and explores the impact of family on their offspring. The novel begins in 1934 in East Texas (the "another time" of the title) and concludes in Austin, Houston, and the Texas Hill Country in the part entitled "Now." In the first third of the novel we meet two couples: Mary and Albert Allen and Tom and Frances Henderson; in the second part of the novel we follow the relationships of their offspring Julia Allen and Jim Henderson, who grew up together. Julia is now married to Hardin Chambers, and Jim Henderson is married to Jo. Hardin Chambers and Jim are law partners. All through college Jim and Julia are pals, almost brother and sister: Julia introduces Jo to Jim, and he finds Hardin for her. They deny their true feelings for years in much the same way their parents did. In "another time," Mary Allen and Tom Henderson, her doctor, almost had an affair—should have had one, it turns out. In the second two-thirds of the novel Julia and Jim Henderson complete the cycle that almost began with their parents. Late in the novel, in Houston, Jim and Julia come together for the lovemaking that should have happened years before.

If *Now and Another Time* is not sharply focused and always clear, Hearon's next novel is. *A Prince of a Fellow* is the story of Avery Krause, a "frizzy-haired, washed-out princess looking for a prince. Some ordinary prince on a limping horse, to carry me off to his leaking, rented castle. . . . No one special; after all, I am nothing fancy" (1). At thirty, Avery may be hoping to find a prince but she gets only frogs. "You never learned. Each time you shut your eyes convinced the frog you kissed would turn. If not this one, then the next one. Green, bloated bastards all of them puckering up those slimy lips in fraud" (166). Avery runs a radio talk show on "Pasture Radio," a tiny station out in the Texas Hill Country town of Prince Solms (a disguise for New Braunfels, the most German of all the Texas German towns). She is having an unsatisfactory affair with the mayor of San Antonio, a king of frogs, who spends much of the time he is with Avery talking about his wife and sons. Before him, she had been enamored of another fraud, an actor back in Kentucky where she was a drama teacher. He said his name was Charles Henry David, but Avery says, "To his delight, people could never remember whether he was Charles David or David Charles. I called him Henry; I never knew his real name" (13). Avery, as a drama teacher, "presented illusions as real," and she is not too surprised that the actor does the same to her. Once again, things are not what they seem; everyone is in disguise. Her job on Pasture Radio fits her illusionary world perfectly, for the audience has to imagine the people they hear. On the air, Avery is a princess if her hearers want her to be. For the Germans of Prince Solms, Avery Krause is pure German, but, she says, "I am, rather, as my mamma is, a Swede sitting like a burr in the saddle of a large German family" (4). The radio news is read to the largely German settlement by Otto, who has a heavy Teutonic accent. In reality, Otto is a "a forty-five-year-old Mexican with a Pancho Villa mustache, who works afternoons (out of his lederhosen and into his stiff black suit) as the cemetery sexton" (4).

Avery may well have found her prince in Gruene Albrecht, the Czech writer. Of course it turns out that Gruene Albrecht is really Billy Wayne Albrecht, a German whose father beat his mother to death and who is contemplating suicide when Avery rides to his rescue at the end of the novel. Apart from the disguises worn by Billy Wayne, Avery, and Otto, there is the grand disguise worn by Queen Esther of the Missionary Baptist Church, who is in reality Jane Brown, a local woman educated in the East who was fired from the Prince Solms schools during integration. Jane/Esther went back east and earned a national reputation before returning to Texas to become Queen Esther in the church and a commentator on Avery's Pasture Radio show. Everyone in this novel has a disguise—Willy Vlasic, the congressman from the region, who "dyes his hair and stuffs his jockey strap," the uxorious but wandering mayor of San Antonio, Avery's Swedish mother, and Avery the prince-maker. Hearon says in the introduction to the reprint that, as she was adapting to her new life in a German farmhouse west of Austin, she was "leaving behind between hardcovers the world where nothing was what it seemed, where every face and voice masked a very different identity, where even the past dissembled and deceived, where even the very dead refused to stay put. Leaving behind the first novel to employ my fascination with disguise" (xi).

If we skip forward to *Footprints*, a novel written two decades after *Prince*, we see a deepening of tone not evident in such works as *Hannah's House* or *A Prince of a Fellow*, novels sharp and ironic tonally and thematically. In *Footprints*, as the main characters attend the funeral of an old man who received their dead daughter's heart, we are witness to Hearon's handling of death and parental loss, not subjects at the center of the early novels. Nan and Doug Mayhall attended their daughter's funeral, and now they are attending the funeral of the man who got her heart when she was killed in a car crash:

> I couldn't help but think how Douglas was going to suffer during the preacher's funeral at the idea that his girl was being buried all over again. I could picture the big satin-lined casket, the elderly man (in reality only fifty, Douglas's age) in his black suit and stiff high-collared white shirt, his red heart-stitched tie and red pocket handkerchief on view. Banks and banks of long-stemmed roses fanning out on stands. And the specter of the young girl also gone. (189–190)

This passage from *Footprints* shows us a Shelby Hearon more chastened by life than the one who wrote *Armadillo in the Grass*. She can do more with her style. In the passage above, Hearon moves from the sadness to the funeral to the speculations on heart-transplant science back to the suffering of Douglas Mayhall—all in two paragraphs. Hearon gives us an economical glimpse into her scientific expertise, but what is most important is that she is able to capture the unspeakable sadness Doug and Nan feel at the funeral of the heart recipient. Nan, who made it her business to watch a transplant, has even more reason than Doug to suffer over the questions she is asking. And that suffering is muted but clear to the reader. By the 1990s Hearon's style had become a supple instrument in her hands. She could still do the comedy, the satire, the ironic situation, but along the way, she managed to master the kind of writing that bespeaks her humanity.

Back in the 1970s, while still finding herself as a stylist and learning to live as a femme sole, Shelby Hearon took on the contract job of helping to write former congresswoman Barbara Jordan's autobiography, the book which followed A *Prince of a Fellow*. Hearon's job was to tape Jordan's recollections, edit the tapes, and fill in spaces from other sources to flesh out Barbara Jordan's reminiscences. It was a job that paid instant cash—$30,000, reportedly—but not one that did anything to advance Hearon's reputation as a novelist.

Her next book, *Painted Dresses*, is one of her most highly regarded works. It is the parallel story of Nell Woodward, the painter of dresses, and Nick Clark, a scientist dedicated to disproving the idea of scientific determinism, an idea foisted off on him by his family of scientists. Nell and Nick do not meet until well into the novel, and their love story takes place only toward the end. But each character is searching for meaning—one in art, one in science. Each is pondering the matters of free will and predestination, of choice versus determinism. In her search, Nell divorces her husband and leaves her son behind to go to Santa Fe and become a painter. Nick struggles in a loveless marriage after his mean-spirited brother tricks him into marrying one of his cast-offs. He experiments with rats in an attempt to disprove a predetermined life. Nell is exercising her free will in leaving her family and painting the dresses that lead to her success as an artist. Her paintings are all versions of her at various stages of life. Nell might be hard pressed to explain their symbolic meanings, but she sees intuitively that their emptiness is a sign that she has not yet filled the dresses that represent passages in her life. As Nick says when he sees her paintings at the end of the novel, "I expected paintings; instead they are you."

There is much more to the novel than the simple story of Nick and Nell in love. Hearon questions Darwinian and Lamarckian biology, Presbyterian determinism; she probes her recurring themes of appearance versus reality and the disguises we wear to get us through life—or to hide from ourselves. The novel is dedicated to Bill Lucas, the philosophy professor Shelby Hearon married in 1981, the year of the novel's publication. She and Lucas met in 1978 while he was working toward a Ph.D. in philosophy at the University of Texas. After their marriage they moved to White Plains, New York, when Lucas took a job at Manhattanville College.

Following her pattern of novels in pairs, Shelby Hearon's seventh novel, *Afternoon of a Faun*, complements *Painted Dresses* in that it presents us with characters in pairs whose relationships are made clear only as the novel nears completion. First we meet Jeanetta, who is about to learn, on her fifteenth birthday, that Finis and Betty Mayfield of Paducah, Kentucky, adopted her immediately after her birth. Up to now, Jeanetta has led the charmed life of a Barbie doll. Her parents dote on her, and Betty considers her daughter almost a little sister. The knowledge that she is not the biological child of the Mayfields is devastating to Jeanetta, for she is ill prepared to accept that things are not what they seem. The person paired with Jeanetta as a central figure is

Harry James, a disturbed young homosexual whose do-gooder parents unthinkingly gave him the name of a celebrity bandleader and left him to shift for himself as they pursued liberal causes. The Jameses both look like Rose Kennedy and are always referred to as the Rose Ks by Harry, now in disguise as Harry Roncevaux. He meets the third pair, Ebie and Danny Wister, a childless couple from Kentucky who are on Holiday in Aspen. Ebie is pregnant and tells Harry that she had a daughter who died at the age of four. Harry "takes up" with the Wisters and follows them back to Paducah where Ebie has her baby, puts it up for adoption, and leaves for her father's home in Louisiana. The father, as eccentric as any character in this novel of eccentrics, lives as a recluse in one room of a decaying southern mansion and runs a network of tax protestors. Ebie dies in a fire there, Danny marries a woman named Louise, and Harry moves on again to Bennington College. Fifteen years pass and Danny meets Jeanetta, a student in a summer music camp, figures out that she is the child of Danny and Ebie, and invites Danny up to pick his daughter out of the assembled musicians at a concert. Danny zeroes in on the wrong girl, is sure that she is his daughter but doesn't want to meet her, and goes away. What Harry learns is that one never really knows who one's parents are—"not the ones who had you or the ones you adopted, could pick you out of a crowd. They could pass you on the street and never know you were theirs. Anybody else could be more kin. . ." (207).

After her marriage to Bill Lucas and her move to New York, Shelby Hearon, not surprisingly, sets her next novel partly in Texas and partly in New York. Hearon is preoccupied with place and with people on the move in search of themselves. New York is new ground for Hearon and provides her with a fresh venue to make her own. In *Group Therapy*, Lutie Sayre, the main character and narrator, goes from Austin to take a job not far from where Hearon and Bill Lucas were living in Westchester County. Lutie is a familiar Hearon character. She is naïve, canny, intuitive, and smart. A sociologist with a degree from the University of Texas, Lutie, ever the naïf, rents a trailer and moves her furniture to New York because she has an interview at Vassar. When she says "Yes, ma'am" to the chair of sociology interviewing her, she is turned down for that job and has to take a temporary position at SUNY–Purchase. In characteristic fashion, Lutie begins building a nest there. As one of her self-help projects, she begins making trips into New York City to take part in Joe Donaldson's group therapy sessions. She and Joe fall in love, and Lutie finds herself providing her own informal group therapy for Joe and his two sons.

Lutie, a sociologist with a specialty in matrilineal descent, understands Joe and his boys, but she has never come to terms with herself, her mother, and the two eccentric aunts she visits in Savannah, Georgia, halfway through the novel. All are obsessed with keeping up appearances: the mother is wedded to the University of Texas and virtually "married" to Dr. Pinter, the administrator she works for at the university. Her aunt in Savannah denies to Lutie and the world that her clergyman husband shot himself and insists that he died of overwork because of an integration issue in the church. The Rutledges, two sisters who are chief benefactors of the church, more or less drove Lutie's uncle to suicide, but since they help provide for Lutie's aunt, they must be deferred to. All of these "therapies" help Lutie to solve the problem of her self and to recognize what Joe told her early: nobody changes but we can find better ways to be who we are. In the final scene, Lutie notes that even though nobody changes, "you had to make provision for the fact that they changed in relation to you" (272). Lutie and Joe understand each other better, and there is hope that they will make a success of their "group."

The next two novels, A Small Town and Five Hundred Scorpions, represent slight departures from Hearon's usual plots, but many of her favorite themes are explored. A *Small Town* is different from Hearon's other novels in that it is essentially the story of a small Missouri town. Much of the history of Venice, Missouri, where the great earthquake of 1811 took place, is seen through the eyes of Alma van der Linden, who goes from little girl to mature woman in the course of the story. Alma's life is strange even by small-town standards. Her grandfather and his brother, both physicians, live at opposite ends of town and don't speak. Her father and mother barely speak, and she suspects her father of having a mistress—she even goes so far as to follow him and spy on him for days. As a teenager, Alma seduces the high school principal, marries him after his divorce from the town librarian, and bears two children. When a visiting scientist comes to town for an extended study of the seismology of the region, Alma begins an affair and is found out by her now-adolescent children.

As this synopsis shows, there is much plot movement in *A Small Town*, and this brief summary barely tells the full story. There is a myriad of characters, dark secrets held and revealed, even a murder late in the novel. Everything that can happen to Venice happens except the predicted quake that might rend the Mississippi River asunder as the great New Madrid quake did in the early nineteenth century. But a massive emotional quake is just under the surface of Venice, and the novel resonates with all the shock waves. As in most of Hearon's novels, it is the journey, not the arrival, that matters. And along the way in *A Small Town* we get a great deal. And even if many of the characters are not fully developed—Alma's mother, Hydrangea Pickens, the twins named Reba and Sheba, Alma's older sisters, Louis Le Croix (Alma's husband), and the adulterous geologist—they are such sketches as good fiction is made of. And the scenes of the novel are equally arresting, even if some of them are not fully fixed in the overall plot. Yet, despite the stuttering of the plot, *A Small Town* is a satisfying novel. The themes that Hearon treats so often—the effect of earlier generations on later, the question of free will versus determinism, the act of putting on disguises to protect our inner selves from an outer world, and the often disastrous relationships of mothers and daughters—are here handled in an intelligent way. Alma is a full character, and even though the others are not as well developed, what we see through her eyes tells us the stories of a small town.

Five Hundred Scorpions hardly seems like a Shelby Hearon novel at all. Set mostly in Mexico during a scientific expedition, the novel has as its main character Paul Sinclair, a lawyer from Virginia who pulls up stakes and slips away from his wife and two sons almost under cover of darkness to join the Tepoztlan project. He literally sneaks away from home by leaving some cryptic notes to his wife and sons and disappearing into the heart of the Mexican jungle with a pair of female anthropologists whose goal is to show that the woman-centered culture of the region destroys the men.

The person who recommends Paul to Dr. Helena Guttman is Paul's old college nemesis, Todd Stedman. Todd had been expelled from Princeton over a minor cheating scandal, and it turns out that the person who turned him in was his friend Paul Sinclair. Now it is payback time, and Todd hopes Paul Sinclair will be ruined by the Mexican experience and that Paul's wife, Peggy, will fall into his arms. Todd's attempt to seduce Peggy and render Paul a cuckold neatly plays against what is going on in Mexico where all the men in Tepoztlan seem to be cuckolds at the same time they are cuckolding others. Paul's role in Mexico is to get close to the men and study the sexual mores of the males of the village, though he is never quite told the full import of the study by the two female anthropologists. Further, his own hopes to seduce the alluring Dr. Guttman are as unrealized as are Todd's to seduce Peggy.

When a huge earthquake hits Mexico City and Tepoztlan, all the five hundred species of scorpions of the region are unleashed.

Paul is bitten and almost dies, and Peggy comes to the rescue. Nothing between them is resolved, but at least Paul has had his fill of adventure and may have survived the midlife crisis that sent him south of the border. The characters peopling this novel are well drawn, and the exotic setting is, as is the case with all of Hearon's novels, carefully rendered and realistic. The theme that so often governs all others in Hearon's work—things are not what they seem—is layered and relayered in this novel of treachery and disguise and mystery. Mexican culture is a mystery to the anthro-pologists, to Paul, and, it would seem, to many of the local peo-ple. Though a real departure from Hearon's usual concerns, *Five Hundred Scorpions* is a success structurally, stylistically, and the-matically.

Owning Jolene, winner of an American Academy of Arts and Letters Literary Award, finds Hearon on familiar ground again. Set largely in San Antonio and centered on the life of a smart young woman narrator, *Owning Jolene* is among the best of Hearon's novels—sentimental, ironic, affecting. It is also Hearon's funniest novel partly because Jolene spends her early life being kidnapped by her parents in the most imaginative and fan-ciful ways. Her father, Turk Jackson, who sells oil-field equipment, wants her to have a normal life, so he keeps snatching her from her mother, who wants anything but. When Turk has Jolene, Midge Temple perpetrates her kidnappings in an array of disguis-es—once dressing up as an exterminator. Midge always takes Jolene to some Texas suburb, sets herself up as a piano teacher, and tries to hide in plain sight. Then Turk tracks them down and takes Jolene away. At one point, when the parents reach a time of stasis, Jolene spends several years with an uncle and aunt, a pair of con artists cut from the same bolt of cloth as her mother.

As a late teenager, Jolene escapes from her family and strikes out on her own. She begins a love affair with a well-known painter and becomes his favorite model. The lover is Henry Wozencrantz (but in true Hearon fashion he is a victim of disguise, for his mother raised him as Henry Kraft and only later did he discover who he really is). Jolene longs for anonymity, but Henry paints her nude, and she ends up as the featured subject in a successful show in San Antonio that becomes the subject of a *Newsweek* feature—Jolene is even on the cover.

Jolene, despite everything done to make her otherwise, is an honest and sensible young woman. She finally takes charge of her life and decides that she is the one to "own" Jolene. She also provides a commentary on the ability to exercise free will and not to be a victim of familial determinism. Jolene may be a little too canny for one so young, but she is a youthful version of the women Hearon admires, women who take their lives in hand and win out against serious odds. The many disguises of the novel are typical Hearon, for once again we see how life is a series of masks that we wear to make our way to sanity.

Owning Jolene was followed in 1991 by *Hug Dancing,* another Hearon novel about a woman breaking the ties that have bound her and striking out in another direction. The novel opens "They lived happily ever after" and ends, "Once upon a time." In between, we witness the courtship and marriage of Cile Tate and Drew Williams. Of course Cile has a husband and Drew a wife, and the disentangling of the two marriages is as much a part of the story as the entangling of their lives. Cile is married to a Presbyterian minister, a man of predestination and determinism and a discounter of free will in this life, or at least in Cile's. When she tells him that she is leaving him for Drew, he announces it from the pulpit of his church before she can tell her teenage daughters or alert anyone in the congregation. A mean trick played by a mean man, a man who has his eye on a member of the congregation and who is in her bed—or she his—before Cile's footprints are out of the yard.

Drew is married to a Dallas socialite and is the father of two sons, also teenagers. Cile and Drew's mother become friends, and

Lila Beth Williams introduces Cile to her daughter-in-law, Mary Virginia. Cile and "Emvee" meet weekly so their children can play—or whatever teens do. When Cile finally meets Emvee's husband, she is startled to recognize him as her old high-school sweetheart, then going by the name of Andy. (Mary Virginia has made him change his name because she can't bear to be married to someone sharing a name with the singer Andy Williams.) Drew and Cile begin a love affair almost immediately, and after many slips and struggles manage to marry and "live happily ever after."

The action takes place in Waco, Texas, the citadel of Texas Baptists, where Baylor University has long prohibited "hug dancing" as the first step on the way to fornication. Though the main characters in the novel are Presbyterians—as Hearon is—there is a strong overlay of Baptist disapproval as Cile and Drew move from marriage to adultery to marriage. For a time, Drew gets cold feet, but love prevails in the end. Admittedly a romantic story, *Hug Dancing* is more, for we meet some of Hearon's best-drawn characters, we have a plot that is tight, and there is much to think about as the novel moves toward "Once upon a time."

Life Estates, Shelby Hearon's thirteenth novel, is the parallel story of two friends, widows in their fifties, who are in the process of adapting to life without husbands. Sarah Rankin and her husband Nolan had already moved into separate rooms before his death, and Sarah had begun to create a separate life for herself by establishing a wallpaper shop (Rooms of One's Own). Her friend Harriet is widowed when her husband Knox Calhoun crashes his car into a tree. Harriet's life was centered on her marriage—"It seems like I spent all day getting ready for him to come home in the evening" (77). But Sarah confesses that she didn't really take to marriage: "it was the institution that rubbed me the wrong way" (77). Sarah also suffered because Nolan's ideas about sex were rudimentary and didn't include her as more than his personal sex toy.

The working title of this novel was *Friends for Life*, but *Life Estates* may better describe what the novel is about. Each of the widows has a life estate in her husband's will, with the estate passing to the children on her death—a normal way of doing things in the legal world. But, as Sarah points out, "Life is a life estate" (78), something we are granted temporarily and that passes on to others when we die. The novel is about mortality, for Harriet learns that she has a tumor in her chest, and Sarah learns from her doctor-lover that her friend for life has but a short time to live. Harriet dies, and Sarah finds happiness—another life estate—with Will, her late husband's physician. (Years before, Will had refused to treat Sarah, for he knew even then that his attraction was too strong; now, all these years later, they are free to live out their "life estate.")

Set partly in Mineral Springs, South Carolina, and partly in East Texas, *Life Estates* is one of the few Hearon novels that doesn't have the strong sense of place that marks most of her fiction. But the plot is clear and well ordered, and the flashbacks fill us in on the early lives of Harriet and Sarah, when they were in school together, when they went swimming in their Rose Marie Reid swimsuits, and when they reveled in their "girlhood of corsages." Now widows with children, they look back over life and are willing to admit how many of the girlhood expectations were never fulfilled. Harriet learns toward the end of Knox's life that he had a lover. In one of the funny scenes in this otherwise sad novel, Harriet discoverers that the woman is a country club friend. She tumbles to this at a dance and confronts the woman, who runs from the room in tears. Harriet follows her to the powder room in a fury and pulls out the gun she has bought to protect her from the crime wave that she imagines is sweeping East Texas. Her friends run into the restroom, see her drawn gun, and all pull out their own guns: "Jo spied the gun in my bag . . . and pulled out a big .38 from her satin purse. Then every member of the Birthday

Club opened her bag and all of us had guns! We had ourselves an arsenal—five .38s, six .22s, and one Tec-9" (147). No blood is shed, but Madge, the other woman, moves to Houston.

The year *Life Estates* was published (1994), Shelby Hearon was divorced from Billy Joe Lucas, her husband of eighteen years. The following year she was married to William Halpern, a cardio-vascular physiologist, and went to live in Burlington, Vermont, where Halpern, a Ph.D., taught at the medical school of the university. Whether Hearon's marriage to a cardiovascular specialist encouraged her to write a novel about a heart transplant is not clear, but it is likely that Bill Halpern was helpful to her in some of the research she did for *Footprints*, a novel about a transplant and about the "heart transplants of parenting," as she wrote in an inscription to my copy of the novel. Part of her research for *Footprints* involved Hearon witnessing such an operation in Houston. A stickler for research, Hearon, who says she spends at least four months learning about the setting of her novels, obvi-ously devotes the same kind of research time to other aspects of her fiction. As evidenced by *Footprints*, Hearon knows not only about heart transplants but also about the effect of them on the donor families and the recipients.

The novel opens at a barbecue in Texas where recipients and donor families meet. Nan Mayhall and her husband, Douglas, are there because their daughter's heart is now in the chest of a black minister from Texas. Nan is reluctant to be celebrating this event, but Douglas feels himself in the presence of daughter Bethany when he sees the Reverend Calvin C. Clayton. One of the strug-gles between Douglas and Nan is the amount of grief each feels for the daughter who was killed in a car wreck at twenty-two. Because Nan doesn't take great pleasure in meeting Calvin C. Clayton, Douglas thinks he is the only one who misses their daughter. That is the chief struggle between them at the present moment, but there are others. Douglas, a professor at an Ivy

League university, is an eminent brain researcher. Nan, who stopped short of the Ph.D. degree in paleontology to be a "married woman," is clearly a minor character in her husband's orbit. Even though he often introduces her to colleagues as "a naturalist in her own right" (31), it is clear that her research and her interests are secondary. As the novel opens, she finds herself, at forty-nine, playing a minor role in the eyes of all who see her. She has borne two children—Bert, a son in the dangerous profession of cave diving, and the late Bethany. She is a faculty wife to a distinguished husband who has already had one affair and is on the verge of another. The second affair, with an English professor who "empathizes" over the loss of Bethany, is serious because Douglas thinks the younger woman can get pregnant and give him a replacement for the dead daughter. When Doug's stepmother warns Nan that Doug "is going to want to start over" (112), Nan calls him on the phone and screams "IF YOU MAKE A BABY, I SWEAR I'LL COME UP THERE AND TEAR YOUR ARMS LOOSE FROM YOUR BODY AND BEAT YOU SENSELESS WITH THEM. DO YOU HEAR ME?" (114)

Later, when Bert is feared killed or injured in a scuba-diving accident, the full measure of Doug's grief is made clear. Bert dismisses himself "as the one who survived," and Doug erupts and tells them about his own life as the one who survived when his brother Walter was killed. Doug's father tried to wipe out all trace of Walter Mayhall and make Doug the focus of all his protective efforts. Doug was "the one who lived," and he found the burden almost intolerable. Doug tells Nan and Bert, "I had nothing left of my brother. They stripped the premises and burned his memory to ash. Now your mother is trying to do the same thing with your sister. I mention that I've talked to the preacher . . . and your mother moves the length of the East Coast in order not to hear me. If I say Bethany, if I even say my girl's name, your mother starts in about something that's been dead since before the mind of man. Digging up some creature nobody would give a fuck about if it wasn't deader than history" (171).

In the final chapter, the Reverend Clayton dies and with him Bethany's heart. After the Reverend Clayton dies, Douglas says, "YOU DIDN'T EVEN THINK OF BETHANY." Nan says, "Our daughter was already gone, Douglas, she died at Thanksgiving" (191). The novel ends on a sad but reconciliatory note as Doug and Nan drive west of Houston to the ranch that Doug was raised on. Things will never be the same for either of them with Bethany gone, but they understand "the heart transplants of parenting"— and themselves better than they did.

Hearon's fifteenth novel is *Ella in Bloom*, the story of a forty-nine-year-old woman still trying to please her mother. Ella Hopkins lives in the New Orleans suburb of Metairie, Louisiana, and writes her mother back in Austin, Texas, about the wonders of her rose garden, about her life of teas and country clubs. Ella has created the perfect garden around her perfect small house with its brick fence laden with roses. Ella's roses are not the unofficial roses of the common rose gardens, but odd specimens from Denmark and England and far-flung lands of the rising sun. Her letters home read like pages from the Smith and Hawken garden catalogs. But the whole world Ella creates for her mother is make-believe. She and her gawky but brilliant and talented daughter live in a run-down shack in Old Metairie with a yard that is usually a swamp. Ella barely makes a living as a plant sitter and caretaker for rich people on vacation. She is an expert on roses but has none. The roses she invents for her mother come from what she learns from Henry Legrand, the rosarian of a local tourist attraction.

Ella ran away from home as a late teen with the no-good but attractive Buddy Marshall, who, we learn late in the novel, first slept with her perfect sister, Terry. Terry married R. Rufus Hall, an up-and-coming young Austin lawyer who fitted her mother's notion of the ideal husband for her favorite daughter. Rufus (or Red as he is known to himself and Ella) was the man Ella was closest to in her teen years. Red/Rufus married the perfect Terry, and the happy pair is living in a plush section of Austin with two fine sons. But one must remember Hearon's main themes: things are not what they seem, and we are all in disguise. Terry starts an affair with Skip Rowland, a West Texas rancher who is a double for Buddy Marshall, and she is killed when her chartered plane crashes on a visit to him. At the funeral and at Ella's mother's birthday party later, we learn how little Ella counted for in her mother's life and how much the perfect daughter mattered to her. But Ella wins in the end when she and Red become lovers and decide to live happily ever after—and this time things are what they seem.

Along the way, we meet a couple of Hearon's best characters. Ella is rounded and believable. She is Lutie Sayre, Jolene Temple/Jackson, and Avery Krause come to maturity. She is Bananas Foster of another time. She is the character Shelby Hearon has been working toward all these years. Ella's daughter Robin (who has renamed herself Birdie) is Jolene and Lutie and Avery in an early stage—and she will turn out to be her mother some day. But not Agatha Hopkins, the grandmother who lives in a world of her own devising, one as false as the world of Ella's letters. Not only are the characters good, but the settings are up to Hearon's high standards. Waterlogged Metairie comes alive; the house Ella and Birdie live in is real to us; and the rose gardens—real and imaginary—emit odors sweet.

The world and life of Shelby Hearon in all its permutations is to be found in these fifteen novels. The band of intelligent women we meet are extensions of the intellectual and intelligent Shelby Hearon, the star student who never forsook learning. We also see the Shelby Hearon who married three times and underwent all the emotional turmoil that intelligent women have been going through in the final third of the twentieth century.

The final assessment of Shelby Hearon the novelist is not in. Unquestionably, she is the finest woman novelist to come out of Texas. To say that is to insult her—and women writers in general—because separating women writers from men seems to be a false division. She is one of the finest writers to come out of Texas, and if a history of Texas literature is ever written, Hearon's place in it will be secure. But is it possible that a history of Texas literature will not be written since Texas writers are American writers and most resent the limiting regional label. Hearon is a Texas writer, but she is a great deal more, for her themes and characters transcend any regional label. And, in the middle and later stages of her career, Shelby Hearon has often abandoned the Texas locales that caused readers and reviewers to see her as typically Texan. It might also be noted that even in the novels with a strong regional sense, the characters could just as easily be shifted to Ohio or California or any other place in the country. Place is tremendously important to Shelby Hearon, but she is as keen a regionalist when writing about New Mexico or New York as she is when writing of Austin or Waco.

Character and theme matter most to Hearon the novelist. Other limiting labels that have been affixed to Shelby Hearon concern her use of female characters as protagonists. She is often called a writer of "women's fiction," a "mother-daughter" novelist, or writer about women struggling to be free of tradition. These labels are both true and false, for they have blinded some readers and critics to what Shelby Hearon is really about. True, her major characters are mostly women, and she does feature a number of mothers and daughters in states of struggle or moments of reconciliation; true, she does depict women who are fleeing the nets of marriage and seeking to determine themselves as individuals. But it must not be forgotten that the characters Shelby Hearon brings to life on her pages are easily substituted for you or me. If a reader cannot put himself or herself in the place of the main character, the literary work is a failure. If a woman cannot see her own life in, say Pere Goriot or Henry Higgins, if a man cannot see himself in characters like Emma Bovary or Carol Kennicott, the fictional character has not really come alive (Sinclair Lewis once remarked that Carol Kennicott is Red Lewis.) In all of Hearon's novels, we make a mistake if we do not see ourselves in Bananas Foster or Avery Krause or Nan Mayhall. While it is true that Hearon's women are real women facing real women's problems, they are also humans sharing the human condition with both sexes. As the poet Betsy Colquitt has noted, all intelligent people are feminists, and intelligent readers of Hearon's novels hardly fail to put themselves in the place of the characters that live and grow in her novels. And while in this time and in this place, Shelby Hearon is very much a "mid-list writer," I think her reputation will grow as critics pay serious attention to her in future years. She is much better than her present reputation indicates. She is a fine stylist, an intelligent observer of life, and a writer devoted to making characters live. People who reread Shelby Hearon are always more impressed with her work than those who come upon her for the first time and see only the simple stories of women fighting free of marriages and families and predetermined roles. Hearon writes about all of us, and I think she deserves a place among the superior observer/narrators of twentieth-century American life.

The Poetry of

Betsy Colquitt

6

ood poetry makes the familiar seem new. True poetry
must, as Pope says of true
wit, tell us "what oft was thought but ne'er so well expressed."
The poems in Betsy Colquitt's *Eve—from the Autobiography and
Other Poems* do exactly that and more. Not only are the "oft
thought" things in Colquitt's poetry "well expressed," but the
"Eve" poems even offer new thoughts. New in that the author
turns the stories we learned from Genesis and, in more cases than
may be healthy, from Milton upside down. Adam is no longer the
first human on earth. Eve is. Eve names the plants and animals,
invents the wheel, baskets, pottery. And then Eve finds Adam in
the strange soil of Eden:

> suddenly this strange soil breeding
> scarabs quickens, gives
> as finger comes forth and i take it,
> hand, arm coming free of burying earth
> . . . .

> he is clay-coated and ugly,
> his strange umbilical linked still
> to his source. unwife
> i discover midwifery.

And then Eve "informs him our geography," "teaches him My language," and names him: "adam i say, man."

In the beginning, Eve awakens in the garden and begins making sense of the world in which she finds herself. By naming things around her and by naming herself, she helps to create herself. Naming things, discovering things, inventing things, awakening to the world, Eve seeing her image in a stream says, "*eve, i say, hawwa, the living one,* and i am" ("am-ing"). And from this point on, Eve remains hawwa, the archetypal woman and mother and repository of wisdom. As she tells the girls of Plymouth Prep School millennia later and toward the end of her autobiography: "Try being Eve, the first woman, the world / your world," and when they ask her why, she says, "Because you are *Hawwa's* daughters, / and I am."

New. Fresh. Different. Colquitt's history of the world is the obverse of the universe seen by the church fathers. The myths we grew up with, myths developed over the past four thousand years, were sung and told and written by Jewish, Christian, and Muslim "fathers." Men. The stronger and more dominant sex. Except for the Virgin Mary and the shadowy non-virgin Eve, women have had no central roles in the myths that dominate our world. And Mary is a late, non-scriptural figure in only one segment of the Judeo-Christian-Islamic mythology. Her veneration, almost completely a Catholic phenomenon, began during the early Middle Ages. In the Bible, she is a vessel for the transporting of God's son from the heavens to the earth. Even Jesus has little to say to her or about her. Woman has always been "the weaker vessel" of the Judeo-Christian-Islamic mythology. (Remember Paul's letter to

Timothy: "I permit no woman to teach or have authority over men; she is to keep silent. For Adam was formed first, then Eve; and Adam was not deceived, but the woman was deceived and became a transgressor.") Eve was the easily seduced weaker partner in the Garden of Eden. Her weakness caused Adam to be the greater sinner. It was his responsibility to look after himself as well as Eve—weaker physically and intellectually and morally. Despite all we have learned about what Ashley Montague calls "the natural superiority of woman," some theologies still subordinate women to men and make men responsible for teaching wives and daughters "the steep and thorny path to Heaven." After all, a woman preacher, Dr. Samuel Johnson says, is like a dog that walks on his hind legs: "It is not done well, but you are surprised to find it done at all."

Betsy Colquitt is right when she says that all intelligent people—men and women alike—are feminists. But the feminism that underlies all of Colquitt's work is not the easy, reactive, thoughtless, knee-jerk expostulations that lead to the burning of undergarments and the bashing of males. Hers is a feminism of responsibility. It is the more thoughtful feminism that realizes that women are equal, if not always in stature, certainly in wisdom and in the sight of God. It is a feminism that puts the responsibility for moral and ethical action on both sexes alike. It admits the possibility that women and men are equal in their wrongdoings, that great crimes are as possible at the hands of women as of men, that neither sex has a corner on justice or mercy or revenge or undistilled evil.

The old shibboleths that women are passionate, unreasoning, reacting, tender, and irresponsible will not hold up in the world as defined by Betsy Colquitt. From the Garden of Eden to the Middle Ages and the veneration of Mary to a present where wars are fought to defend "womanhood," we have accepted patriarchal dogma. Colquitt will do no such thing. Her poems all begin with

the idea that all ideas, all saws and maxims "would be scanned."
And scan them she does in the three parts of Eve—from the
Autobiography and Other Poems.

The Eve poems are divided into two parts; the first, "garden,"
traces Eve's thoughts from her awakening in the Garden of Eden,
through her discoveries of creatures, language, and implements to
her finding Adam, to her meeting the snake—also a "she"—to the
sudden changes in the garden and the ultimate abandonment of it
for the larger world. In the second section of the Eve poems—
"History"—we follow Eve down the ages as she comments from
her unique feminine—and feminist—perspectives on the world as
it developed after "the Fall," if indeed it was a fall and not the evolution of all life as seen in one immortal woman's life.

The Eve story is engrossing because this new and radical
worldview comes to us through eyes and voice unused before by
writers and thinkers. The recent popularity of Dan Brown's The
DaVinci Code and the commotion it has caused among theologians
and feminists and general readers was presaged by the ideas in
Betsy Colquitt's poems about the first woman. The fifty-seven
poems in "Eve" form a long continuous narrative spoken by a
woman—actually Woman—moving from awakening awareness to
calm acceptance to world-worn wisdom. The best way to think of
"Eve—from the Autobiography" is as a novel/poem that develops
as the character Eve develops. And as Eve grows in knowledge
and wisdom, the language of the poems moves from simple to
sophisticated. Catching the reader almost unaware, we hear the
voice of Eve move from the staccato utterances of the early poems:

> and rushing to grow, meander,
> the honeysuckle, its scents,
> flowers fattening bees, the honey
> vining now from crowded combs
> time is present, only, always.

> i know no tenses, nothing
> but the constancy of flowers . . . .("day scene")

to these lines from "Perspective" near the end of the second part of "Eve":

> Then suppose Whitehead's interwoven perspective
> is true, that nothing is independent and symmetry
> of the law of cause/effect is law more than theory—
> then past, present, and future bind
> almost to Ptolemy's harmonics, and
> nothing is ever singular, alone and nothing is ever lost.

Not only are the ideas in Eve's head simple in her early life and complex four thousand or so years later, her language—Colquitt's language, we must remember—develops similarly. This is one of the glories of "Eve—from the Autobiography," and it is certainly apparent in all her poems: style and tone and voice follow story and theme. Only true poets accomplish that marriage.

The twenty-four poems in this section comprise Eve's reflections on life from the Garden of Eden near the Tigris-Euphrates Valley to the Big Bend of the Rio Grande Valley—the final poems are "Kafka at Santa Elena" and "In the Big Bend–20th cent. CE." The second poem in the second part, "Entering History," opens:

> I begin again but not as in the beginning.
> Far now from Eden, I enter history . . . .

Eve begins by a recapitulation of her history (herstory?) and then says

> I come to understand my role as instrument
> for keeping, change, the woman's part to be,

act, join past to recurring presents.
Entering history I begin this journey.

Slowly, it becomes clear that Eve is the spokeswoman for all of us, not just women but men also. It is she who is charged with telling mankind's long trek from the paradise of the first garden to the present-day valley of the Rio Grande, a garden still unspoiled, still new to the long history of mankind. But suddenly we know that one time is all time, that we live in a world of "recurring presents." In "Letter to Cain," she says, "I would like to know how your city / planning goes, when the mall opens" and then tells him

> Your father ages, talks sometimes
> of trying for social security.
> Perhaps we'll leave this land,
> move to Babel.

The juxtaposition of past and present echoes modernist poets like T. S. Eliot (cf. "Unreal City" in *The Waste Land*) who shift time backward and forward without comment. In "Eve" we see Cain, doomed to wander, live in a world of city planning and malls. Adam considers social security. And haven't we all moved to Babel, the fabled city of noise and incommunication? But biblical time passes, and in "Separations" she grieves for the death of Adam, for "Abel long buried," for Cain and Seth and all who grow old. All except Eve, who lives in what John Keats calls "slow time":

> I know myself hawwa, the living one
> schooled by Eden, to learn by other pasts,
> to live in many presents,
> each past, each present, rich
> in loss, hurt, wonder, marvel.

Then down the centuries Eve observes and participates in the cir-
cling years and centuries. She visits Machiavelli, answers a query
from *Who's Who*, visits Emily Dickinson in "Alias Mrs. Adam."
(Dickinson, in a letter reprinted as epigraph, calls herself "Mrs.
Adam," mentions that there is no record of Eve's death in the
Bible, and asks "and why am I not Eve?" Of course she is; we all
are.) Eve watches Schliemann dig, sees Sigmund Freud, Franz
Kafka, St. Francis, joins the lecture circuit to visit the girls at
Plymouth Prep, and once remembers Adam while she is at a
supermarket, sees him mirrored in an old man "Once easy in
homespuns, he stifles now / in double knit of polyester, / this old
man fashioned far from garden."

So Eve moves eternally through the world of slow time,
doing, observing, reflecting, teaching, being. In our "fast time,"
she rests at Santa Elena Canyon:

> I home here, journey when I please,
> am needed, receive many visitors,
> plan to stay, the long ago garden I seek
> in time, story, change, in self, selves
>   wholeness never complete—
> always to seek, try to make,
> perhaps to be again in this place
> where I am, have my kiva,
> this Santa Elena where I am
> begin again and again.

Always seeking, always Hawwa, always Woman.

Besides the "Eve" poems, the book, *Eve—from the
Autobiography* contains "Honor Card" (1980), and, in a third section divided into five parts, a collection of forty-two poems
arranged in four parts, as well as fifty-five uncollected or hitherto
unpublished poems. The subjects range across art, literature,

travel, marriage, domesticity, nature, and religious-philosophical speculation. The poems in the two final sections are not as person-centered as the "Eve" poems, but then since all poems are filtered through a personality, it is perhaps more accurate to say that Colquitt's filterings in these final two segments are impersonally personal. There is none of the confessional whine that mars some romantic and much immature modern poetry; no "I fall upon the thorns of life, I bleed." Even when we sense that Colquitt is commenting on things close to her—marriage and family, for instance—she maintains a distance from the personal. Despite the number of marriage poems in the second and third sections of the present volume, all reflecting Colquitt's conviction that marriage is a form of unarmed combat, the distance is such that we can never be sure that the marriages in question represent her own experience, though it would be hard to conclude otherwise. The first of the marriage poems in the "Honor Card" section will serve as an example of Colquitt's restraint. In "The Lie and Truth of This Land," a poem that uses the images of "wars and alarums" to signify the vicissitudes of married life, we see a couple embarking upon a marriage—or a martial campaign:

> Bonded, trothed, we foraged separately,
> each army wanting provender and uncomfortable
> in bivouac.

But time passes, skirmishes are fought, and by the end of the poem there is a peace—however temporary:

> our armies mainly easy at armistice
> and rarely foraging, commissaried now
> mostly from home.

As many of her other marital poems show, the circling "left and right through cul-de-sacs" that is marriage is never easy. As

Colquitt has pointed out, "marital" and "martial" are matters of reversed letters only.

Too much explication may destroy the pleasures for the reader, who will certainly want to savor the poems without the intercessory ramblings of a critic, but it is hard not to keep pointing out the small miracles that Betsy Colquitt has wrought. There are the delightful poems celebrating the lives and deaths of E. E. Cummings, Robert Frost, T. S. Eliot, and William Carlos Williams in the five sections entitled "of some recent dead" in "Honor Card." The poems mimic and play off the most famous lines of the dead poets. Here is one:

> how do you Mister Death
> like e. e. cummings at you
> coming with lyrics and love into
> your really enormous room
> coming wide-eyed and word handsome.

Cummings is captured perfectly: the tortured syntax, the wide-eyed blue-eyed puddle-wonderful language that marks this most romantic of modern American poets.

One has only to compare the wit and frivolity in "of some recent dead" with another poem in "Honor Card" to see Colquitt's range. The elegy "For Frank, Lost in the China Sea" compares the young man's death with Icarus falling into the sea off Crete and, in tranquility, remembers the man:

> Now in Texas season
> gaudy with Judas,
> orchards in flame,
> pears in communion dress,
> I hear of that plunging moment
> and would speak his Icarian
> unlegended descent

sharpening in blunt words
feeling not of kin-grief
but keen at loss of him
once student, then pilot and dead.

The half-dozen or so famous elegies in English hardly surpass this memorial to Frank "once student, then pilot and dead." Colquitt's poem has dignity and sharpness of observation and restraint. In this poem, as in all Colquitt's poetry, the overflow of emotions is always recollected in—if not tranquility—at least in distance and controlled passion.

Even in the final poem in this volume, "Return," which I take to be occasioned by the sudden death in 1991 of Landon Colquitt, the writer's husband, the restraint is complete though the reader can hardly hold back the tears. In the poem the speaker addresses the dead man as she imagines (dreams) him suddenly home. She tells him that if he returned, she, "surprised, glad, / would hold you like life, / warm your hands, feet, cold body" and then

after you supped and I fed
on the marvel of your presence,
you'd tell me how it was
your sudden leaving,
how you called—think you did—my name
but I didn't answer. So swift it was,
the way things go with the heart.

After he has told her where he had been, "news of this strange place," they would dream

you that you were home
I that your dream was true.

As is the case with all Betsy Colquitt's poems, the language of "Return" is new and fresh and sometimes startling. It performs what Conrad says is the artist's role: "Above all to make you see." The style is modern (to call it modernist or postmodern is to use terms "too often profaned") in that Colquitt proceeds as often by indirection as by direction—the topic is often only suggested by the analogue. In "non. pro," the speaker at "three and fifty" sees life in terms of football; three and ten (third and ten yards to go) is optimistic,

> but three and fifty's no metaphor
> in this real, undaylight saving—

> clock ticking, odds rushing
> to dark as time runs down
> to the two-minute warning,
> the final time out.

In this poem, as in all the others in the collection, the language is clipped and taut, catching the tempo of fleeting life that modern man—"Yea, and woman, too"—bemoans. The finality. The uncertainty. The "withdrawing roar" of Mattew Arnold's "Sea of Faith." In such a world, the cryptic must pass for commentary; if life's rhyme and reason are obscure, the soft rhymes and rhythms of poetry seem out of date. The new poetry must be as harsh and disjointed as our thoughts, or at least seem to be. And capital letters must be husbanded for use.

In poem after poem—far too many to explicate here—Betsy Colquitt sums up the world she has lived in (and brightened) for more than seventy years. Long after most poets have used up what the Anglo-Saxons called their "word-hoard," Betsy Colquitt is still finding new ways to make us see. Many of the poems in her most recent collection—almost all of the "Eve" poems and many of those in "Uncollected and New Poems"—are new within the decade before publication. And she continues to write. Her career defies the cliché that poets burn themselves out early. It's true that Samuel Taylor Coleridge and William Wordsworth, though they lived to be old, lost the "the visionary gleam" and the "inner joy" before age forty. And Lord Byron and Percy Bysshe Shelley and John Keats—Dorothy Parker's "trio of lyrical treats"—died young. But Frost and William Butler Yeats maintained the spark almost to the end. Sophocles was writing *Oedipus at Colonus* at ninety. And Betsy Colquitt gave birth to "Eve" long after many have retired to Highgate.

A proper introduction to a writer should begin with a biographical sketch, but I have saved the exterior facts of Betsy Colquitt's life for last because her poetry comes so much from an inner life that biography seems an afterthought. I can think of few writers whose work appears so little influenced by surroundings, even though a number of the poems in this collection center on Fort Worth and a few of them speak of home and family. Still, Colquitt has so refined her experiences that each piece takes on its own life, a life strangely apart from the writer. Born Betsy Feagan in a house on Berry Street almost within sight and sound of Texas Christian University in Fort Worth, Colquitt has spent almost all of her seventy-odd years in the shadow of TCU. After taking her B.A. (magna cum laude) at TCU in 1947, she studied for the M.A. (1948) at Vanderbilt University, which still had about it the aura of Robert Penn Warren, Allen Tate, and that band of agrarian poets, novelists, and critics who had decamped a few years earlier. Between 1948 and 1954, she taught at the University of Alabama at Montevallo, the University of Kansas, and the University of Wisconsin. In 1954, she married Landon Colquitt and joined the English faculty at TCU where her husband was a mathematics professor.

During her years (1954–1995) on the TCU faculty, Betsy Colquitt published scores of poems, books, scholarly articles, and reviews—while finding time to be mother to two daughters, one a physician in Texas, the other a professor of English in California. Despite not having taken the Ph.D., usually a requirement for senior rank, Colquitt became a full professor in her department and was the first recipient, in 1982, of the Chancellor's Award for Distinguished Teaching. For almost thirty years, she was editor of *Descant,* one of the state's most respected literary journals. Her work as writer, teacher, and editor earned her grants from the Frost Foundation and the Texas Commission on the Arts and the recognition of being listed in *Contemporary Authors, Who's Who of American Women, Directory of American Scholars,* and *World Who's Who of Women.* The best way to summarize Betsy Colquitt's influence on her world may be to quote from one of her most popular poems, "poetry and post, Texas." In the poem, the speaker, obviously judging a high school poetry contest, comes across a West Texas boy with "the gift":

> he's never seen a daffodil
> nor does Pecos flow like Avon,
> yet this marvelous boy manned of language
> visions his landscape whole
> it's not enough to judge he's won:
> he's by God a poet, and Post
> and all West Texas
> can never be proclaimed again
> the same.

Betsy Colquitt has made a difference, and those of us who read her "can never be proclaimed again the same."

Boom Town:

A Romance of the Oil Patch

7

In art and literature in Texas, most of the romance has involved the Alamo and independence from Mexico, ranch life, cattle drives, settlement of the West, and Indian battles. Even after oil was discovered at Spindletop in 1901 and oil became important in the state's economy, there was no great outburst of literary and artistic interest in the industry. In the folklore of Texas oil, the roughneck, the wildcatter, and the instant millionaire took on romantic proportions, but the fiction about black gold can almost be counted on one hand. Karle Wilson Baker's *Family Style* (1937), Mary King O'Donnell's *Quincie Bolliver* (1941), Jewel Gibson's *Flowing Gold* (1950), non-Texan Edna Ferber's *Giant* (1952), William Owens's *Fever in the Earth* (1958), and Tom Pendleton's *The Iron Orchard* (1966) all depict the life and romance of the various strikes, though Jett Rink's oil strike lacks the romance of Bick Benedict's cattle empire in *Giant*. Terry Pringle's *The Tycoon* (1990) tells of the depression of the West Texas oil patch of the 1980s. There is a scattering of folktales of the oil and a good bit of oral history. Mody Boatright and William A. Owens edited a number of folktales about the oil industry, as did Boyce House in *Were You in Ranger?* (1935) and his story of Spindletop, *Oil Boom,* House treats the oil strikes in a rollicking and romantic way. House, a Fort Worth journalist best remembered for a number of books of Texas "brags," was hired as technical advisor for the movie *Boom Town,* still regarded by many as the ultimate film about Texas wildcatters and oil strikes.

Boom Town captures all the romance it is possible to imagine about the oil boom. This popular 1940 film starring Clark Gable, Spencer Tracy, Claudette Colbert, Hedy Lamar, Frank Morgan, Chill Wills, and Lionel Atwill is both a melodrama and a romance. It also espouses all the virtues of unbridled capitalism and laments the restrictions imposed by governments and lawyers and small thinkers on captains of the petroleum industry. It takes its characters from hardship to success, back to poverty, and on to great riches. It exposes the temptations overnight millionaires are given to and then sees them back to virtue. It is supremely a work of romance. That is, it has a hero who is larger than life; it is filled with deeds of derring-do; and it pictures the hero winning and losing and winning his lady fair.

The literary critic Northrop Frye says that western literature for the past fifteen hundred years has moved from myth to romance to realism to irony. Today, he says, the prevailing form is irony. Romance, he argues, has not been a major form in five or six hundred years. And yet, we are surrounded by romance in sub-literary fiction, in mainstream fiction, in films, on television, and in commercials that fill the airwaves. We still love a hero, we still admire lovers, both requited and unrequited. We love the swashbuckling romantic hero who drinks and wenches his way through the pages of uncounted romances. According to Frye's *Anotomy of Criticism,* the way to tell whether a work is myth, romance, realism, or irony is to look at the hero. If the hero is a supernatural figure, we are witnessing myth; but "if superior in

degree to other men and to the environment of other men, the
hero is the typical hero of *romance* whose actions are marvelous
but who is himself identified as a human being" (33 passim).

In the film *Boom Town*, we find such characters. Big John
McMasters cannot leap tall buildings in a single bound, but he
can woo a maiden, subdue a woman, win in a fistfight, and bring
in a gusher where no gusher is suspected. And, God knows, he is
a manly man. A hero. A lover. A man of broad appetites and vast
dreams. He corners the petroleum market, overwhelms the virgin
bride who has come west to marry Square John Sand, and makes
and loses several fortunes in his "little two hours traffic on the
stage." Big John is played by the same heroic figure who, a year
earlier, had portrayed "that will o' the wisp blockade runner
Captain Rhett Butler" and wrapped his arms around the tiny
waist of Scarlett O'Hara and swept her off her ladylike feet.

The character played by Clark Gable is the central hero of
the film, but the character played by Spencer Tracy includes many
of the hero's characteristics. What starts out seeming to be a
"buddy movie" soon turns into a story with a hero and his sidekick. Though Square John is his friend's equal in many ways, he
falls short in at least one important aspect: he is unable to win the
heart of the maiden. He never wins a heart as far as we know but
is always in the subservient position of the unrequited lover who
is much in the shadow of the hero. At other times Sand becomes
the almost-hero of his own story. Square John has loved and lost,
one of the marks of the hero of romance, and the torch he carries
for Beautiful Darling Betsy is as "massy as a club"—another mark
of the romantic hero. And when left on his own, he is as able as
Big John McMasters to amass a fortune in the uncertain and
highly romantic world of the wildcatter. And he does not always
lose when the two of them resort to the manly arts of fisticuffs.
But, no matter his triumphs, he is still "Shorty." He is clearly a
secondary figure to Big John McMasters. In true sidekick fashion,

he tries to pull the hero's chestnuts out of the fire by proposing marriage to stunningly beautiful and desperately tempting Karen Vanmeer as played by Hedy Lamar. He does this not only to save the marriage of the woman he loves but also to protect the big fellow from the clutches of a woman whose role in life is to seduce and destroy. (It is interesting to note that nine years later Hedy Lamar was chosen to play the role of the biblical world's most notorious temptress when she was cast opposite Victor Mature in *Samson and Delilah.*)

The sidekick role has been with us from the start of written literature, from at least as far back as the Sumerian epic *Gilgamesh*. *Boom Town* has more than one sidekick—two act as clowns and one is the knight errant's loyal squire. Modern film almost always has the sidekick as a comic figure, and the writers of *Boom Town* spared no expense in having both Chill Wills and Frank Morgan as humorous characters. Chill Wills plays Harmony Jones, the crackshot cook, and Frank Morgan is Luther Aldrich, the stuttering, sputtering, gesticulating oil-field supplier. Wills played a version of the Harmony Jones role in movie after movie, and after his death, Slim Pickens took over the role. Frank Morgan raised bombast and confidence trickery to a new high in such roles as the Wizard in *The Wizard of Oz* and as Baby Snooks's father opposite Fanny Brice on the "Maxwell House Coffee Hour."

The function of the sidekick is to throw the hero into high relief, to feed him lines, or to show cowardice or stupidity in counterpoint to the main character's fearlessness and courage. The sidekick is often a wily servant type so familiar from the Roman comedies or a bumbling braggart like Falstaff—Frank Morgan does a variation on the Falstaff character here. Tracy is almost always the serious and intelligent aide-de-camp to the hero. In some ways he plays Horatio to Gable's Hamlet. He is the man who is "not passion's slave." John Sand's main role is to show

McMasters in relief, though at times he is near to the buddy role in his equal partnership with the main man.

It is also a feature of romance that we find a number of the stock characters of early drama, some going back to Roman times. In any given romance, we are also likely to see the saucy servant, the braggart soldier, the parasite, the fallen woman, the innocent maiden, the confidence trickster, the joker, the femme fatale, and the conniving villain. All of these characters show up in the romance of the oil patch that is *Boom Town*. Betsy Bartlett is the virgin, the Maine schoolmarm who has been teaching poetry to dolts for too long and has come west to find her man on the lawless frontier. She is wide-eyed but more canny than we think at first. But like all women in romance, she is a pushover for a hero. She meets Big John, eats a meal, visits a saloon, and marries him. All in one night. Then she becomes "the little woman," totally dependent on her man, willing to follow her man to the most malaria-ridden tropics after he has stupidly flipped a coin and thrown away an oil field. Of course she realizes that life was better and more authentic before they were rich. We get echoes of the good time when we hear of Burkburnett, Whizzbang, and Ranger. Those three boomtowns are objective correlatives for the good old days before the McMasterses go off to Tulsa and New York, before the femme fatale is introduced into the plot by the evil Harry Compton (played by horror star Lionel Atwill). It may be true, as the song says, that if you can make it in New York, you can make it anywhere. But we all know better as we watch *Boom Town*. New York is corrupt. Real life and real love exist better in Burkburnett, Whizzbang, and Ranger, all places where McMasters, Betsy, and Sand were poor, at least part of the time. Remember the scene in the plush limo when Gable is dressed like a dandy even to gray suede gloves? When he exits the car, we see "the look" cross Claudette Colbert's face. It is a look that we will come to know well before the movie is over. It is that look of hurt and disappointment, a look that so many movie simps seemed to live by. Betsy's look not only signals her awareness that Big John is trifling with Karen Vanmeer but that disaster lies just across Park Avenue West. We see the same look when she, McMasters, Sands, and Luther Aldrich are touring the cracking plant and Karen shows up. It is not long before the simpering smiles and hurt looks are replaced by the embarrassment that follows her attempted suicide. Her chagrin precedes by minutes another reference to Burkburnett, Whizzbang, and Ranger. Claudette plays the Patient Griselda, a Boccaccio story made most famous in Geoffrey Chaucer's "Clerk's Tale," but one replicated by simpering stars down through the history of film—the one described by Willie Nelson and Waylon Jennings as "A good-hearted woman in love with a good-timing man." And, to extend the country-and-western motif for a second, we know that she will "stand by her man."

She stands by her man in the film no matter what, but in James Edward Grant's 1939 *Cosmopolitan* short story, "A Lady Comes to Burkburnett," she is on the point of leaving Big John and Burkburnett following one of his episodes at Spanish Eva's and just before the fire that is handled with such drama in the film. In the short story, the fire burns for fifty-three days—not the short time that it burns in the movie. But in both film and story it is put out by the two heroes getting close to the well behind a tin shield and dropping nitro into the hole. This is one of the most romantic scenes in the movie, for two heroes risk almost certain death as they creep toward the fire behind a few millimeters of metal braced by a few two-by-fours. What they are doing can't be done. But they do it—to great applause. Big John's heroism, however, is not what keeps Betsy near home and hearth. It is only when Big John loses the field on a turn of the counterfeit coin that Betsy knows she must stay with him even if it means washing clothes on a rub board and living in a tarpaper shack in the middle of Central America. In the story by James Edward Grant, the narrator says of Betsy when Big John comes in broke and grimy after quenching the fire:

> Of course Betsy didn't leave Big John then. It was one thing to walk out on a man because of another woman; to walk out proudly, asking nothing and leaving a man who was a millionaire. But when he came home, where she was packing her clothes, she didn't need words to know that he had been hit a bad body blow. That made it different; she wouldn't leave him when he needed her.

James Edward Grant's "A Lady Comes to Burkburnett" shows how a man and a town can be transformed by the appearance of "a lady." Grant (1902–1966) was supremely at home in the romance genre, for he had been a pulp writer of the thirties and went on to do a great many things in film, where he was almost always associated with the romance form, with the tall, laconic hero. He wrote and produced *The Great John L.,* and he was writer and director of John Wayne's *The Angel and the Badman.* His handling of romance heroes can be seen in the series of John Wayne films that he wrote or co-wrote: *The Sands of Iwo Jima, Flying Leathernecks, Big Jim McClain, The Alamo, The Comancheros, Donovan's Reef,* and *McLintock.* (Remember Chill Wills in some of these works, especially as a kind of Harmony Jones in *McLintock?*)

In a James Grant story or movie, the good woman is likely to win out. Gail Russell makes the Duke lay down his guns in *The Angel and the Badman,* just as Betsy will subdue the mighty John McMasters. When his wild oats are sown, he will no longer be interested in women such as one found at Spanish Eva's or sirens like Karen Vanmeer. It will take a while, but, like the Patient Griselda, she will win in the end. The lady does in romance literature. In Betsy's early scenes, she brings up the Arthurian matter of knights and ladies when she poses as the fair Elaine to McMasters's Galahad and/or Mordred. We are tipped off early to the roles the two will play throughout the film. He is the knight with a touch of rascality; she is the lady who will finally steer him onto a proper path for a knight of the Round Table. By the end of both movie and story, we see the happy ending of romance. In the story, Betsy stands outside Big John's office as the two Johns prepare for their last fistfight: ". . . no woman had ever been so happy! She started home—home where soon would come a husband who could whale the daylights out of her." Don't talk to me about the death of romance in the modern world.

The lady trumps the strumpet. Karen in the film is the embodiment of the most beautiful woman in the world, as publicists actually called Hedy Lamar. She was the film world's Helen of Troy. To heighten her beauty and her dark side, she is, in the film, almost always photographed with shadows around her and a glow of light spotted on her. She is dark and sultry, she is dangerous, and she is so seductive that no hero—a Big John or a Samson—can stand a chance against her. Only Sand, who is still so besotted by Beautiful Darling Betsy that he will never hear a siren song, can withstand the wiles of Karen. It is as if Sand, like Odysseus, has had himself tied to the mast and his men's ears plugged with wax as he sails by the sirens. He can hear the song, but he can't be seduced.

One of the interesting contrasts between Grant's short story and the film is that Karen's name is changed from the story's Steenbeck to Vanmeer, more Dutch sounding than German perhaps. And since Hedy Lamar was chosen to play the role, the vamp is translated from blond to dark. In the story, Karen Steenbeck is beautiful enough in an ash-blond, regular-featured, poised way. And she has a magnificent figure. But her physical attraction is only lagniappe; she has a mind. No mature man could resist a fine intellect wrapped up in a provocative body. It was miserably easy to see how Big John McMasters could go overboard for Karen Steenbeck.

Don't tell me that the prose of the story that furnished the plot of the film does not demand an epic of romance. There is no Harry Compton in the short story, but in the film he sets his protégé on John McMasters to undermine his efforts to capture the petroleum world from New York City. (Incidentally, in Grant's short story, the New York scenes are really in Washington, D.C.) When we first see Lamar, we are alerted to her wiles and get a glimpse of the Delilah character she was to play nine years later, a plant, a high-priced whore out to ruin this Samson of a wildcatter. It is not altogether clear as the film moves forward that she is still the creature of Compton. She may be simply the mistress-in-ordinary to Big John. She may have no more connection with Compton. Or maybe she does. We never know for sure.

Apart from the characters of romance fiction and film and the overheated plot line, there are other elements of romance in the film. There is the icon of the wildcatter. Once oil began to be a factor in American life, there was the kind of rush to find it that had consumed the country during the California gold strikes. While it is true that most oil was probably found by geologists with maps and cores and test drillings, the romance of the oil field was to be found in the wildcatter, a man who could "smell" oil, who could taste the dirt of a field and say, "we drill here." The wildcatter begged, borrowed, and stole the pipe and the rig needed to prospect for oil. He is heir to the old-time gold prospector with a pick and a pan who senses gold "in them thar' hills." Clark Gable and Spencer Tracy are wildcatters, almost as romantic in folklore as the cowboy. They smell oil, they drill based on instinct, and they steal Luther's pipe and cement. They are reminiscent of such famous real characters as Dad Joiner and H. L. Hunt. And of the late Glenn McCarthy, who billed himself as the King of the Wildcatters. McCarthy was probably the model for Jett Rink in

Giant. Such men as Hunt and McCarthy swung a wide loop—Hunt maintained two families simultaneously and spent some of his vast fortune sponsoring right-wing causes. McCarthy built the famous and lamented Shamrock Hotel in Houston in 1949, perhaps the high point of Texas vulgar. It had seven shades of green, just like the hotel that Jett Rink built. These were legendary figures, larger than life, and like the heroes of romance, characters much more able than we are—the kind of romance heroes that Northrop Frye talks about in *Anatomy of Criticism.*

No proper oil movie would be complete without the runaway gusher and the flowing gold covering jubilant roughnecks and wildcatters. And then the fire! One reason that oil-field movies work better than oil-field fiction is that we can witness the gusher erupting from the earth and see the drillers dancing around in the oil as pieces of the drilling rig collapse around their heads. We can see the oil millionaires driving around in their Rolls Royce touring cars and their Deusenbergs and Pierce Arrows. We get a glimpse of the formerly poor Oklahoma Indians with a fleet of cars, and we see wildcatters who never owned a suit of clothes now dressed like the Prince of Wales. One of the great cartoons from Texas oil days shows a woman standing outside her shack as the gusher comes in and oil pours over her and her dirt farmer husband. She says, "I wonder what time Neiman Marcus closes?" We love the romance of the suddenly rich, and we love the romance of the rich person who loses a fortune if we know he is likely to make another one as soon as the next Burkburnett, Whizzbang, or Ranger hits.

And the fire. No oil-field film can ever be made that does not include a fire, and not just a little dab of a blaze but a fire that threatens to burn up the world. And then the wildcatter or a professional like Red Adair comes in with the nitroglycerine to blow it out. Of course, in films at least, nitro is so volatile that one drop spilled on the ground can create an explosion that will rock the world. I know nothing about nitroglycerine, but I know in movies where oil well fires break out, it is the only thing that will blow the fire out and it is the one element that is likely to kill all hands before it can be got into the ground.

All these things work well in film, but they are not that dramatic in books. That explains why there are only a handful of oil-field novels and hardly any that are memorable. And I am a little at a loss to explain why there are not more films that show the romance of the oil patch. Or maybe the dearth of great oil-field movies comes from the success of *Boom Town*. Maybe Gable, Tracy, and company said it all.

The Function of Criticism and the

Criticism of

Regional Literature

8

R eaders and critics of regional
literature find themselves in
a favored, or to use modern
critical jargon, "privileged" position. They are not bound by what
the most modern critics call "theory." They are not overcome with
jargon-like terminology for the simplest of things, nor do they
have to impress readers as far away as France with a full grasp of
Jacques Derrida or Michel Foucault. Both readers and critics of
regional works agree that they are reading novels, poems, plays,
and nonfiction and not "texts," that "set of indeterminate meanings that come to life in the mind of the reader/perceiver" (E.D.
Hirsch, *Validity in Interpretation*, 24). For another thing, the
regional author has not "disappeared," and it is considered fair
play to talk about her life, her plots, her meanings, and the place
from whence she comes. Finally, for the regional critic, it is per-
missible to assume that the book or poem or play means more or
less the same thing to any intelligent reader.

I agree with the reader-response critics when they say that we
all read works differently based on our biases and experiences.
(One shouldn't dismiss Ralph Waldo Emerson's comment that

"'Tis the good reader that makes the good book." But I don't agree with Terry Eagleton that "the true writer is the reader" and that "the readers have now overthrown the bosses and installed themselves in power" (*Literary Theory*, 85). In discussing Stanley Fish's brand of reader-response theory, Eagleton says that Fish sees reading not as a "matter of discovering what the text means, but a process of experiencing what it does to you" (85). (How, one cannot help but wonder, is this very different from the "impressionistic" criticism so reviled by twentieth-century critics?) In any case, critics of regional literature, while admitting that the reader plays a role in apprehending the work, take a more balanced view of the reader, the writer, and the text. Readers of—and commentators on—regional works tend to be what Dr. Samuel Johnson called "common readers" and not theoreticians and philosophers and ideological terrorists.

In the last thirty years, when English departments have gone to war over literary theory, critics and readers of regional literature have remained above the fray, so impossibly old-fashioned that nobody expects them to line up with either the New Critics, the structuralists, or the poststructuralist deconstructionists. Regional readers and critics still rock along in the old ways of reading and seeing: first, figure out what is being said—a step scorned by the newest critics—and then decide what it means and how it makes its point. As readers, we become involved with the text; as critics, we discuss those things in the text that may invite clarification or commentary. Readers of regional literature—all common readers, I hope—love poems and plays and novels and stories. They read for entertainment and enjoyment and enlightenment. For them, the text is not a thing to be fought over. It is not merely a document of ideology or a device to be used to enhance a career.

I am so impossibly old-fashioned as to think that the role of the critic is to make literature accessible to the common reader and not to "valorize" criticism itself. In the preface to *The Nigger*

of the Narcissus, Joseph Conrad says exactly what his job as a novelist is: "by the power of the written word to make you hear, to
make you feel—it is, before all, to make you see." Well, I submit
that it is also the role of the *critic* to make you see. It is not the job
of the critic to be a political philosopher or psychologist or scientist or historian or literary artist. The critic, whether she is a book
reviewer for a local newspaper or a contributor of articles to
learned journals, has as her first duty "by the power of the written
word . . . to make you see." To explain the unexplained. The use
of psychology or philosophy or linguistics or history or even science is legitimate in the explication of literature. But we must
always remember that the role of the literary critic is to annotate
the literature so that the reader, common or uncommon, can see.
The literary critic is not, as Geoffrey Hartmann and others have
argued, a producer of a parallel belles-lettres in his writings.
(Harold Bloom calls his critical work *The Anxiety of Influence* a
poem.)

Nor is the literary critic charged with effecting a political
change as do the terrorists with tenure who espouse
Marxism/Leninism/Stalinism, who attack dead white males, and
who call out for a revolt on campus against the privileged human-
ists. But Alvin Kernan says in *The Death of Literature,*

> Deconstructors show the emptiness of literary lan-
> guage and texts, Marxists show how the works of litera-
> ture have been used as the instruments of power to estab-
> lish the ideology of one or another dominant class—
> "Shakespeare as Hegemonic Instrument"—while femi-
> nists demonstrate literature's use of the past wrongfully
> to suppress the female. In this way literature has been
> emptied out in the service of social and political causes
> that are considered more important than the texts them-
> selves, to which the texts are, in fact, only means to a
> greater end. (212–13)

This is where we are today in the world of literary criticism, and it is of more than passing interest to consider how we got here. It is necessary, I think, to go back to the beginnings of the romantic movement—a movement, I contend, that is still underway. It seems clear to me that we are now in the decadence of the romantic period, an era of literary and intellectual history that began in the middle of the eighteenth century with the redefinition of God and continues through what we are now calling postmodernism. We are still defining and redefining God—first as Nature, then as Art, Science, Humanism, Language, or Politics. As Morse Peckham argued forty years ago in a *PMLA* article titled, "Toward a Theory of Romanticism," the essential feature of romanticism was the overthrowing of a world view that had existed since Plato. From Plato to Kant, thinkers had seen the world as a mechanical unit—made perfect, functioning perfectly, though not perfectly understood. From Kant forward, intellectuals have seen the universe not as a static entity—a machine—but as an organism constantly in process, constantly being defined. God is no longer the bewhiskered old man that William Blake calls Nobodaddy. In the first flush of romanticism, God was redefined as a benign Nature.

That first blush of romanticism ended when mature reflection taught Alfred Lord Tennyson that Nature, that is, God, was red in tooth and claw. Reflection taught Thomas Hardy to see God/Nature as a force without conscience or consciousness. Hardy hoped that God was in a state of evolution and might, ages hence, develop a conscience and a consciousness. A. E. Housman calls God "whatever brute and blackguard made the world," and William Ernest Henley challenges to battle "whatever gods may be."

The redefinition of God that is at the heart of romanticism is still going on today. We are still searching for meanings. Nothing much has changed philosophically since Immanuel Kant's day. It is also true, I think, that literary criticism has followed the various redefinitions of God that inform our age, our post-Kantian universe.

One of the quickest ways to see how literary criticism follows prevailing modes of thought is to contrast the critical writings of Dr. Johnson with those of Samuel Taylor Coleridge. Dr. Johnson was a practical critic who saw it as his business to point out things to the reader that the reader might miss. Coleridge was a theoretician who sought correspondences between the literary work, the mind of man, and the universe. Coleridge, like his fellow romanticists, saw the universe as an organic entity like a flower or a tree. It is in a state of growth and change, leading, possibly (probably?) toward death. It is unlike the mechanical universe of Dr. Johnson, which was like a watch and, therefore, not in a state of growth and change. Coleridge was concerned with the organic character of literature and of nature and with the way the mind worked to produce literature and thought.

Except for Matthew Arnold, who sought to replace God with Art and Culture, the years between Coleridge and the New Critics were mostly given over to Johnsonian practical criticism or the much castigated "impressionistic criticism" that the New Critics associated with Walter Pater.

But T. S. Eliot, William Empson, John Crowe Ransom, I. A. Richards, Cleanth Brooks, Robert Penn Warren, and a small army of rebels and agrarians ushered in the "New Criticism" in the 1920s and 1930s. It was new in that it was philosophically based and reawakened many of Coleridge's ideas. It was rigorous in its devotion to the text, its focus on language, and its dismissal of biography and chronology. It simply didn't matter who wrote the work or when it was written. The work had a life of its own and could withstand the most serious "scrutiny," a term that F. R. Leavis used as the title of his journal of the period.

The New Critics sought to wipe out the impressionistic criticism that had run rampant in the late Victorian period. They

THE FUNCTION OF CRITICISM

tried by close, hard readings to make the text give up its meanings. They favored tradition and the eternal verities. They espoused a return to the land, to the church, to conservative politics. The New Critics swept all in their path and had their way with criticism for half a century. They revised the canons by deifying the metaphysicals and denigrating Percy Bysshe Shelley, and they pondered deep subjects: "Where is the poem?" Rene Welleck and Austin Warren ask in A *Theory of Literature*. It is not an answer to say that the poem is right there on the page, as anybody with half an eye could see. Ah, but what if all copies were destroyed and it existed only in the memory of one reader? What if it is there on the page but nobody sees it for five hundred years? Welleck and Warren taught us that the poem had a life all its own, that it was a "structure of norms" existing in a state of growth and change. Heady stuff. We all quickly realized that we were on the cutting edge of something profound. And for a time we were.

Once New Criticism became the Mother Church of literary study, discipleships arose. The famous critics at Vanderbilt or Cambridge or Louisiana State University or Kenyon or Minnesota or Yale wrote their books and sent out their students with those books in hand. Along with the critical theories went right-wing ideology—oftentimes involving segregation of the races and white supremacy. The young who went forth declared themselves New Critics and set out to reform American literary education. And they did. (*Time* magazine once declared that Brooks's and Warren's *Understanding Poetry* was the second-most influential English textbook ever published. *McGuffey's Readers* were first.)

These antiromantic New Critics—T. S. Eliot called himself a classicist, a royalist, and a conservative—may not have known that they were in the late stages of a movement that had begun before William Wordsworth and Blake were born. They had found something new. They thought that modernism, a literary and artistic movement that ran from shortly after the turn of the century until either 1930 or 1940 or 1945 or 1954, was the start of something big. Actually, it was merely a byway of romanticism. The high modernist age of Eliot, William Butler Yeats, William Faulkner, Thomas Wolfe, and James Joyce lasted only a short time. Its heyday was from about 1920 until 1940. Or maybe shorter than that. But the New Critics have prolonged it by retaining control of graduate English education for decades. When I was in graduate school, if you could solve the "Wasteland" puzzle and knew when the "hyacinth girl" stopped speaking and gave way to "the Wastelander," if, with the aid of Stuart Gilbert's guide, you could read *Ulysses*, and if you could track the parallel paths of Mrs. Dalloway and Septimus Warren Smith as they went about London, then you were ready to take your rightful place in the criticism of modern fiction or poetry. You might even write a dissertation on Ezra Pound and go out in the world as a promising assistant professor. But if you could not do any of these things, you were taken off the "A" list and put into American literature. Or maybe one of the earlier British periods. Or, heaven forbid, you might wind up as a critic of the regionalists.

In the past few years we passed through structuralism, with its plan for a grand universal scheme, to poststructuralism, with all its fellow travelers: deconstructionism, semioticism, reader-response criticism, and the new historicism. These newest critics have found truth in the same way that Ransom et al. did. A few years ago, I was at dinner with Cleanth Brooks, and someone asked him what he thought of the new Yale critics who were at the time sweeping all before them. He expressed disgust. Someone—I suspect it was me—said, "Didn't you do the same thing to your predecessors fifty years ago?" He said, "Yes, but we were right."

The deconstructionists, the catchall name that most now use for the poststructuralist critics, know they are right too. But how can that be? Derrida and his cohorts posit that language is so personal and changing that any coherent meaning is impossible. Harold Bloom says that all readings are misreadings. So if there is no such thing as truth, I might do well to avoid any arguments with the deconstructionists, for as John Ellis says in *Against Deconstruction,* "deconstructionists have generally reacted with hostility and even outrage to any serious criticism of deconstruction and thus to any possibility of an exchange with their intellectual opponents" (viii). After all, it is well to remember that the American branch of the deconstructionist/politically correct movement emanates from the cafes of Paris and Central Europe, the coffeehouses of San Francisco, the free speech movement at Berkeley, the civil rights marches at Selma, and the antiwar riots of Vietnam. The freedom fighters, Weathermen, and chanters of "Hell, no, we won't go!" are now senior faculty at the better universities. These "tenured radicals" (see Roger Kimball's 1990 book by that title) brook no arguments against them. They did not in the 1960s, and they do not now. Theirs was a slash-and-burn movement designed to overthrow the establishment—and after the overthrow they would make a plan for future action.

So, for fear of reprisals from the politically correct, let me back off from any quarrel with the deconstructionists. Let me simply say that I think the whole deconstructionist/politically correct/incommunicability issue is the end result of mankind's redefinition of God. We redefined God, found Her red in tooth and claw, tried to substitute Art, Science, Culture, Progress, and Philosophy for Her, and have finally denied God altogether or have found Him to be unknown and unknowable. If He or She is dead, as Friedrich Nietzsche claimed, we are free to realize ourselves, to become Supermen (or women). Or we would be if we could speak to one another coherently, which the deconstructionists say we can't. Or it may be that God is lurking about in the chaos waiting for the Swiss Superconducting

Supercollider (we cancelled the one we started near Waxahachie) to find It. Or Him. Or Her. Physics, which like economics, theology, and Northrop Frye, sought a grand unifying theory that would answer all questions, has now developed a new physics—the physics of chaos. These "chaoticists" study the order to be found in chaos. I think that is what the deconstructionists are doing. They have given the lie to the order that Eliot, Ransom, and their fellows sought in literature, that armies of social scientists sought in history or geography or economics, that theologians sought in religion. They are seeking an order in the disorderliness of language. And, what scares me, they are waiting around to create a political New Order when the present society collapses, but, as in the 1960s, we don't know their plan. Like the New Critics, they have sent their disciples forth with copies of Bloom's *The Anxiety of Influence,* Paul de Man's *Blindness and Insight,* Derrida's *Of Grammatology,* Stanley E. Fish's *Is There a Text in This Class?* Jonathan Culler's *Structuralist Poetics,* and any one of a dozen "texts" for the times. It may be that the present-day disciples are less monolithic than those of my generation; in my day, we could label ourselves New Critics and let it go; nowadays, one declares himself a Bloomian and engages in "strong readings," or a Stanley Fisher and carries a copy of *Is There a Text etc.?* clutched firmly under her arm. Modern criticism, like modern linguistics, has become a series of cults, each headed by a Pied Piper acting like an academic Jim Jones.

The ideological literary critics of our age may be stirring up theory, but what they are not doing is spending much time on literature. And that is another worry that we old-timers have. The deconstructionists are philosophers and politicians, not bookworms. It is now possible to go all through the more prestigious graduate schools and read little more than Derrida, de Man, Martin Heidegger, Foucault, Fish, Jacques Lacan, Ferdinand de

Saussure, Bloom, and J. Hillis Miller. In fact, given the heavy jargon that these luminaries use to mystify the commonality, one might not have time for much else in a graduate career. Robert Alter says that "the most central failure" of the modern critical theoretical schools "is that so many among the whole generation of professional students of literature have turned away from reading" and insist "that daily newspapers, pulp fiction, private diaries, clinical case studies, and imaginative literature belong on one level, that any distinctions among them are dictated chiefly by ideology" (*The Pleasures of Reading in an Ideological Age*, 10–11). Imaginative literature is much lower on the graduate-school scale than the jargon-riddled criticism that prevails.

Maybe what troubles me is that I am a bookworm and expect all my friends to be Bookworms. If I mention Mr. Fitzwilliam Darcy and his ten thousand pounds a year, I expect all my colleagues to know that I am referring to *Pride and Prejudice*. What does it matter to me that "logocentric discourses try vainly to fix some original or final term that can never be reached" (Elizabeth Freund, *The Return of the Reader*, 2). This is philosophical speculation. What does a bookworm care about *différance?* What do I care that a reader-response theorist challenges "the privileged position of the work of art and seeks to undermine its priority and authority not only by displacing the work from the centre and substituting the reader in its place, but by putting in doubt the autonomy of the work and, in certain cases, even causing the work to vanish altogether" (Freund 2).

I don't argue that the act of reading is not participatory. I realize that I am helping to establish the story and the themes when I read a novel or a poem. I remember my Wordsworth and Coleridge, both of whom told us again and again that we half create the world we live in, that "we receive but what we give." I know I don't get exactly the same thing from Judy Alter's *Mattie* as someone from the plains of Nebraska would. I suspect a person from San Angelo or Midland sees some things in an Elmer Kelton novel that I might miss. Will I see exactly the same things in Bruce McGinnis's novel *The Fence* as someone from Comanche County might? But regardless, it is still McGinnis's novel and, given its 272 pages and its several ounces, I can't make it "vanish altogether," as Elizabeth Freund says I perhaps should.

My whole problem may be that I am not of a philosophical turn of mind. I am the sort who can only spend a short time wondering whether a tree makes a noise when it falls in a deserted forest. I may be fit only for the criticism of regional literature. It is a dead certain fact that I feel at home pondering the geography, history, folklore, and popular culture of the place I have chosen as my home country. Maybe all I can do is try to make someone see. It is not my job to tell the reader that no communication is possible because of the ultimate fluidity of language. My job is to bring my bookworm credentials to literary works of this region and hope they won't vanish altogether as I sit there reading them.

But those of us who devote our lives to the criticism of regional literature are not exactly like those more ponderous professors that regional critic Don Graham calls "the English majors." We are reading for the common reader, to use the term that Dr. Johnson invented and Virginia Woolf made a part of our currency. The people who read Elmer Kelton and Judy Alter and Bruce McGinnis and Benjamin Capps, who read all the Panhandle writers that I admire—Doris Meredith, Walt McDonald, Loula Grace Erdman, and Al Dewlen—don't want to read commentary alleging that the books and their authors have vanished. That language is incapable of communicating anything at all. That the novel you just read is not a novel, not a fiction at all, but a text. And that it is a lie because the writer is a right-wing, wrong-thinking, privileged, male-chauvinist pig. Readers of Meredith and Alter and McGinnis and McDonald still like to talk about what they have read, and if they can't find someone to talk to, they like to read the comments of some other flesh-and-blood human who has also read that book.

I won't deny that in the criticism of a regional writer a little deconstructing may take place, a little history and politics and geography may not be amiss, and it might not hurt to fit some of these non-canonical texts into the canon—if there is still one left in this age of the critical terrorist. We in the hinterlands have always been accused of wanting an unchanging canon and wanting to keep inflicting *Silas Marner* on the unsuspecting innocent forever and forever. I have never advocated a frozen canon. I want Benjamin Capps's *A Woman of the People* to take its rightful place alongside F. Scott Fitzgerald's *The Great Gatsby* as one of the best novels ever written in America. I want Walt McDonald and Betsy Colquitt to be accorded the status they deserve as major contemporary poets. I am not a conservative canonicist. I think the canon, like the flower or the tree or the universe, should be in a state of growth and change.

But I think a lot of strange things. I think the deconstructionist/reader-response/semiotics critical schools are on their last legs. There are too many attacks against them now. Alvin Kernan's *The Death of Literature*, David Lehman's *Signs of the Times: Deconstruction and the Fall of Paul de Man*, John Ellis's *Against Deconstruction*, David Hirsch's *The Deconstruction of Literature: Criticism after Auschwitz*, Roger Kimball's *Tenured Radicals*, and Dinesh D'Souza's *Illiberal Education: The Politics of Race and Sex on Campus* are but a few of the books that have begun to attack the excesses of the multiculturalists, the politically correct, and the theory-oriented faculty members who dominate the "best" English departments.

I think we may see a return to sanity in criticism that will allow us to read Elmer Kelton without apology. That will allow the kind of criticism that helps the common reader to hear, to feel, and above all to see. I am almost led to think the romantic movement that began with Kant and passed through the optimism of Wordsworth, the pessimism of Hardy, the existentialism of Hemingway and Fitzgerald, to the fragmented nihilism of Donald Barthelme and Thomas Pynchon may be nearing an end. But I won't be so naïve or bold as to wonder "what rough beast, its hour come round at last," is even now "slouching" toward Kalamazoo—or Houston or Amarillo or Commerce—"to be born."

PART II

Folklore

and

Texas Culture

The Uses of Folklore

9

E ducation is a wonderful thing for disabusing us of prejudices and smoothing off our rough edges. Historian John Lukacs said on a recent television program, "prejudice is the beginning of knowledge." And in many cases, our prejudices are the foundations of who we finally become. And some of those prejudices happen to be accurate. It is not a prejudice nor is it inaccurate to say that we learn the important things of life from the folklore of our culture. Most of those crucial things come to us in the oral tradition—but sometimes in poetry, song, and aphorism. Most of our main attitudes are shaped early in life—at our mothers' knees, to use the folk saying. A few years ago *Newsweek* Magazine devoted a cover story to children's brains, and the scientists quoted in the story more or less confirmed what ordinary people have always known—that as the twig is bent so grows the tree, another bit of folk wisdom. The scientists claimed that the brain of the child either develops skills in the first years or shuts down certain faculties. Language skills are developed between birth and about ten years of age, and if a child is told stories, read to, and talked to, chances are he or she will develop superior language skills. In recent years, some child psychologists have begun to experiment with something they call narrative therapy, encouraging children to turn happier events of their lives into stories to help them work through fears and neuroses. In *The White Album*, Joan Didion says, "We tell stories in order to live." Stories get us close to those root matters of life that make us the people we are. Here is a famous story:

> A certain man went down from Jerusalem to Jericho and fell among thieves, which stripped him of his raiment and wounded him and departed, leaving him half dead.
>
> And by chance there came down a certain priest that way, and when he saw him he passed by on the other side.
>
> And likewise a Levite, when he was at that place, came and looked on him and passed by on the other side.
>
> But a certain Samaritan, as he journeyed, came where he was, and when he saw him, he had compassion on him,
>
> And went to him and bound up his wounds, pouring in oil and wine, and set him on his own beast, and brought him to an inn and took care of him.
>
> And on the morrow when he departed, he took out twopence and gave them to the host and said unto him, Take care of him and whatsoever thou spendest more, when I come again, I will repay thee. (Luke 10:30–35

That is a very simple story. It makes a point about loving one's neighbor, about ethnic prejudice, and it does so without venturing into the abstract. It is, as you know, a parable Jesus told in response to a lawyer who asked, "Who is my neighbor?"

This 166-word story is a complete course in ethics and morals and love for one's fellow humans. There have been, since this story was first told, thousands of books on morals, thousands of university courses on ethics, and millions of sermons on the love that the Greeks called *agape*. But not a single one of them has sur-passed this story about what Wordsworth calls "that best portion of a good man's life, / His little nameless, unremembered acts / Of kindness and of love." The story Jesus tells the lawyer has been told in one form or another for as long has mankind has been on the planet. It is a folktale. It was a folktale before Jesus told it and fixed it in scripture. And the chances are good that you learned the parable first as a folktale, that is to say, you heard the story—as a story—long before you read it in the New Testament chapter ascribed to St. Luke.

The story we now call "The Parable of the Good Samaritan" should serve as a model for contemporary storytellers. And short-story writers. In fact, some forgotten literary critic calls the story told in chapter ten of the Book of Luke a perfect short story. It entertains, it speaks to universal issues, and it reflects the cul-ture of a time and a place. Those of us who write and tell stories would do well to imitate the Parable of the Good Samaritan. It teaches economy, attention to detail, and the art of showing rather than telling.

For the folklorist and the cultural historian, there is even more to the story. There is also a lesson about Mideastern preju-dice of the time, about the anti-clericalism of Jesus, about the prejudicial casting out of a whole ethnic group—the Samaritans. Cultural historians use such tales, as well as songs and myths and customs, to recreate in large part the world of the past. Much of what we learn about the past is not found in the history of events, official history as written by servants of the king or queen—echoes again of those famous dead white males we hear so much about. But the real history of the world is found in the lives of ordinary people. The modern French school of cultural history—they call it *"mentalities"* history—has produced a number of works showing how much we learn from the ordinary people of past ages. Of course cultural historians can't interview the folk of days long past. And the folk did not leave written records. The folk, often seen as simple people, are sometimes extraordinarily complex and have left a record in a trove of stories, songs, beliefs, jokes, customs, and superstitions that are with us today in one form or another.

Their stories existed in the oral tradition for centuries and millennia before being transcribed by antiquarians of the seventeenth and eighteenth centuries. Incidentally, the term "folklore" did not appear in the language until the middle of the nineteenth century. Among the early recorders of folktales were two German philologists named Grimm. They were in the Black Forest researching philology and kept hearing tales from the peasants—the folk—who were acting as linguistic informants. The folktales the Grimm Brothers published were an afterthought, but we remember Jacob and Wilhelm Grimm not so much for telling us about the sound changes of consonants but for the stories they published. Interestingly, many of the stories told by the Brothers Grimm came from French tales that moved to Germany during the Huguenot diaspora in the reign of Louis XIV. But the French tales told by the Huguenots were not even directly from the oral tradition as folktales are supposed to be; most came from a book published in 1697 by Charles Perrault called *Tales of My Mother Goose*. It is only with Perrault that we begin to get closer to folk sources for the tales we know so well, tales that form the bases for many of the stories we hear from childhood on. The tales of Mother Goose did come from French peasants of the seventeenth century, and those peasants got them from their forbears, who got them from their forbears, who got them from . . . .

Those stories that lasted in the oral tradition for centuries often changed with generations to reflect changes in culture, but the stories that came down the corridor of the years offer us valuable insights into the nature of stories, the nature of storytelling, as well as the role that stories play in shaping our lives, our moral positions, and our religious convictions.

Those tales contain the wisdom to be found in simple, common stories about unspectacular lives—stories like the Good Samaritan, which, like so many others, was told to us early in life. And the things we learn at our mothers' knees are never completely eradicated by scientific training or by throwing the cold light of reason upon our beliefs.

The Irish poet W. B. Yeats says in "Among School Children" that "blear-eyed wisdom" does not come "out of midnight oil." Wisdom comes from our careful reading of the book of nature, from our reflections on life, and from the stories we absorb early and never are able to put aside. Jesus knew that the wisdom imparted by stories could quickly and clearly summarize "all the laws of the prophets" (Matthew 22:40).

Many of the stories you hear everyday are part of our folklore, of our common culture, of the common wisdom that passes from generation to generation in the oral tradition. The job of the folklorist is to help preserve the wisdom of the ages that has been passed down from person to person and from culture to culture. The folklorist is almost any person who has an interest in the stories and songs and language of the past. The folklorist knows that wisdom really does derive from our folklore. It is our folklore that we live our real lives by. If Joan Didion's assertion that "We tell stories in order to live," means anything, it means that we recognize our parts in the greater life and wisdom of the world and must recount it to make sense out of our lives and our culture. The stories we "tell to live" are folktales or legends or anecdotes or jokes or narratives of things we have seen and remembered. Tales that express our families or our clans or our class or our culture. The Texas writer William Humphrey, who has always seen himself as a southerner rather than a westerner, says that every southerner has a "book of books," a "collection transmitted from father to son of prophecies, legends, laws, traditions of his origins and tales of the wanderings of his tribe." The southerner, Humphrey says, must be conscious of the power of story, for

in his time he is priest of the tribal scripture, to forget any part would be sacrilege. He treasures the sayings
of his kin. . . . If he forgets them, he will be forgotten. If
he remembers, he will be remembered, will take the place
reserved and predestined for him in the company of his
kin, in the realm of myth, outside of time. (*The Ordways*,
36)

Not only the southerner has a duty to his clan to remember
the stories and retell them, many American Indian bands had an
official historian to keep the memories of the people alive, to
learn and keep the history and to retell the tales of the tribe. One
of the most interesting examples can be found in Texas novelist
Benjamin Capps's great novel, *A Woman of the People*. Capps's
novel is about Comanche life toward the end of the nineteenth
century, a time when the Comanches and other Plains Indians
were being overwhelmed by the Anglo world and herded toward
reservations. One of the members of the small Mutsani band of
Comanches focused on in Capps's novel is an old man named
Storyteller. Like Humphrey's southern storytellers, he carries the
history of his small band in his memory. When his time comes to
die, he passes the tribal history—that is to say the lore passed
from generation to generation—to the young captive white girl,
Helen, the "Woman of the People" of the title. Her name now
becomes Storyteller, and it is her duty to be what Humphrey calls
the "priest of tribal scripture." At this point it might be well to
point out that Humphrey's "priest of tribal scripture" is more
often a priestess than a priest; as everybody knows, it is frequently women who are our "rememberers," our storytellers, and our
transmitters of culture.

Certainly those things that we learn before we can read are
usually learned from our mothers. They teach us our folklore by
way of nursery rhymes, games, and tales of the family, and they

retell the tribe's history of the world. They teach us folklore, which is, after all, the wisdom—and folly—of all the ages. Folklore, as I keep repeating, is what ordinary people figured out across the eons without the benefit of science or other revealed knowledge. It is the compendium of all our beliefs and behaviors. Most of what we still believe about the important things in life have been with us for centuries and is little changed by science or philosophy or history or technology. Despite all the scientific advances in the history of the world, all the folk truths still apply. We are no farther along than our earliest ancestors in solving our real human problems. Neither medicine nor mathematics nor philosophy has made it possible for us to find ways to ward off change, chance, mutability, and death.

Folklore is our common sense and common wisdom. Someone has defined common sense as that faculty which teaches us that the earth is flat. Well, the interesting thing is that the earth *is* flat. Anybody who really thinks that we can hang upside down on a ball without knowing it—and without falling off—is either a fool, a scientist, or an abstract thinker. The fact that the earth is an oblate spheroid with a strong gravitational field is meaningless to all but scientists. If you remember John Donne's line "at the round earth's imagined corners," you may get some hint of the convergence of science and common sense early in the scientific age. By Donne's time, the roundness of the earth was an accepted scientific fact, but in order to make sense of "the real world" you had to imagine corners, you had to imagine flatness, you had to imagine an earth-centered universe. In order to get along in ordinary life, one does not need to know whether the earth is round or flat or whether the earth goes around the sun or vice versa. You may remember that Sherlock Holmes did not know and did not want to know whether the earth went around the sun or the sun around the earth. Such knowledge would clutter up his mind and keep him from the more important considerations of life. The folk have always known that the earth is at the center of the universe. To think otherwise is to move from reality into abstraction. Here is another abstraction *v* reality conundrum: To think that two objects—say, a feather and a cannonball—will fall from the Leaning Tower of Pisa at the rate of thirty-two feet per second per second is an abstract absurdity. Common sense will tell you that the cannonball will fall faster. And it will. Unless you put it in a vacuum, which nature abhors, and which you, as a child of nature, ought to abhor also.

More than forty years ago I watched a Walt Disney television program with a man of middle years and his ten-year-old son. The man and I talked through much of the program while the child watched. Something on the screen caught my eye, and I asked the little boy what it meant. He explained that objects propelled into space would remain there in orbit. The father said, "Everything that goes up has got to come down." When the child tried to explain the science of extra-gravitational flight, the father said, "Shut up. I told you: 'whatever goes up has got to come down.'" It ended there. I felt embarrassment at knowing someone so backward and so adamantly ignorant of modern science. Now, all these years later, I realize that what the father said was true. Whatever goes up must come down is sound in a real, observational sense if not in a scientific one. If you don't believe me, throw some object as high in the air as you can and see what will happen. Unless you throw it to the edge of what Donne calls the sublunary sphere, it will fall back to earth—possibly with a resounding crash. Now, ask yourself which gravitational truth is most immediate to you. Is it embodied in the folk phrase "all that goes up must come down," or is it in some theorem compounded by Walt Disney or Werner von Braun or whoever figured out that it is possible for objects to find an equilibrium between earth and high heaven? So, to repeat, folklore is compounded of all those real things that real people face as they go through real life. And our folklore provides most of our stories. Even if we steal them from books, we may find that folk sources predated the printed word by centuries, perhaps even millennia.

Without romanticizing them too much—as the Germans, the Irish, and the Scandinavians have done—let me talk a second about who the folk were and are. They are the people who learned everything the hard way. Learned it from one another. Starting, as I keep repeating, at their mothers' knees. The folk are not necessarily illiterates who transmitted everything orally —they are not always those "mute, inglorious Miltons" of Gray's country churchyard poem. Once we thought of the folk as unlettered peasants, or so the early folklorists defined them. But since the industrial revolution, the folk come from the proletariat and the bourgeoisie, and most of them can read—not well enough to suit an English teacher, of course. But many of the folk in America and Europe and much of Asia have been reading for more than a century. Sometimes the folk are found in ranks of the great capitalists. Don't forget Henry Ford's dismissal of history as "the bunk"—a folk attitude if I ever heard one. And when folk attitudes are found among politicians, we call it populism. You must remember that the Latin word for "folk" is "populari" meaning "of the people," hence the term "popular culture," which is simply folklore of live people. Think back to the George C. Wallace American Party; it was one of the larger folk movements of the twentieth century. Also think about Ross Perot, a man who became rich without becoming sophisticated. He is a paramount example of folksiness applied to modern politics. But among intellectuals and persons of a scientific and rational disposition, the folk are the scorned of this earth. Scorned for their ignorance. Scorned for their superstition. Scorned for their refusal to see the limits of gravity—or to believe in gravity at all. Scorned for their practices and pleasures—scorned, as the country song says, for their "Red

necks, White Sox, and Blue Ribbon Beer." But the scorn
heaped upon them should not come from the folklorist or from
the storyteller. And certainly it does not come from me, for I
grew up among them and, to use a folk phrase, don't want to be
thought of as "gettin' above my raising." Therefore, I marvel at
the achievements of the folk down through the millennia. I am
more impressed with the development of cloth than with the
discovery that objects can orbit in space. Can you imagine how
long it took—and how important it was—to figure out that
plants can be beaten and shaped and woven into a soft, flexi-
ble, supple, long-wearing material to protect people from the
cold and the heat. The development of clothing causes such
advances in our culture as space travel to seem trivial. NASA
can congratulate itself on television about the landings on the
moon and most recently on the red planet Mars, but when all
is said and done, does it really matter in our everyday lives
whether there was ever water on Mars? Isn't the invention of
cloth more important? Everyone can think of other processes
that evolved over the years that are so startling that the concept of the Superconducting Supercollider seems insignificant.
Try to explain how this government project started and abandoned near Waxachachie, Texas, a few years and several billion
dollars ago, could tell me about the wisdom of the ages. When
billions of dollars were being sought, everyone heard that the
Superconducting Supercollider would unlock the secret of the
founding of the universe. Nonsense. We were told the same
thing about the landing on the moon, about the Hubble
Telescope, about the Mars landing. Nonsense! Nothing that
really matters about life—about birth, love, marriage, human
relations, and death—will ever be discovered by scientific
inquiry. We are taught in school and college that science has
rendered common sense obsolete. That our immediate ancestors were primitives and our distant ancestors brutish savages.
Technologically speaking, that may be true, but speaking about

the important aspects of life, we have not moved much beyond
the ancients. Yeats says the only subjects for poetry are sex,
death, and immortality. Thus it is and thus it has always been.
In Process and Reality, Alfred North Whitehead says "all philosophy for 2,500 years has been footnotes on Plato." What
Whitehead says is hard to deny. As Whitehead knew, when you
come down to it, there are only two ways to look at reality in
this universe: Plato's way (later appropriated by St. Paul),
which says that life is a dream from which we will someday
awaken. In this life, we see through a glass darkly, but someday
we will see face to face, or as the old gospel song puts it, "farther along we'll know all about it, farther along, we'll understand why." The other view of what constitutes reality is
Aristotle's, which says that what you see is what you get.
Nothing new has been said about those positions. Another
thing the ancients figured out is that if you make it past childhood and don't meet with an unfortunate accident or contract
a fatal disease, you will live to be about seventy. Despite
longevity tables, these words found in the Old Testament have
not been superseded:

> The days of our years are threescore years and ten;
> and if by reason of strength they be fourscore years, yet is
> their strength labor and sorrow; for it is soon cut off and
> we fly away. (Psalm 90:10)

At my age—and I am out of warranty—I find that a hard
piece of folk wisdom. But it is enduring. Our only hope is to be
found in the same psalm a couple of verses down: "So teach us to
number our days, that we may apply our hearts to wisdom" (Psalm
90:12).

As I argued earlier, it is unlikely that wisdom will come to one
from scientific experiment, from historical research, from literary
criticism. I am not saying that the doors of wisdom are closed to

scientists, historians, or literary scholars. But I am saying that wis-dom—the second word in the very useful and meaningful com-pound "folk-wisdom"—comes the same way that knowledge and wisdom have always come to the folk. By experience and obser-vation and reflection, by pondering sex, death, and immortality, by listening to the wisdom of the storytellers who preceded us, by the direct application of common sense. Oliver Wendell Holmes says, "Science is a first-rate piece of furniture for a man's upper chambers, if he has common sense on the ground floor" (*Poet at the Breakfast Table*).

And the folk are either endowed with or have by long trial and error garnered a store of common sense. And what are we to do with that store of hard-earned common sense? Are we as folk-lorists—and please remember that we are all folklorists—simply interested in collecting the flotsam and jetsam of past ages as idle curiosities? So, are all us folklorists out merely to recapture songs and tales and customs and rekindle some form of romantic nationalism? Are we out to preserve what the Utah folklorist Jan Harold Brunvand calls "fast vanishing relics"? Are we mainly interested in recreating Shaker villages and Ozark blacksmith shops so we can make our folk centers into Disney-style theme parks? I agree that it is important to preserve the "fast vanishing relics," to encourage folk crafts and to recreate folk villages. But I think all those reasons for the study and preservation of folklore are less important than the use of folklore to see how our ances-tors read the "great book of the universe" and how they made sense out of their lives and taught us homely ways to make sense out of ours. And for keeping alive the stories that express the uniqueness of whatever culture we inhabit.

Wallace Stevens says that "the maker"—and I suppose he means the poet or storyteller or fiction writer—that the maker has "a rage to order words. . . ." And much of that rage for order can be seen in mankind's desire to preserve what T. S. Eliot calls "withered stumps of time." We give different names for those "withered stumps of time" depending on how they are recorded or preserved. For the folklorist, the stumps appear as legends, songs, myths, tales, anecdotes, *objets d'art*, games, customs, and so forth. For the historian, the stumps are records, letters, and documents. For the folklorist, legends are the history of the folk; folktales are the short fiction of the folk; and myths are the religion of the folk. In an unlettered culture, the only way to preserve the religious laws, to record the cosmology, to explain the origins and practices of religious life is to develop myths. Think for a second about the Greek myths, and you will see how a people transmitted their religious beliefs.

Now think for a minute about the short stories you have read and see how closely they parallel the folktales you have heard. In Ecclesiastes we learn that "there is no new thing under the sun," so if you learned in your English classes that Edgar Allan Poe or Guy de Maupassant or Boccacio or somebody "invented" the short story, forget it. The short story has been with us as the folktale for as long as we can imagine. Even Aesop was a latecomer to short stories.

As long as there have been mothers, as long as there have been knees, as long as there have been children, there have been stories—not always short fiction, but folktales, folk rhymes, legends, myths, anecdotes, jokes, superstitions, customs. Embedded in those tales—no matter how simple—there is often folk wisdom, perhaps the only wisdom we have when you come right down to it. Think of the wisdom to be learned from "Mary Had a Little Lamb": "leave them alone and they'll come home, wagging their tails behind them," the worrying child is told. That applies to so many things that we labor and sweat over, things over which we have no control, things that will come home if we leave them alone. Often it is all that a parent can do with children; you simply, at some point, have to learn folk wisdom and leave them alone and hope that they will come home "wagging their tails behind them." And if they come home after a period of dissipation, maybe the best lesson to be learned is found in another folktale, one best known from scripture. In that tale, a lad has fallen deep into degradation and decides to return and ask for forgiveness; he says:

> I will arise and go to my father, and will say to him, Father, I have sinned against heaven and before thee, And am no more worthy to be called thy son; make me as one of thy hired servants. And he arose and came to his father. But when he was yet a great way off, his father saw him, and had compassion and ran, and fell on his neck, and kissed him. . . . the father said to his servants, Bring forth the best robe, and put it on him; and put a ring on his hand, and shoes on his feet. And bring hither the fatted calf, and kill it, and let us eat, and be merry. For this my son was dead, and is alive again; he was lost and is found. (Luke 11: 15–32)

The folk wisdom of that story, which also appears in Buddhist mythology, needs no comment.

Let me confess that I am not a religious person. But I find the Bible to be almost a full compendium of the folklore of our tribe—myths, legends, tales, poems. By tribe I mean those of us in Judeo-Christian tradition—even if we are not orthodox in our beliefs. I find that the authors of the Scripture read the great book of nature as well as it has ever been read. Little of the wisdom of that Scripture—and of the great book of folklore—has been superseded.

In 1623, Galileo said that the universe is a grand book "which stands open to our gaze." Galileo's grand book was written in the language of mathematics, and he said if a person did not have knowledge of circles and triangles, the book was closed and one was "wandering about in a dark labyrinth." But not everyone will agree that the great universal book is written in mathematics. For some it is written in nature. Robert Boyle, writing not long after Galileo, said, "I should be content that the world should think I had scarce looked upon any other book than that of nature." And Shakespeare, a contemporary of both Boyle and Galileo, speaks of "the book of fate" and "sour misfortune's book." (And Heaven knows it is both!)

But whether the great book is the Bible, the Bhagavad Gita, the Koran, or some other sacred text, it is almost certainly a compendium of the great book of life, of nature, of folk wisdom. It is no accident that we use the book as a metaphor for life. We "turn over new leaves," declare ourselves to be "open books," and threaten others with such statements as "I can read you like a book"—a phrase, in my experience, often spoken by wives to husbands.

I submit that life is a great book, and that we are all assigned to read it. The philosopher reads it one way, the historian another; the scientist in terms of circles and triangles; the clergyman in terms of parables, commandments, and proverbs; the folklorist in terms of myths, legends, tales, and songs. I am concerned here with the folklorist, specifically the storyteller. What we learn from folklore will make our reading of the grand book valid. Long before anyone had ever heard of postmodern reader-response criticism, Emerson wrote, "'Tis the good reader that makes the good book" ("Success"). And we ought to teach ourselves to be the best readers of the book of life that we can be. And as storytellers, we must shape our material so that our readings of the great book of life can be transmitted to those who hear us. As storytellers we are influenced by what we learned at our mother's knees. And it is our duty to "report the cause aright" with the same directness, the same clarity, the same underlying wisdom that we find in the parables of Jesus and the other great storytellers who have gone before us.

Texas: Land of Myth
and Legends

10

Texas is truly a land that has long struggled to live up to its myths and legends. Its heroes are outsized and its villains are deeper and darker, and, yes, often more romantic than those of other places. For most of its history, it was the biggest state in the nation. It was one of only two republics that came to statehood. In fact, it was the only one: California briefly proclaimed itself the Bear Flag Republic, but that was no more a nation than such fanciful creations as Fredonia and the Free State of Van Zandt. But here in Texas, the old-timers created a true nation with a navy and an army and a set of ambassadors. The French even established a legation in Austin in a building that still stands. That the state existed under six flags is true and real, and one of those flags was the Lone Star, which still flies over the capitol and other public buildings today.

The Texas of myth and legend is a compilation of all the lies, legends, literature, superstitions—and, yes, history—to be found in the tales, songs, movies, jokes, brags, booster pamphlets, and media hype about the Lone Star State. The Texas myth is everything you have ever heard about Texas. That it is the biggest, best, driest, hottest, coldest, dampest, dreariest, sunniest, windiest state in the union. That its people are the friendliest and most honest. That they are crude, crooked, mean, cantankerous, litigious, and murderous.

The great Texas myth is made up of many small myths. Or as the anthropologists say, little traditions inside the big tradition. Here are some examples that we all recognize: the noble savage; the rude, land-grabbing frontiersman; the free-range cowman; the wildcatter; the rich vulgarian; the lazy Mexican; the gunslinger; the athletic ignoramus; the leggy and vacuous cheerleader; the wheeler-dealer; the outlaw; the lawman; the songwriter; farmer and bracero and planter. And these are just the heroes and villains. There are also the beasts of legend: longhorns, vinegaroons, javelinas, wild boars with tusks four inches long, tarantulas, sidewinders, coyotes, and armadillos. And the plants of story and song: palmetto, pine, cactus, wiregrass, Johnson grass, salt grass, gamma grass, stinging nettle, oak wilt, Spanish moss, mesquite, and scrub oak. All these creatures are in a vast land with a mythical climate, a land beset by drought, hail, hurricane, tornado, wind storm, dust storm, and mud storm. At one end Texas is Calcutta; at the other, the Gobi Desert. And always there is wind, wind, wind across desert and mountain and coast and plain; red land, black land, sandy land, grassland. As Pappy O'Daniel sang it back in 1938:

> You can be on the plains or the mountains,
> Or down where the sea breezes blow,
> But you're in beautiful Texas
> The most beautiful place that I know.

Texas has too much nature, too many people, too many tales, too many facts for any one person ever to keep straight. At first, the Texas myths and legends seem simple and straightforward.

Then the contrasts come. It's the land of Lyndon Johnson and two George Bushes; Bonnie Parker and Barbara Jordan; Van Cliburn and Bob Wills; Katherine Anne Porter and Candy Barr; seashore, dust bowl, and swamp; the Valley and the Panhandle; the Piney Woods and the Llano Estacado. To quote Ernest Tubb, "There's a little bit of everything in Texas, And a whole lot of Texas in me."

The myth of Texas is hard to trace historically. Too often myth is piled upon myth in random order—one culture flowing into the other, confusing the other. How do you blend the myth of the free-spending crude vulgarian into the myth of Stanley Marcus, the hero of Dallas, importer of Godiva chocolates to a Hershey-bar city? Marcus created the Neiman Marcus Fortnight and the Christmas catalogue with its million-dollar gifts and his and hers airplanes. Marcus came back to Dallas from Harvard and promoted the Neiman Marcus "philosophy" here and across the consuming nation.

But even though the myth is too confused and the tales too tall, one has to start somewhere, and it might as well be at the beginning. Well, not the beginning. Not with Comanches and Apaches and Caddoes and Tonkawas. Not with the area lying astride the border known to Spaniards as Nuevo Santander or missions named San José and San Antonio and Dolores and San Juan. Those things are important to the Texas myth only as they fit into the great Anglo scheme of history and folklore, because the Anglos have so far been the great propagators of the myth. If not *the* beginning, then at *a* beginning. Start with the Mexican state of Tejas almost two hundred years ago. It was a paradise governed by the benign and enlightened sons of Old Spain who resided in the City of Mexico a thousand miles from the Tejas metropolis of San Antonio de Bexar. Americans who were willing to come west and embrace the Catholic Church and swear allegiance to the Mexican nation would get grants for vast tracts of land and lead lives like those California colonials that we see in the Zorro movies. That was the first Texas myth to capture the national imagination. That Texas, the Tejas of Moses and Stephen F. Austin, lasted little more than a decade, and then the hosts—the Mexicans—became, not the benign grandees from Old Castile, but a mob of murderous, lazy, deceptive greasers who were a blight on the land and needed a good dose of gunpowder and Scotch-Irish Presbyterianism. And Andy Jackson—or his surrogate son Sam Houston—was the one to bring it to them. As Arnoldo de León tells us in his book *They Called Them Greasers*, it took almost no time for the Americanos who came to Texas to find that the noble sons of Old Spain were lazy, ignorant, and vicious. They were obstacles to progress and prosperity and would have to be subjugated if Texas were ever to join the civilized world. So the Texicans revolted.

First there was the slaughter at the Alamo in which a band of hard-eyed Texans stood off a barbaric army led by a cruel dictator for what Lon Tinkle calls the "thirteen days to glory." As Travis and Bowie and Davy Crockett fought off the self-named Napoleon of the West, one Antonio Lopez de Santa Anna, Sam Houston and a ragtag army retreated and retreated and retreated all the way to the bayous of what is now Houston to lie in wait for the all-conquering Mexican army. There, under trees dripping with Spanish moss, Sam Houston and Deaf Smith and Emily Morgan, "the Yellow Rose of Texas," not only defeated the western Napoleon but humbled him and fed him some serious East Texas crow. Once the yoke of Mexico was thrown off, the Republic of Texas was ready to flourish among the family of nations. And the myth of the Lone Star Republic grew and grew and grew. Everyone in the state under the Lone Star Flag was sure that this new nation would someday rival France and Germany in the world's eyes. The myth of Texas the independent and invincible began. That myth lasted a decade. No. That is not true. The republic lasted a decade, but the myth survives to this day, for even after the republic failed and was annexed to the United States, Texas the invincible was celebrated in story and song. And even after Texas seceded from the United States and was forcibly restored to the Union, the myth persisted. And persists.

As we view it from the twentieth century, the Texas of the Confederacy hardly ever existed. Texans never had to writhe in the agony of Yankee subjugation the way the rest of the South did. It was hardly any time before the U.S. Army was helping Texas to rid the plains of the marauding Comanches. It is true that Texas supplied a higher percentage of her sons to the Confederacy than any other state and that a quarter of them were killed or incapacitated, but Texans simply rose above the facts— and the defeat. That was not hard to do, for the population of Texas during the Civil War was relatively small, and almost immediately after the war, the population boom began. Rebels and Yankees alike poured into the Lone Star State following 1865, and the people who had the drive to go west after the war were not the same kind of people who remained at home to lick the wounds left from the rebellion. Texas was the frontier, and frontier-seekers are not the sort of people who spend time in looking backward and lamenting their lot. Because of the population explosion—Texas doubled in size between the war and the turn of the century—the state bounced back more rapidly than any other southern state. And that strong sense of recovery and purpose has also become a part of the Texas myth.

Cotton was king, but it was cattle that powered the post-Civil War myth of free-range, cowboying Texas, the myth that persists to this day in the movies and in the popular imagination. The Texas of the Great Cattle Empire offers an interesting note on Texas mythmaking. The Cattle Kingdom lasted for barely thirty years, but, to this day, the image of the bowlegged cowpuncher and the longhorn overshadows all others—and not just in the movies. Because there were indeed hard-case cowboys and gun-fights and trail drives, because the plains were filled with buffalo and Indians acting as a barrier to westward expansion in Texas, because the dime novelists from the East found Texas romantic and wild, the myth of the Texan as lawless, heroic, laconic, tire-less, fearless—and male—grew and grew. The quick-draw novel-ists, many of whom never ventured west of the Susquehanna, per-petuated the myth that Texas started with an all-male cast of Confederate veterans and homegrown rangers who drove the Indians from the land, pointed the cattle north, and made short work of horse thieves, rustlers, and tinhorn gamblers. "It was a great land for men and mules," the saying goes, "but it was hell on women and horses." Not to mention Comanches, Mexicans, rustlers, and tenderfeet from the East.

The idea of the West, and Texas, as a place where young men of adventurous spirit came into virgin land and made westward expansion possible by romantic acts of derring-do has been seri-ously questioned by the New Western era historians led by such revisionists as Patricia Limerick of the University of Colorado. In her *The Legacy of Conquest,* she rebuts Frederick Jackson Turner's thesis that the frontier closed in 1890, attacks the western myth of benign exploration, and focuses on the damage done to Native Americans, Mexicans, Chinese laborers, and women in building "a playground for young men." But despite the New Western his-torians, despite the voluminous writings of Limerick, Albert Hurtado of Arizona State, Donald Worster of the University of Kansas, Richard White of the University of Washington, and Howard Lamar of Yale, the western myth will never go away. It is the dominant myth of Texas to this day. Texans might have been willing to let go of it once oil was struck and the state began being urban rather than rural, but Hollywood had too good a thing going to let the cowboy myth die. And, as Don Graham points out in *Cowboys and Cadillacs: How Hollywood Looks at Texas,*

Texans who had never seen a longhorn or worn a high-heeled boot were taught to see themselves as Hollywood did. Cowboy hats, boots, spurs, lariats, and rodeos started appearing from Texarkana to Port Arthur, from Baytown to Bonham. By the thirties, every boy who grew up in those parts of the state that lived and died by cotton and rice and pine trees and petroleum saw himself as Hoot Gibson or Buck Jones or Gene Autry or Bob Steele or Tex Ritter—just as grown men of the fifties began looking inward and seeing John Wayne, an Ohio native who became the ultimate Texan in the state's most enduring myth. The fact that the Duke was born in the Midwest and spent his childhood and adult life in L.A. does not negate his ultimate "Texanness."

Almost as enduring as the cowboy myth is the one that glorifies the oilman. When oil was struck at Spindletop in 1901, there was nothing western or cowboy-like about it. Oilmen from across the country flocked to the Beaumont area, as did muleskinners from the Piney Woods, cooks from small town cafes in Deep East Texas, and a parade of farmers, plowboys, timber workers, fishermen, and merchants. But there were no cowboys. At least, not for a long time. The strikes brought in at Kilgore, Longview, and Corsicana were not western. Look at the photographs of Dad Joiner, H. L. Hunt, and the other oil promoters, and you will see snap-brim hats and city clothes. If there are boots, they will be those that lace up to the knee, the kind worn by engineers and lumberjacks. But once the oil boom moved westward toward Burkburnett, Ranger, and the heart of the Permian Basin, the rich oilman myth was superimposed on the myth of the cattleman, and quickly the oil promoter was seen in jeans, sharp-toed boots, and cowboy hats.

The many myths of Texas are like so many drops of quicksilver under our thumbs. Things run together and fall apart and jump aside and skitter dangerously away. It is sometimes impossible to keep the myths separate. The cowboy, the land grabber, the wildcatter, the old-rock ranchman, the wheeler-dealer politician, the big-city developer all blend into one giant Texas type. At least in the myth. In the myth, we catch glimpses of Lyndon Johnson, H. L. Hunt, Shanghai Pierce, Charlie Goodnight, Glenn McCarthy, H. Ross Perot, Trammell Crow, George Mitchell, Billie Sol Estes, and Willie Nelson.

The motion picture *Giant* may tell more about the myth of Texas than any other single movie, book, story, tale, or history. Edna Ferber, whose only acquaintance with Texas, some Texans alleged, was that she once flew over it in a plane, gathers up much of the Texas myth in one volume. Actually, Edna Ferber did visit Texas. Don Graham told me an anecdote about her visit to the King Ranch. The Kleberg family invited her to lunch, but after her views on the ranch and Texas were made clear, the hostess told the server, "Miss Ferber will not be staying for dessert." In his book, *Kings of Texas*, Graham says Edna Ferber is supposed to have based Bick Benedict and his wife, Leslie, on Richard Kleberg and his cosmopolitan wife, Helen Campbell. And certainly the King Ranch, though it is not in the Trans-Pecos as is Bick Benedict's ranch, is the original of the half-million-acre Benedict Ranch. Hollywood took Ferber's words and turned them into some of the lushest visuals ever put on the screen. In scene after scene in George Stevens's cinematic version of Ferber's novel, the Texas of the popular imagination comes to life. The world was taught to see the "real Texas" in the film. The rancher with his half-million-acre spread, the wildcatter who brings in a gusher and becomes a member of the super rich, the inexpressible vulgarity of the green-on-green hotel that Jett Rink builds in Houston, the racism, the wheeling and dealing with politicians over the depletion allowance—these were the staples of the Texas myth as it had developed in the twentieth century. Bick Benedict represents old Texas; Jett Rink is an upstart in the new Texas. But they are merely the opposite sides of the same coin. What Jett

Rink was in the thirties, Bick Benedict's forbears had been a generation or two before—tough, rapacious, and power hungry. And, in the popular imagination, ignorant, provincial, vulgar, lawless, and bloodthirsty.

When James Dean opens the movie version of wildcatter Glenn McCarthy's Shamrock Hotel in *Giant,* all the worst aspects of the Texas myth are borne out. The hotel is the ultimate in Hollywood's Texas vulgar. However, the movie version of the Shamrock opening wasn't all that different from the real thing. *Life* magazine sent photographers to cover the grand unveiling of Glenn McCarthy's hotel, and the rest of the world could look at the pictures of wealth in Texas and be sure that old, wild, romantic, vulgar Texas was alive and well and dancing the Cotton-eyed Joe.

World War II changed Texas immeasurably, but it didn't change the Texas myth all that much. Movie after movie depicted Texans sitting at Salerno or Iwo Jima or Bastogne bragging about how wonderful Texas was. The movie soldier from Texas was a natural son of the men who had chased the Comanches off the frontier, driven the Mexicans out of Texas, built the ranches, herded the cattle north, and struck gusher after gusher all across the Lone Star State. That was the movie Texan, and the myth could have been laughed off as pure Hollywood if Audie Leon Murphy, a farm boy from the cotton patches of Collin and Hunt counties had not become the most decorated soldier of the war—the most decorated soldier of all time. It was all so fitting somehow. It is also fitting that Murphy took his fame as a soldier to Hollywood and cashed in on it. Not as a farm boy from Texas but as a gunslinger. The myth had come round perfectly. Beneath the skin of every Texan lies the cowboy gunslinger. Whether it's killing Comanches or Mexicans or Nazis, the Texan is up to the task.

Once the Indians were herded, the cattle driven, and the law brought to Abilene, the Texas hero found another manifestation on the playing fields of Texas. Davey O'Brien and Sammy Baugh were the first in a long line of football players from Texas to capture national attention. The old myth of gunslingers and wildcatters was being re-lived on Friday nights in high school stadiums and on Saturday afternoons on college campuses. The football mania became so bad that some years ago the state was torn apart by a law that was expressed in the pidgin English phrase "No pass, no play." (The authors of the bill may have thought that the coaches and players and principals and parents and fans of Texas football would not be able to understand a concept if expressed in more complex language.) The football coaches marched on Austin chanting "No pass, no play, no shit"—or something like that. But they failed to reckon with H. Ross Perot, a Texas wheeler-dealer.

Perot came out of Texarkana and the Naval Academy and a job with IBM to take his place in the mythology of Texas alongside the Charlie Goodnights, Bick Benedicts, Jett Rinks, and Audie Murphys. Perot did not blaze a trail for cattle as Goodnight had in the nineteenth century, nor did he wear a gun or strike oil or win medals in the war. He won fame with that most un-Texas of weapons—the computer. By the time of "No pass, no play," Perot had amassed a billion-plus dollars, tried and failed to conquer Wall Street, declared war on drugs and lost, and declared war on a foreign country and won. (He sent in mercenaries to liberate some company employees from Iran.) He was a hero. So in 1992, he decided to attempt to take the United States hostage by threatening to run for president; then threatening not to; then threatening to. His egomaniacal search for the presidency endeared him to many three-piece suits with retro glasses and many matrons with beehives but made him, his ears, and his bad haircut into a figure of fun in the editorial cartoons. He didn't seem to mind. He just threatened to take his country and go home. He didn't fit the myth of the tall Texan, but neither did

Audie Murphy. But he did fit many of the other myths that marked the Texas of the post-World War II era: he was richer than a king; he was a right-winger with military leanings; and he had come from humble beginnings. What Charlie Goodnight had done with cattle, H. L. Hunt with oil, and Earl Campbell with a football, Perot did with computers. He wasn't exactly the "new Texan," but he seemed to be to the "new Dallas." Actually, he was what J. Frank Dobie would have called "out of the old Rock"— that is, he was tough, traditional, and independent. And cussed. His cussedness and his money carried the day on at least one occasion, and "No pass, no play" was enacted into law. It was a grand gesture, but it does not seem to have done much good. While it may still be true that "No pass, no play" is the law of the land, Mojo still reigns in the Permian Basin, and the myth of King Football remains intact. For an outsider's look at Odessa football, clearly a microcosm of all Texas athletics, readers should take a look at H. G. Bissinger's *Friday Night Lights*, a Philadelphia investigative reporter's dismemberment of Permian High School's obsession with football. Bissinger, winner of a Pulitzer Prize for reporting, is not a hero to West Texas.

In the twentieth century, the wheeler-dealers of Texas have evolved into a class by themselves. Inheritors of the cattle baron and gunslinger traditions, these men became the icons of Texas after World War II. H. L. Hunt was the preeminent wheeler-dealer before Perot and T. Boone Pickens appeared on the scene. H. L. Hunt was Texas's first billionaire. He was a perfect type. He was lucky, cagey, and given to wonderful flights of fancy. He made a fortune in the oil fields, apparently had two families going at the same time—one in Texas, another in Louisiana—branched out into right-wing politics of the most virulent sort, and did eccentric things like baking his own bread, carrying his lunch in a paper sack, and singing patriotic songs with his children around the fireside. He also perfected the art of creeping for exercise: he would get down on all fours and creep about his house to the amazement of reporters and family members. He died and left his fortune to his very large family. Some of his children prospered, but two of his sons tried to corner the silver market, went broke in one of the largest personal bankruptcy cases ever filed, and joined their father in the myth of the Texas wheeler-dealer who whipsawed between boom and bust. One son created the American Football League in 1960, and a daughter went very successfully into the hotel business. Her Mansion on Turtle Creek is one of Dallas' legendary hostelries and dining spots.

Political wheeling and dealing reached its zenith with Lyndon B. Johnson, who created legends wherever he went. His first big contribution to Texas mythology came in 1948 when he is reputed to have stolen an election for the U.S. Senate. His last, when he left the presidency over a war that got beyond his control.

The myth of Texas seems at first to be totally male: cowboys, roughnecks, athletes. In the myth, women don't surface at first, except of course for the beauty queens and gun molls like Bonnie Parker. Despite political figures Miriam Ferguson, Oveta Culp Hobby, Barbara Jordan, Frankie Randolph, Sissie Farenthold, Ann Richards, Kathy Whitmire, Annette Strauss, despite writers Mollie Moore Davis, Dorothy Scarborough, Katherine Anne Porter, Karle Wilson Baker, Jewel Gibson, Jane Gilmore Rushing, Shelby Hearon, Betsy Colquitt, Sarah Bird, and Betty Adcock, despite athletes like Babe Zaharias and Martina Navratilova, despite Belle Starr, Emily Morgan, and Candy Barr; despite all the contributions to Texas culture by women, the myth of Texas is still largely all male. Whether that is symptomatic of the treatment of women by historians, journalists, and folklorists or whether it is a part of the Texas tradition of frontier masculinity, it is still true that Texas mythology is great for men and mules, but hell on women and horses. Sad though it is, when women come up in the Texas myth they are either snuff-dipping pioneers who get presented as men-in-skirts or they are Kewpie dolls fit only to lead cheers in high school and grow into the "little woman" on a West Texas ranch. When Clayton Williams ran against Ann Richards he said he found it hard to campaign against a woman. And ex-Texas Ranger Clint Peoples was quoted early in 1990 as saying about Ann Richards's campaign for governor, "I am not going to be part of contributing to the election of a petticoat governor." But maybe the best and most succinct comment on feminine Texas was one that I saw on the board outside a Baptist church in Aubrey that proclaimed "Satan's Rib/Woman's Lib."

It would be nice to say that with the election of Ann Richards the myth of Texas changed to one that gives more dignity to women, to Hispanics, and even to ordinary-sized men. But I am not sure. I fear it is business as usual for the myth. Ann Richards was indeed elected governor, but her election was possibly the result of Clayton Williams's breaking of a masculine code that says you must be courteous to "the weaker vessel" no matter what. If a woman offers her hand, you take it. And Williams broke that code. If John Wayne, Clayton Williams's hero, got crossways with a woman, he might have had to throw her over his shoulder and take her to a bedroom for disciplining, but he would never have refused the proffered hand as Williams did late in the campaign. That is just not done. Ann Richards was a woman, a "lady," and courtesy is required. Never mind that Ann Richards shouldered the manly twelve gauge to hunt the warlike dove, a requirement for a candidate for Texas political office. Manliness was certainly a part of the Williams-Richards race for governor, as it always is. All the old male myths about crime and punishment surfaced—and they are unchanged from the days of Bigfoot Wallace and Sam Houston. Republican Clayton Williams promised to have the youth of the state breaking rocks in West Texas. Democrat Jim Mattox bragged that, as attorney general, he sent thirty-two miscreants to the death house. And Democrat Mark

White, in a desperate attempt to make a comeback from a defeat in 1986 and a poor showing in the early polls, put an ad on TV showing the faces of the eight murderers he had personally put to death during his governorship. He said, "These hardened criminals will never again murder, rape, or deal drugs. As governor, I made sure they received the ultimate punishment—death. And Texas is a safer place for it." And don't forget: all the candidates promised to "get tough on crime" with "no new taxes." This is Texas to the core. Build thousands of new jail cells. And swear not to raise taxes.

After Richards' election it seemed that a new day had dawned and Texas had decided that a woman's place is in the Dome. But a short four years later, Ann Richards lost to George W. Bush and found herself doing potato-chip commercials on television. At about the same time, Gib Lewis, under indictment for misdemeanors involving, among other things, a trip to Mexico with a female not his wife, was reelected as speaker of the Texas house with only one dissenting vote. Of course you and I know that the allegations against Mr. Lewis are politically motivated dirty lies. But would such lies have hurt Ann Richards? And I wonder if Ms. Richards could have been elected if she had admitted—as Clayton Williams did—that she made youthful trips to the border "to get serviced."

Maybe I am wrong about masculine myths dominating in Texas. Maybe more women will find a place in the Dome. I doubt it. Texas masculinity is all around us. George W. Bush, while campaigning for president, was seen shooting at doves, the old campaign ploy that Ann Richards used. Bush downed a killdeer by mistake and let himself in for some minor razzing by the media. As president, the younger Bush has fought hard against the image that his father was saddled with, that of being a wimp. He took the war to the Middle East and said to the terrorists, "Bring it on!" He made his celebrated landing on the aircraft carrier dressed in the battle garb of a warrior. His speeches have all been challenging and warlike, and he walks with his arms hanging out from his body in the stance of the tough guy. The fact that he was born in Connecticut and educated at Yale and Harvard Business School has been left behind, and he is depicted as an old Midland boy now most at home on a ranch at Crawford in Central Texas. He hunts and cuts brush on his hobby ranch and does all the things that a good old boy should do. His critics claim that his Texanness is a veneer and recall his unsuccessful campaign for a house seat. He is supposed to have asked a West Texan for directions to the ranch of a potential contributor and was told to drive to the first cattleguard and turn right. Bush is supposed to have asked what kind of uniform the cattle guard would be wearing.

To go back a ways: If Clayton Williams had not refused to shake with Ann Richards, he might have been elected governor. If he had run for a second term, George W. Bush would have stayed in Dallas and kept going to Texas Ranger games as general partner. At the end of Bill Clinton's term some other Republican would have run for office against Al Gore, Rick Perry would not be governor, and Tom DeLay would not own and operate the Texas legislature. If those events had happened, King Karl Rove would have had to find us another president. And a new set of myths and legends about Texas would be in play.

Small-Town Texas

I I

If you walk the streets of small Texas towns like Palo Pinto in Near West Texas or Winona in Deep East Texas, are you walking into a past of sweet nostalgia or are you looking at the final stages of decay in rural and small-town Texas? Clearly, twentieth-century Texas has gone from rural to urban. The 2000 census shows that half of all Texans live in a dozen cities. And this dozen does not take into account large cities like Abilene or Lubbock or Beaumont. Census figures also show that small towns are getting smaller the farther away from metropolitan areas they are. People, young people especially, see little reason to stay in Strawn or Union Grove or Swinton. City lights beckon the young, and small towns have older and older populations. Many decry the demise of the small town, and all across the state, and the nation for that matter, people are trying to figure ways to make the small towns attractive. A few small towns experience growth because of a new industry or a recreational phenomenon. Granbury, the county seat of Hood County, experienced a new spurt when the Brazos River was dammed and Lake Granbury became a developer's paradise. Now Granbury, while still small, has an active downtown with an opera house that puts on a dozen shows a year, a theater that features live music on weekends, a first-class restaurant or two, and a town square that is the envy of many small towns in Texas. But for every Granbury, there are scores of county seats that, like Palo Pinto, are falling into disrepair and shrinking in population.

Not many small Texas towns are replications of America's Norman Rockwell serenity. Too many are sinkholes of suffocation like we see in Larry McMurtry's *The Last Picture Show*. In his famous "Ever a Bridegroom" essay, McMurtry admonishes Texas writers to turn their backs on the simple pastoral of the countryside in favor of the more complicated life of the cities. But there is hardly anything simple and pastoral in McMurtry's first three novels about life in and around his native Archer City. At best, his message is mixed, for he pictures his own Archer City as a place of sin and gossip and degradation, not anything like the calm pastoral of some idyllic place like Gilbert White's Selborne. But by the time he wrote "Ever a Bridegroom" in 1981, he had taken his own advice. After his first three novels of ranch and small-town life published between 1961 and 1966—*Horseman, Pass By, Leaving Cheyenne*, and *The Last Picture Show*—he had indeed shifted his narratives to Houston. Then to other places like L.A. and Las Vegas. As far as a reader of McMurtry's novels could tell, he had taken his advice and done what so many small-town people had done: he had moved to the city. McMurtry lived in Fort Worth and Houston and Washington D.C., for a good many years before returning to the small town of his youth. In his fiction, it is only in *Texasville* (1987) and *Duane's Depressed* (1999) that he comes back to the small Texas town that looks and smells like his native Archer City. And then even later in life, he himself moved back to that dusty, dreary North Texas town of Archer City to live and operate his famous store-front bookstores. In an interview, he more or less deplores some of the drawbacks of small-town life and says he needs a pied à terre in a big city if for no other reason than to get away for a decent meal from time to time. Word has it that on weekends he travels from Archer City to stay in the Worthington, Fort Worth's finest hotel. Now, if rumors are correct, he has moved again, to Tucson, Arizona.

Like McMurtry, mankind seems always to have suffered from the town-versus-city dilemma. Thomas Jefferson's ideal was of a nation made up of virtuous farms and villages. Benjamin Franklin was a confirmed city dweller. When Dr. Samuel Johnson was saying, "When a man is tired of London, he is tired of living," Oliver Goldsmith was remembering "Sweet Auburn, Loveliest village of the plain." These are only eighteenth-century examples, but the struggle between city life and bucolic or pastoral life predates the eighteenth century by a couple of millennia at least. The Greeks who lived in city-states longed for the innocence of Arcadia, though the cities of ancient Greece were hardly larger than our mid-sized towns. In fact, Aristotle thought the ideal city should have no more than 5,000 people—not counting, of course, women, children, and slaves.

In Texas, like the rest of America, we have never been able to make up our minds. We have always alternated between idealizing city life and idealizing small-town and country life. During America's early years, rural life and small-town life were still part of our ideal existence, but by the middle of the nineteenth century, Midwestern author E. W. Howe's *The Story of a Country Town* blasted small-town America as rife with backbiting, prudery, gossip, ruined reputations, restricting provincialism, and all that ran counter to America's ideals of freedom. Later in the century, Texas novelist and poet Mollie Moore Davis's *Under the Man-Fig* showed the small costal town of West Columbia as a place where old men meet under the man-fig tree to destroy reputations with gossip and half-true tales. By the latter half of the nineteenth century, Americans from small towns, notably Mark Twain and

William Dean Howells, settled in New England cities. And Ulysses S. Grant, from a small town in Illinois, ended his days in New York City. At the same time, cities were being pictured as places of evil by Stephen Crane's *Maggie: A Girl of the Streets* and Lincoln Steffens's nonfiction *The Shame of the Cities* and Jacob Riis's *How the Other Half Lives*. Nevertheless, Boston still laid claim to being "the hub of the universe." (Actually, Oliver Wendell's Holmes's phrase was "the hub of the solar system" and was tinged with irony, but Bostonians deleted the irony and altered the phrase.) And at the end of that century William Sidney Porter, who had spent part of his life in the small town of Austin, Texas, was writing about New Yorkers in *The Four Million*, an ironic title that contrasted the elite four hundred members of New York society with the masses who lived among them.

Carl Van Doren identified some unpleasant twentieth-century depictions of small-town life in 1921 as "The Revolt from the Village." Van Doren notes that many twentieth-century writers were taking issue with the old ideal of the small town or village as a place of sweetness and innocence. Earlier writers often saw the small, postcard town as a place of rural and small-town virtues where man's best nature could flourish. Many writers of the Jeffersonian persuasion agreed with Thomas Gray's ideals expressed in "Elegy Written in a Country Churchyard," where village Hamptons were "guiltless of their country's blood," a place of sweetness where "the rude forefathers of the hamlet lay." Early rural writers failed to see the repressiveness and stultifying conformity.

Today, we are in a reactionary period, back again to the rose-colored view of small-town life. *Time* devoted its December 8, 1997, cover to many Americans' escape from the cities to small-town life. In certain parts of the country, "white flight" accounts for the rapid growth of suburbs and small towns. In other places, people seem to be fleeing pollution, traffic gridlock, high real estate prices, crime, and overcrowded schools. Today's wide-spread use of the personal computer allows many workers to spend only a few days a month in an office; therefore, many work at home—and home might be a farm or a small town forty or fifty miles from the office.

But it may be that the newest love affair with small towns is not really what it seems. Are these urbanites ready to immerse themselves in the culture of the small town? Or have they brought city ways with them? Are they eating in the home-cooking cafe on the square? Buying clothes from the local dry goods store? Having their hair done at the local beauty parlor? Or are they shopping from catalogs, going to the city for entertainment, hairdressing, and "real" culture? In short, are they bringing a ready-built enclave with them, or are they ready to join the small-town life that Carol Kennicott found so torturing in Sinclair Lewis's *Main Street* or that Letty Mason was overwhelmed by in Dorothy Scarborough's *The Wind,* a 1925 novel set in and near Sweetwater, Texas? I suspect that they are idealizing small-town life and will ultimately find it as flat and dull as Carol Kennicott did.

And besides, many of the people *Time* writes about are not going to what are generally considered small towns; they have retreated to cities of twenty thousand or so. And some of the towns are not all that far from great cities. Two things are necessary to qualify a place as a small town in Texas: size and distance from a metropolis. Ganado and El Campo are far enough from Houston and Victoria to qualify, but Manor and Elgin are too much in the orbit of Austin to count. Goldthwaite and Dilley and Jacksboro and Clarksville and Woodville are small towns. If we look at McMurtry's own Archer City, we can see what small-town Texas is all about. We can see the past and the present of those places in a context that makes sense when we talk about city versus town. In Archer City, the county seat of Archer County, there is indeed a courthouse, but the best meal that can be offered is at the local Dairy Queen. (See McMurtry's *Walter Benjamin at the Dairy Queen.*) In Archer City, movies have to be rented from the video store or bought from a catalog. The old Royal Theater, site of "the last picture show" that Duane and Sonny and Charlotte Duggs attended, is a ruin. There are, according to *The New Handbook of Texas*, forty-nine businesses and about twelve hundred people. The town is twenty-five miles from Wichita Falls, just far enough away to make travel a consideration. In McMurtry's *The Last Picture Show*, back when even the Royal was still showing movies, it was necessary for Sonny to drive Ruth Popper to Olney, another small town nearby, to go to the doctor.

In Santo, Texas, the three hundred or so residents buy all their necessaries at Thornton's Mercantile, which sells feed, seed, veterinary supplies, hammers and tongs, and a thousand pairs of work gloves. The mercantile also offers frozen food, canned goods, panty hose, Crayolas, suede jackets made in China (cost $19.95), a drug counter full of remedies from aspirin to Super Polygrip for slipping dentures. To see a movie, Santo citizens have to drive past the county seat of Palo Pinto into Mineral Wells. There the movie is $3.50, but to go to a really good movie in a new theatre, it takes a drive of an hour all the way to Weatherford where the cost of a show is $7.50 and rising. The football is six-man in Santo, and one small house near downtown has two sheep penned in what looks like a quarter-acre yard.

Nobody is quite clear how to define a small town. *The Oxford English Dictionary* says that a town is smaller than a city but larger than a village, which is larger than a hamlet. In this country we have neither hamlets nor villages. Our smallest unit is the town, and our desperation for growth always makes us think of towns as cities in the making. When Miami, Florida, declared itself a city, it had 343 voters, which would have made it illegal in present-day Ontario or Quebec, where a town must have fifteen thousand citizens before it can declare itself a city. In France, the word *cité* denoted a town that was the seat of a bishopric, and size did not enter into the definition. In Spanish, the word *ciudad* is used for either town or city, whether the place be as small as Ciudad Acuña (formerly Via Acuña) or Ciudad Juarez with its million or more population. In 1930, the U.S. Bureau of Census defined some population areas as "rural non-farm" and said that such places must be outside cities and have populations of more than twenty-five hundred.

To further confuse us, many small towns use "city" as part of the name—Archer City, Colorado City, Karnes City, Wolfe City, Orr City. But we are not fooled. We know a town when we see one. We know that a town has a distinct culture and that moving from town to city or from city to town will subject us to culture shock.

When we go "out and about" in a small Texas town, we will be in a world where beauty parlors, paper-napkin cafes, skating rinks, domino parlors, barber shops, civic clubs, pool rooms, drive-ins, filling stations and railway stations and bus stations are cultural institutions in ways they are not in cities. Life centers on what we learn at the beauty shop or down at the garage mechanic's or at the parts house. These small-town cultural institutions are gathering places for the transference of culture and the retailing of gossip in a way that they are not in the city. City dwellers, by the way, do not go down to "the parts house," but to Auto Zone or Pep Boys. In small towns, the auto dealerships are regularly called "the Ford house" or "the Chevrolet house," but nobody in Houston or Dallas ever calls the dealership "the Ford house," and the very idea of visiting the "Lexus house" is ludicrous.

People who really live in small towns, who are not camping out to escape the crime and crowding of the cities, live in a world where Friday night in the fall is football night, where waitresses are always called by their first names, but the schoolteacher is

"Miss," whether married or single, where the Kiwanis meet on Thursdays and the Lions on Tuesdays in the town's main restaurant, in the banquet room, where funerals follow customs long outdated in the cities, with open coffins, processions to country churchyards out from town, more sermons at the graveside, followed by a large dinner in the fellowship hall of the First Baptist Church. The local druggist practices a little medicine, and the beauty shop may dispense more news than the weekly paper.

It is true that small Texas towns are no longer as cut off from the larger world and the big traditions as they once were. Television has had its homogenizing effect, and better roads and faster cars have made trips to the city easy. That is why distance is as important as population in determining what a small town is. If a town is within fifteen or twenty minutes of a city, there is little chance that the small-town culture of fifty years ago can survive. The picture show closes, and the young people go to the city for movies; shopping at the local grocery gives way to the city supermarket; the doctors move on, and health care is now handled by the city hospital. In short, the small town becomes another suburb and loses its identity. In North Texas, Carrollton and Grand Prairie and Arlington have long since been swallowed up by what is now called the Metroplex. In the mid-fifties, Arlington, Texas, had a population of about twenty thousand, and now it is the second largest city in Tarrant County with over three hundred thousand residents. And towns like Keller and Roanoke, which once had lives of their own, are now part of greater Fort Worth. The same is true of Tomball and Alvin and Friendswood in the Houston Metro, or Manchaca and Oak Hill in Austin. Hardly anyone in Austin is clear where Manchaca is, but from time to time the Manchaca Fire Department will hold a chili supper to raise funds.

With more and more urbanization, our views of town life are best seen in novels and memoirs set in an earlier time. William A.

Owens's second volume of autobiography, *A Season of Weathering*, recaptures a rapidly passing institution of the small town, the dime store. In the twenties Owens got a job at S. H. Kress in Paris, and part of his education came from the time he worked selling the notions that are now found in bubble packages at Wal-Mart. The major dime store chains like Kress, Woolworth, Ben Franklin, and W. T. Grant weren't found in the smallest towns, but M. E. Moses, T. G.and Y., and Duke and Ayers were as prevalent half a century ago as Wal-Mart is today. Small-town businessmen complain bitterly about the damage wreaked by Wal-Mart. Local dry goods stores, dime stores, and hardware stores closed their doors in the face of the inevitability of Wal-Mart. The same thing is happening more and more with locally owned cafes as pizza joints, KFC, Dairy Queen, and McDonald's crowd out the mom-and-pop eateries. In the town of Marlin in Central Texas, the Wal-Mart store came just long enough to kill off the local businesses and then when its own trade lagged, closed the store and left the town in a worse state than it had been in before. Tiny towns like Maypearl and Venus and Grandview may be lucky in that they are too small to attract a Wal-Mart. That lets the small grocery stores and the occasional parts house survive.

If a town is far enough away from a metro area, if the town is too small to lure Wendy's and Wal-Mart, we may still get a glimpse of the culture that is so perfectly pictured in Larry McMurtry's first three novels and in William Humphrey's *Home from the Hill* and his memoir of Clarksville, Texas, in the 1930s, *Farther Off from Heaven*. And in Rockdale, the original of the small town that Sam Tucker lives near in George Sessions Perry's *Hold Autumn in Your Hand*. Even today when the towns have Wal-Marts, we can still travel there and see the small Texas town as it used to be, and still is to some extent. We see the class structure —rich farmers and ranchers, bankers, doctors, lawyers, merchants at one end. In the middle are store clerks, teachers, a handful of white-collar workers. The two bottom rungs are made up of the working-class whites and, finally, the minorities. These towns present a wide-angle shot of small-town Texas. The young people endure high school, long to imitate the pool shark Abilene and the pool room owner Sam the Lion in *The Last Picture Show.* They look up to the town's rich man the way the citizens of Clarksville did to Captain Wade Hunnicutt in *Home from the Hill.* They play football on Friday nights, go to church on Sundays if they can't get out of it, and long to escape to Fort Worth or Wichita Falls or Texarkana or Austin. The older people are either comfortable in their town ways or restlessly looking for thrills to dampen the prudery and provincialism of towns like McMurtry's fictional Thalia, Texas.

In small-town Texas, institutions are slow to change despite the incursions of Wal-Mart and McDonald's. "Beauty operators" still fix hair, unlike the loftier city hairdressers and cosmetologists. The funeral director is still likely to be called an undertaker, and the burial plot is often in a graveyard. The businessmen still meet once a week or more with the Kiwanis or Civitans or Lions or Optimists. The Masonic Lodge may still be the most distin- guished building downtown, and the Odd Fellows, Knights of the Pythias, and Elks may still rent space up over the hardware store. And even though there may be a "Ford house," shade-tree mechanics still buy replacements at "the parts house." The Pep Boys have not arrived, nor has the Nissan dealership, unless the Ford house has taken on some of the foreign lines.

Reputations still hang by a thread, and the sexual revolution came slowly and carefully, if it came at all. Dope fiends are few, homosexuals are not open, and bastards are still talked of in whis- pers. There is a good chance that the small town will, at least once a year, throw an old fiddlers' convention, celebrate the yam or the black-eyed pea, and have a Fandangle or some form of pio- neer days. Coffins will be opened at funerals, and mourners are expected to pass by the coffin. Oftentimes ladies of the congregation will reach in the coffin and rearrange some article of dress. And there is always commentary on the skill of the undertaker: "Don't she look natural?" or to quote the George Jones song, "First time I've seen him smile in years." Old men still sit on the lawn of the courthouse or play dominoes in the back of the store if there is no domino parlor. Cards are pretty much forbidden to all except the reprobates who play poker or the high-toned women who play bridge. Preachers and preachers' wives and preachers' kids still behave in the patterns expected of them: the kids in semi-revolt after a certain age. (See the fine Texas novel by Terry Pringle called *The Preacher's Boy*). The waitresses still call you "Hon," and the local café is a kind of coffeehouse and gentleman's club before the lunch rush comes in.

The small town ideal still lives in Jayton and Spur, in Baird and Putnam, in Dilly and Cotulla, in Timpson, Tenaha, Bobo, and Blair. There is at least one good paper-napkin café where customers, mostly men, gather to drink innumerable cups of bad coffee and befog the air with cigarette smoke. (Non-smoking areas are still not common in Texas small towns; if they do exist, they may be a couple of corner tables not three feet away from the smokers.) In Jacksboro's The Green Frog, the waitresses call you by your first name if they know it, point out your flaws, make jokes about your size, and pour you a cup of coffee and move on, knowing that you have already had breakfast and are just here, as church people used to say, for the fellowship. Joyce Roach tells of a café owner in Jacksboro back during the fifties worrying that integration might open his place of business to minorities. He says to a canny old cattleman, "What would you think, J. B., if a colored came in here to eat?" The old rancher thought a minute and said, "I'd say it would serve him right."

The cafés open early for the workingmen and women who have to be on the job by seven. The retirees and small shop owners are not far behind the workers. The retirees kill time almost up till the lunch rush, long enough for "the wife" to get the house cleaned up and some dinner on the stove. (Dinner is still at high noon in Texas small towns.) As the day wears on, the beauty shop fills up, the parts houses and garages and filling stations do business and double as social centers, and the "quiet colored end of evening fades." There is not much action at night among the older folks. They stay at home in recliners and watch sitcoms and sports on television. The young, when they get to driving age, often circle the town square, trolling for dates. One of the great narratives about small-town life is in Don Walser's song about his Mercury, a car he owned back in Lamesa, Texas, in the fifties. He had a cut-out muffler and a "monkey knob" on the steering wheel with a picture of a naked woman in the knob's Plexiglass circle. As the boys circled the square one way, the girls drove around in the other direction. And when you saw someone who took your fancy, you reached down and pulled the wire that operated the muffler cut-out and "you could hear the Mercury roar."

In small towns they still "drag the square" on Saturday nights, paint Seniors '03 on the railroad overpasses, climb the water tower as a lark, drink whiskey out of brown paper bags in the pool hall or domino parlor, refrain from talking dirty in front of the womenfolks, make the youngsters say "Sir" and "Ma'am" and, echoing Merle Haggard's song about Muskogee, Oklahoma, USA, think "football's still the roughest thing on campus."

Folkways of

the Arklatex

One of the corners of Texas that has its own distinct culture is the region around Texarkana, which is the heart of an area called the Arklatex. Businesses and Chambers of Commerce in Northwest Louisiana think of Shreveport as the heart of the Arklatex, but the real cultural center is Texarkana. The term Arklatex may very well have been invented in Shreveport, for it is the biggest city in the region, and the television stations in Shreveport always bill themselves as broadcasting to the Arklatex. But culturally the region is much less like Louisiana than it is like Texas, Arkansas, and southeastern Oklahoma. In fact, a better name for this region would be Arkoklatex, but since nobody calls it that, we are stuck with the name Arklatex for this Texas equivalent of the Southwest's Four Corners where Arizona, Utah, Colorado, and New Mexico come together.

The Arklatex is a world in itself while still remaining a part of the four states that comprise it. What you find in the Arklatex is not at all foreign to what you will find in many parts of the South. Nevertheless, it is a kind of mini-state, partly because it is so far from the various capitals—Little Rock, Austin, Oklahoma City, and Baton Rouge. It is also a borderland and has many of the characteristics of other border cultures. In Texarkana it has a capital city that straddles a state line, and there are not as many of those as you might think, at least of the size and importance of Texarkana. Like Bristol, Tennessee/Virginia, or Juárez/El Paso, Texarkana has unique qualities. Hardly anybody who lives in Texarkana can remember, except at tax time or when wanting a drink, where he lives. Of course as you drive down State Line Avenue, the thoroughfare that divides Texarkana into its two halves, some things become clear. There are liquor stores on one side of the street and Baptist churches on the other. And since Baptists don't drink in front of one another, the proximity to the stores is always distressing to the Texas side.

And there is probably nobody who lives in Foreman, Arkansas, who does not have relatives in Tom or Moon or Haworth, Oklahoma. Or Dekalb and Marshall and Gilmer in Texas. Or Caddo Parish in Louisiana. An amazing number of Arkansas residents have Texas license plates on their cars and trucks. In short, these borders don't really exist for people who are residents of the state of the Arklatex. Of course if you want to buy beer on the Texas side or in Little River County you have to cross State Line in Texarkana to get to Arkansas or make your way into Oklahoma to buy 3.2, which is weaker but will still give you a headache. Thousands of people live in one state and work in another and sometimes forget which state is which. Many live in one, work in another, and shop in a third or fourth. Back in the 1940s even the Phantom of the Texarkana Moonlight Murders was a multi-state killer. And who knows where Huddie Ledbetter was born—somewhere near Mooringsport, but was it Louisiana or Texas? No matter: he served prison sentences in both states. First, Texas Governor Pat Neff pardoned him after Leadbelly wrote him a song. Later he was set free in Louisiana by Huey Long's protégé, Governor O. K. Allen, because of Leadbelly's famous song,

"Goodnight, Irene," in honor of Irene Allen, the governor's wife. Huddie Ledbetter, who lived for a time in Bowie County under the name Walter Boyd, was discovered by two famous Texas folklorists, John and Alan Lomax, who promoted him—and some cynics say exploited him. He was buried in 1949 in the Shiloh Baptist churchyard near his birthplace in the Arklatex.

Leadbelly was by his own admission a champion cotton picker, guitar picker, timber cutter, and railroad spike driver. All would have stood him in good stead in the Arklatex, for this was cotton country. And timber country. And a place where the railroads led from the east to the west. It was also river country, with navigation all through this country before the railroads killed off many other kinds of traffic before committing suicide themselves. Incidentally, the Red River provided a good deal of transport, and a generation ago there was a drawbridge at Ogden on Highway 71 about a dozen miles north of Texarkana. Historians in the Arklatex and beyond document the rise and fall of Jefferson as "the Gateway to Texas." This port on Caddo Lake was second only to Galveston during its heyday, and Galveston in an 1840 immigrant's pamphlet was called "the New York of Texas."

Music plays its role in the Arklatex. If you remember the song that was popular back in the television folksong craze, "Them Old Cottonfields Back Home." In that Mitch Miller favorite, there are lines that say, "It was down in Louisiana/Just about a mile from Texarkana." There may be geographical incorrectness in those lines, but culturally Texarkana is just about a mile from far Northwest Louisiana. A little older and almost forgotten is the country song that depicted the perfect Arklatex sweetheart: "She's my Texarkana baby/Do I love her lawdy law/Her pappy came from Texas/And her maw from Arkansas." Even older is one that admonishes the prospective bridegroom not to marry an Arkansas lass. It says, "don't marry none of them girls from Arkansas/But marry you a girl from Tennessee/Eat cornbread and 'lasses and sassafras tea."

What is it that ties this state of Arklatex together? It is the people and the climate and the soil. The people were traditionally white Anglo-Saxon Protestants and African Americans who descended from the slaves brought here by the plantation owners to grow cotton in the river bottoms and on the well-watered plains. Cotton became king by 1830, and by 1859 Bowie County alone was producing about seven thousand bales a year. In 1850 blacks outnumbered whites 1,641 to 1,271, and in 1859, county slaveholders paid over a million dollars in taxes on 2,269 slaves. It is no wonder that when the vote for secession was held in 1861, the vote was 208 for and 15 against. And there were many parts of Texas that opposed secession as strongly as the Arklatex espoused it.

Cotton was the main crop in those antebellum days, and the people who grew it were not from New England. They came from the South. And that southern migration continued—and continues. After the Civil War thousands of southerners went west. One of the pathways was through Miller County, Arkansas, onto the black, waxy prairies of East Texas and on toward Dallas or down toward the Big Thicket. Another principal route, one that goes back well before the Civil War, was from the Lower South across Louisiana and down through Nacogdoches toward the cotton lands along the Brazos and Trinity rivers. But obviously not all of them kept going. Many stayed in Miller County, Arkansas, and Bowie County, Texas. In fact, until 1836 or so Bowie County was thought to be a part of Arkansas and not a part of Texas.

The culture of the Arklatex ties the various counties and parishes together—language, customs, food, stories and songs, religion, ethnicity, and politics. And those are areas the folklorist likes to consider as much as he does political definitions. In the area of food, this is the land of the church potluck. Go to one and you will see the foods that are eaten all over the Arklatex. Congealed salads, English peas, biscuits, fried chicken, pork barbecue, potato salad, cornbread, slaw, dressing and gravy, Seven-

Up cakes, pineapple upside-down cakes, and pies, pies, pies. If you want the short course in the food that is at the heart of the Arklatex, visit Bryce's Cafeteria on the Texas side of Texarkana. The whole picture is there. Everyday they produce a whole iconography of Arklatex cooking. There are pies with the calf slobber rising three inches above the filling. They even make spinach that is not only edible but good. This used to be pork country and chicken country. Unlike the Texas brisket infection that is spreading into this country and across the South where they should know better, barbecue to southerners always meant pork. It was as God intended. In early days southerners didn't eat much beef because a cow was not as easy to manage as a hog, and the killing of a cow involved a great deal more work than the killing of a hog. And hogs don't give milk except to other hogs. This country produces neck bones and liver, collards and rape, fried corn, green beans cooked in enough hog fat till they are medium brown and completely limber. People in this part of the world eat chitlin's and pigs feet and oxtails and chicken feet, if worse comes to worst. Most people in the Arklatex were past middle age before they knew you could eat an alfalfa sprout—or broccoli or Brussels sprouts or artichokes. Artichokes were usually thought of as a weed akin to the yucca and were usually called "hardychokes." One Arklatex resident of my acquaintance once remarked, "You know, they is people who eat them things." Imagine! A serious foodlorist could write a book about the cooking native to this region.

The Arklatex has a language of its own—or did until movies and television set about homogenizing it. Things and people are named differently in this region. And sometimes pronounced differently. Texarkana is always Tex-a-canner, and Shreveport is often Shrevesport. Generally, the dialect is southern, and the names follow the patterns of the Old South. But there are a lot of little local tricks. The region is full of people who do their shopping at Wal-Marks. One woman challenged her mother on this local name for Sam Walton's store. She said, "Why do you insist on calling it Wal-Marks? How do you spell it when you write a check?" Her mother replied, "Wal hyphen Mart, Wal-Marks." This woman also grows some beautiful high "geraniums" in her yard, with large blue, white, and pink blossoms the size of soft-balls. Once, this same woman had to make a trip to the eye doctor in Texarkana. She had trouble driving home because she said, "that doctor violated my eyes." During the war her husband drove from the Arkansas side over to Hooks to work in the Red River "Arsenic." Made good money, too.

People and places have names that are not found too often in Vermont or British Columbia. The woman whose husband worked at the Arsenic had a grandmother named Minnie Ola, a mother named Lula May, and sisters named Ola May, Mildred Ola, and Christine Beatrice. And Texarkana native H. Ross Perot's mother was named Lulu Mae. And I am reliably informed that Perot's parents pronounced the name Pee Row, though I don't think the theater named for them is called Pee Row any longer. The surnames in the outlying parts of this region are what you might expect in largely Anglo-Saxon, Scotch-Irish country: Thornton, Glover, Thrash, McDonald, Foster, Edwards, Jones, Brantley, Overstreet, Payne. And the nicknames are brutal—guys named Shorty, Cross-eye, Fat, and Dago. Dago was the nickname of a man named Milledge Deaton. He had no Italian in his background, but his children and grandchildren knew him as Dago as long as he lived. Political correctness was slow to come to the Arklatex, for another person from the Oklahoma side was always called Chink, though there was no Chinese in his heritage. He didn't seem to resent it, and there were no Chinese to be offended in his part of McCurtain County, Oklahoma. In case this sounds like the Arklatex is lagging far behind the rest of the nation in careful use of ethnic slurring, there is a restaurant in Locke,

California, called Al the Wop's. I ate there fifteen years ago, and I looked it up on the Internet last week and it is still called Al the Wop's. So maybe Dago would still pass as a nickname in the Arklatex today.

And the place names. There is Boggy Creek—home of the celebrated monster—and at least three Caney Creeks and a Ticky Creek or two. Modern times have caused residents of the Arklatex to change old names to more thrusting and modern names. Rocky Comfort, once the county seat of Little River County, Arkansas, became New Rocky Comfort before someone decided to name the town Foreman. The present Little River county seat of Ashdown was once Turkey Flats. Wonderful names abound—Tom and Moon and Arkinda and Caney and Bokhoma and Fouke and Broken Bow. Broken Bow, Oklahoma, home of the athletic teams called "the Savages" and the Trail's End Motel, is not—even though it is in the middle of what was once the Choctaw Nation—named for the Choctaws or anything else local. Herman Dierks, the lumber baron, named the town for Broken Bow, Nebraska, where the Dierks family had a lumberyard. Dierks also named a town in Howard County for himself. Dierks, along with Texarkanan T. W. Rosborough, was one of the main timber cutters who laid waste to the Ouachita forests. Rosborough has a town named for himself up between Amity and Greenwood in Arkansas and another in Oregon, where he moved his timber operation after the Ouachitas were cut over. T. W. came back to Texarkana to build himself a mansion to die in. And did. You can read all about this in Kenneth L. Smith's *Sawmill: The Story of the Cutting of the Last Great Virgin Forest East of the Rockies.*

Cotton and timber were central to the development of the Arklatex. It was the shipment of cotton that made the Red River ports so important. Cotton was farmed in the Arklatex on large plantations with slave labor before the Civil War and by share-croppers and crop sharers and day laborers after Emancipation.

Lula May Thornton tells how she once picked cotton on a farm in Little River County back about 1920 that was run by a woman who patrolled the fields on horseback carrying a whip. If one of the workers in this integrated field lagged, the overseer would pop him or her with a whip. Not exactly the work of Simon Legree, but not all that different in some respects.

The population figures have changed since the days of slavery, and now the counties in the Arklatex are roughly seventy-five percent white and twenty-five percent African American. However, there is still one all-black town, Tollette, Arkansas, not more than thirty miles from Texarkana. Such towns are a rarity today, but after the Civil War there were over sixty all-black towns in the country, almost half of them in Oklahoma. Cotton is still grown, but rice has become a serious crop in the Arklatex. And timber still is a major industry, as anyone knows who has ever smelled Ashdown's paper mill or the one in Valliant, Oklahoma.

Get outside the big towns and this is overall and sunbonnet country. I once knew someone in the Arklatex whose total wardrobe consisted of overalls. When he died, his family, most appropriately, bought a new pair of 401s and buried him in them. He never had a use for what he called "waist pants." My friend Dago, also an overall wearer, always dressed in waist pants for funerals—except once. When his wife's ex-husband died, Dago went to the funeral in his work overalls. Once when he was at a funeral in his waist pants, Dago's wife took to wailing at the open coffin and fainted into his arms. His overlarge and unaccustomed waist pants fell to his knees, and one of his stepsons, said, "Why, Dago, you got on flowerdy drawers."

The religion of the countryside is Protestant, though there are Catholics and Jews in some numbers in the cities. Texarkana, which has a good sized Italian population, most of whom came here around the turn of the twentieth century when the railroads came and the timber industry flourished, has two large Catholic churches, one in Texas and one in Arkansas. Until the sixties both St. Edwards in Arkansas and Sacred Heart in Texas had flourishing parochial high schools and grammar schools. There is a small synagogue in Texarkana, and Ashdown's only Jewish family had to drive the twenty or so miles each week to attend, as did other Jews in the region. The late Carl Benson of Waldo, Arkansas, was, as he always said, half Jew, half Baptist, and since the synagogue was too far, his family had to make do with one of the several Baptist churches in Waldo. Nowadays, with the rise of Tyson and Bo Pilgrim and the surging Hispanic population, a good many of the rural and small-town Baptist churches have become Iglesias Bautistas. And like the rest of America, the Hispanic population of the Arklatex is increasing. In the entire state of Arkansas, Hispanic population is up 377% since the 1960 census.

The country may have been religious, but churchgoing never had a bad effect on freewheeling politics of the Arklatex. A sheriff in one of the nearby counties conducted a long love affair with a local doctor's wife. An open affair. On two occasions, the doctor shot the sheriff—sounds like a song title—both times putting the lawman in the hospital. Once the high sheriff of Blank County had to have a load of birdshot picked out of his rear end, and everybody in the county knew it. Nevertheless, he kept getting re-elected until he was too infirm for dalliance and enforcement. Harry Ashmore, longtime editor of the *Arkansas Gazette,* wrote in his bicentennial history of Arkansas that the citizens of that state always "displayed a pronounced tolerance for boodling by public officials." Ashmore quotes Roy Reed of *The New York Times* as saying that there is "an inverse relationship between . . . political peccadilloes and the stringency of professed religion" (Ashmore, 192). Reed says, "The Protestants, many of them barely two hundred years from the northern austerities of

Scotland and Ulster and now Southerners through geographic happenstance, enjoy it as a forbidden fruit, as a country preacher enjoys sex."

I won't go too far with this mixing of politics and Protestantism, but many politicos have become beloved and often elected officials despite some boodling and sexual peccadilloes. The history of the Longs of Louisiana bears this out. And the Longs fall into the broadest definitions of the Arklatex, coming from Winn Parish, which is on the outer fringe of the National Weather Service's Arklatex. Besides, Huey practiced law in Shreveport for ten years and his son, Senator Russell Long, was born there. And Governor Earl, Huey's younger brother, became a beloved officeholder despite his long love affair with the exotic dancer Blaze Starr.

The Arklatex has produced its share of celebrities and has seen some desperate acts. Bonnie and Clyde were gunned down outside Arcadia, the Phantom terrorized Texarkana, and the Monster of Boggy Creek became a star of story and film. Maya Angelou grew up near Stamps, Arkansas, and H. Ross Perot was born in Texarkana, Texas. Scott Joplin was born near Linden, Texas, and grew up in Texarkana. He became a whorehouse piano player there and went on to become the king of ragtime and the composer of the Pulitzer-winning opera, *Treemonisha*. Country singer Tracy Lawrence is from Foreman. Johnny Mathis and Don Henley of the Eagles from Gilmer, and the East Texas String Ensemble from Nacogdoches. Nacogdoches is almost too far away to count, but since the ensemble is my favorite country group, I mention them. Besides, country music lived and flourished in this area. Between 1948 and 1960, "The Louisiana Hayride" from fifty-thousand-watt KWKH in Shreveport was in the same league as the Big D Jamboree and just a cut below the Grand Ole Opry and Chicago's National Barn Dance. Hank Williams and Kitty Wells and Johnny Cash and even the late

Elvis played on "Hayride." And then there is a notable saxo-
phone player who was born in Hope, Arkansas, but turned to
politics at an early age.

Texas Sidekicks

Texas is often thought of as the land of the hero. Men like Sam Houston and Stephen F. Austin and Charlie Goodnight and Lyndon B. Johnson are all larger than life. In the movies, great portrayers of Texas life were heroes like John Wayne, Clark Gable, Spencer Tracy, Gene Autry, and Randolph Scott. The history of Texas is the history of great men and great movie stars. But where would these heroes be without the sidekicks who supported them? For every Charlie Goodnight and Oliver Loving, there was a Bose Ikard, the black cowboy who is buried with Loving in the cemetery in Weatherford. For Lyndon Johnson there was John Connally, at least for a while. And in the movies, where the sidekick had a more prominent and visible role, for every John Wayne or Gene Autry there was a "Gabby" Hayes, a Smiley Burnett, a Walter Brennan, a Slim Pickens, an Andy Devine, and a Chill Wills. Even Willie Nelson has a longstanding sidekick in Paul English— "I guess Buffalo ain't geared for me and Paul."

In Texas and elsewhere, you can't be a hero if you don't have a sidekick, and this has been true down through history. Sidekicks go way back in history—to the Sumerian epic *Gilgamesh*, to the Old Testament. What do you think Ruth is telling Naomi when she says, "Whither thou goest I will go also"? (Smiley Burnett probably said those same words to Gene Autry when they hooked up.) Beowulf had several, King Lear had his fool, Prince Hal's main sidekick was Falstaff, and Hamlet had Horatio to brood at. And don't forget Don Quixote and Sancho Panza, Holmes and Watson, Sam Rayburn and Lyndon Johnson, Lady Bird and Liz Carpenter. George W. Bush and Karl Rove.

Of course the famous Texas Ranger Lone Wolf Gonzaullas didn't have one; otherwise they wouldn't have called him Lone Wolf. (Of course they called the Lone Ranger "lone," despite his never being ten feet from his "faithful Indian companion.") But I wonder about Lone Wolf Gonzaullas. I wonder who he told stuff to so he could become famous. Maybe there was a Mrs. Lone Wolf to help him circulate his exploits. Somebody had to tell the world the famous words LWG said, words like "It ain't but one riot, is it?" LBJ had his Lady Bird or his Walter Jenkins or his Jack Valenti to report his famous sayings. After all, one of the main jobs of the sidekick is to brag on the hero.

But the sidekick has other duties. It is his job to gather the faithful retainers: "Gabby, round up some of the boys and meet me at the Rim Rock Canyon." Or Tom DeLay to Rick Perry, "Round up the legislators and let's gerrymander the state." He also has the duty of making jokes at the hero's expense to keep him from getting a case of hubris. King Lear's sidekick, called simply "Fool," got away with a lot more than mere jokes. I have heard Walter Brennan and Chill Wills come down pretty heavy on the Duke. A lot heavier, I'll bet, than John Connally ever came down when he was sidekicking LBJ. Connally may have been more like Hamlet's sidekick Horatio, who let Hamlet make the jokes. All he did was listen, agree, and stand ready to report Hamlet's "cause aright to the unsatisfied."

As I said, the sidekick has been around forever, but it took western movies to refine being a sidekick into art. Everyone old enough to remember the Saturday afternoon movies knows what I am talking about, but the young may not remember such famous actors as Gabby Hayes, Smiley Burnett (AKA Frog Millhouse), Dub "Cannonball" Taylor, Al "Fuzzy" St. John, Raymond Hatton, Fuzzy Knight, Russell "Lucky" Hayden, and Max "Alibi" Terhune. All were sidekicks to more famous B-western stars—such luminaries as William Boyd, Gene Autry, Roy Rogers, Johnny Mack Brown, Sunset Carson, and Al "Lash" Larue.

The sidekick as a dramatic type was not, of course, an invention of grade-B westerns, though the name "sidekick" became a household word—or bunkhouse word, I should say—from these movies. But the Roman playwrights Terence and Plautus set many of the standards for the western sidekick. Before they wrote the lines and stage directions for fools and faithful retainers, sidekicking was a pretty informal business (remember Ruth and Naomi). The Romans, sticklers for organization, set some formal traits and established certain sidekick character types that have lived to this day—the clever parasite who lives by his wits, the *Miles Gloriousis* (or braggart soldier), and the cowardly, sly servant capable of coming through when the plot demands it. Shakespeare's greatest sidekick is Falstaff, but his plays—the comedies, the tragedies, the histories, even the comical-pastoral-historical-tragical—all abound with early versions of Gabby Hayes and Russell Hayden. And what is the bumbling, faithful, childlike, irresolute Dr. Watson but parasite to the great detective of 221 B. Baker Street?

The dramatic and literary reasons for using a faithful retainer type are almost too well known to go into. The hero's best attributes are always made to seem even better when he is contrasted with a fool, a clown, a dolt, a coward, or a lummox. Frequently, the sidekick is extremely useful in that he provides a loyal and sympathetic ear for the protagonist; that makes it possible for the audience to know what the hero is thinking and planning to do without the author having to resort to the artificial device of the soliloquy. A stupid or naïve sidekick is a great aid to a stupid or naïve audience, and what Shakespeare and Herbert J. Yeats of Republic Pictures thought of their audiences is no secret. And for comic relief, it works better to have a regular, onstage character be funny than to rely on drunken porters and casual passersby. And finally, a hero just needs somebody with him because it's no fun to slay a dragon by yourself or do some daring deed and have nobody to turn to and say, "Don't get excited, Gabby; it's all in a day's work."

The western stars of the teens and twenties used sidekicks more sparingly than did the stars of the thirties and forties. William S. Hart, who began making movies in 1914, used his first sidekick, Lucien Littlefield, in 1925 in *Tumbleweeds.* In 1924 Pee Wee Holmes played a similar role for Jack Hoxie. Such silent stars as Hoxie, Hoot Gibson, Fred Thompson, and Ken Maynard sometimes used sidekicks and sometimes "played a lone hand," as western writers like to say. The first western movie sidekicks apparently did not play the low comedy roles that we associate with Gabby Hayes and Smiley Burnett. I say "apparently," for many of the movies of the teens and twenties have been destroyed or lost, and film histories don't always make much of the minor roles.

It took talking pictures to bring B-westerns about Texas and the West into their golden age, though some producers and distributors argued that sound in B-westerns would never go over. Some of the early Ken Maynard and Hoot Gibson movies were made both as silents and as talkies, and the silents were, in some areas, more popular. The problem with sound in westerns grew from the outdoor recording difficulties. Once Hollywood learned to put the sound over the action, hoofbeats began thundering across silver screens, old-timers took to saying things like, "Dagnabit, Roy," and cowpokes started warbling like mocking-birds. Warner Baxter sang in the first *Cisco Kid* movie in 1929, and Ken Maynard, a silent star, took up singing and fiddle playing in his sound movies. Hoot Gibson, who was of a humorous and satiric turn of mind, parodied Maynard in one movie by having his boys sit around the campfire loudly yowling songs out of tune. But one of the most important things about sound was that it made it possible for the comic sidekick to come into his own and become one of the main features of the B-movie.

By the middle thirties, such actors as Hayes, Burnett, Cannonball Taylor, the two "Fuzzies"—Knight and St. John—Russell Hayden, and Raymond Hatton were featured in the movies and listed prominently on the theater flyers of films pro-duced on Hollywood's poverty row by such companies as Republic, Mascot, Monogram, and Grand National.

The greatest and most durable of all the comic sidekicks was George F. Hayes, born in Wellsville, New York, in 1885. Hayes had been acting in the silent movies and had been in westerns as a fumbling father for several years. He was usually the single par-ent of the beautiful girl who was enamored of the cowboy hero. And it was his incompetence that was about to cause him and the girl to lose the ranch—usually to a guy in a black hat named Kincaid. In 1935 he was cast in the first William Boyd *Hopalong Cassidy* film, and as that series developed from filmings of Clarence E. Mumford novels into the patterned series it was to become, Hayes became Hoppy's regular sidekick. He was a garru-lous blowhard named Windy Holliday. "Gabby," the name that identifies him to all fans of cowboy movies, came later. In the Hoppy movies he was first paired with James Ellison and, later, with Russell Hayden as Cassidy's co-sidekick. Ellison and Hayden played "lovers and lusty bachelors" in the manner of the Squire (the Knight's sidekick) in *The Canterbury Tales*. The handsome

Lotharios fell in love often and deeply and got themselves called "you goldarned young whippersnapper" by Windy about three times a reel. To their young squire, Hayes played the foolish braggart soldier stereotype—old, bearded, enthusiastically absurd, but reliable and brave in clutch situations.

Hayes's beard was a part of his comic equipment, for no actors in a B-western wore facial hair unless for dramatic purposes. Villains wore pimp mustaches, but the full beard alerted the audience to the comic nature of the character. He was either a prospector, a father, or an all-purpose "old-timer." There are almost no pictures of George Hayes without his beard. Roy Rogers told that Hayes once grew tired of the beard after many years, shaved it off, looked at himself in panic, would let no one see him, and went off into the desert alone to grow it back.

Hayes left the Cassidy company in 1939 and signed with Republic. For legal reasons, Hayes could no longer use the name Windy, so, with Republic, he became Gabby, the name forever associated with him and with a certain type of sidekick. Hayes had been a sidekick under various names before the Cassidy series —in a 1934 Ken Maynard movie, *In Old Santa Fe*—and, as both sidekick and villain, in several John Wayne B-movies (the Lone Star westerns) made by Monogram. But in the Republic work with Roy Rogers, Gene Autry, and others the Gabby character became known to every child in America. Gabby was never identified with Gene Autry the way Smiley Burnett was, but he made several Autry movies. He was Roy Rogers's chief sidekick for a decade beginning in 1939. In fact, in 1945, one of the Rogers's vehicles, *Don't Fence Me In,* was made so that Gabby could be the star. Hayes appeared in very few feature movies, though he was in Texas novelist Barry Benefield's *Valiant Is the Word for Carrie,* and he and Roy Rogers starred with Walter Pidgeon and John Wayne in *Dark Command* (1940). In that movie Roy Rogers says to John Wayne, "Well, as Shakespeare says, 'All's well that ends well,'" to which the Duke replies, "Well, that Shakespeare fellow must have been from Texas. That's what we say down there." This, of course, leaves Gabby Hayes looking curmudgeonly.

Gabby Hayes lived out his last years as the manager of an apartment house he owned in North Hollywood; he died in 1969. Jon Tuska in his book, *The Filming of the West,* says that Hayes remembers none of his stars with affection. The only western actor he seemed to like was second-unit director and actor Yakima Canutt, often called "the king of the stuntmen." Maybe Gabby's life as a sidekick turned him bitter; after all, he was working for journeyman's wages while the Autrys, Waynes, and Rogerses were growing rich doing the same kind of work.

Next to Gabby Hayes, the best-known sidekick of the great days was Lester "Smiley" Burnett (b. 1911), who went to Hollywood with Gene Autry in 1935. Burnett played Frog Millhouse in all the early Autry movies, left Autry for a time to be a sidekick with Roy Rogers and others, and ended up in the last six movies in the Autry series in the fifties. In later years, he was on a television series, *Petticoat Junction,* as a comic railroad engineer.

Smiley Burnett's role as a sidekick was somewhat different from the roles played by George Hayes and other cowboys' companions. For one thing, Burnett was much younger than Hayes and couldn't play the old-timer. He was not the handsome but callow bachelor played by James Ellison and Russell Hayden; and he wasn't an ethnic with innate wisdom like Tonto as played by Jay Silverheels, whose real name was Harold J. Smith. Therefore, all that was left for him to play was the goofy buffoon. He fitted the role, for Burnett as Frog was fat, clumsy, ignorant, and not very bright. He rode a mule with a white circle painted around one eye, had his cowboy hat turned up to the crown in front, and talked and sang in a froglike voice. His main appeal was to children, but that, of course, was true of all these sidekicks—and, for

227

that matter, of all grade-B westerns. There was much of the braggart soldier in Frog, something of the sly servant-parasite, but
mostly he was what Jon Tuska calls a stooge. Tuska, who has no
admiration for Autry's movies and thinks the Autry formula killed
off the western, credits or blames Burnett for stooge types and
holds him responsible for the countless unfunny imitators who
began to appear in westerns after 1935. Some pictures had two or
three of these stooge types in them.

There is no doubt "the Autry phenomenon," to use Tuska's
term, changed the nature of the B-western. Whether Autry is
responsible for the decline of the Saturday westerns is arguable,
but when Texas native Gene Autry became popular, a new genre
of western developed. Ken Maynard had started the trend toward
singing cowboys, but Autry changed the western from an action
story to a musical. In his pictures, singing was no longer inciden-
tal; it was the reason for the movie. The role of the sidekick
changed from the old-timer or the young lover or stalwart Indian
companion to the singer of novelty songs and musical clown.
Burnett, who had been a backup man on Autry's Chicago radio
show, did some of the sidekick work and some of the singing and
clowning, and often a second sidekick of the more traditional sort
was used. (Even Gabby Hayes appeared in some of the early
Autry/Burnett movies.) When Autry moved to Columbia
Pictures in 1947, Pat Buttram replaced Smiley until Gene made
his last six movies of the fifties.

Roy Rogers's movies grew out of the Autry phenomenon, and
the two singing cowboys were by far the most popular B-movie
heroes of the Golden Age. Roy used Gabby Hayes, who had left
the Hopalong Cassidy series, but Gabby was no singer, and Roy
had a number of musical sidekicks—usually his old friends, "The
Sons of the Pioneers." Rogers had formed "The Sons of the
Pioneers" back when he was using the name Dick Weston (his real
name is Leonard Sly). Singing groups became popular in western

musicals, and the singers not only sang but often made up the "boys" who rode to the rescue. Besides Bob Nolan and "The Sons of the Pioneers," there were groups like "Tex Terry and the Cass County Boys," and the Spade Cooley Group. From 1940 to 1946 "Bob Wills and the Texas Playboys" acted and sang in Tex Ritter features, a series starring former Hoppy sidekick Russell Hayden. Wills and the Playboys also made a few Charles Starrett westerns.

Despite the popularity of the singing westerns, the studios still turned out regular non-singing westerns. Such stars as Charles Starrett, Sunset Carson, Johnny Mack Brown, Alan "Rocky" Lane, Don "Red" Barry, "Wild Bill" Elliot, Bob Steele, and the late-arrival, Lash Larue, had their moments on screen. All used sidekicks of one sort or another. Raymond Hatton, an original member of the Three Mesquiteers series, was a good old-line sidekick. Fuzzy Knight and Fuzzy St. John were bearded old-timers like Hayes, and Dub "Cannonball" Taylor was a comic stooge of the Burnett variety. Dub Taylor went from westerns to commercials for Dairy Queen and Hormel's "Chili Fixings." He also made regular features from time to time. His best-known role in the movies was as C.W. Moss's father in Arthur Penn's *Bonnie and Clyde*—he sold out the Barrow gang to former western side-kick Denver Pyle. Another of Taylor's roles was as the father of Newley, one of Marshal Matt Dillon's sidekicks, on the television series *Gunsmoke*.

There were a multiplicity of ethnic characters—Chief Thunder Cloud and Jay Silverheels as Tonto in the Lone Ranger series and the various Panchos of the Cisco Kid series. The last and best-known Pancho was Leo Carrillo, who played the role as the broadest of stage Mexicans. (Away from the westerns for a moment. One of the great ethnic mishmashes was having Mantan Moreland, the black actor, play minstrel show Negro sidekick to the Oriental detective Charlie Chan. It is what one of my friends calls "gelding the lily.")

In addition, some famous A-budget actors played roles in the B-westerns before going on to the relative stardom of major motion pictures. Such actors as Walter Brennan, Chill Wills, and Slim Pickens started in the Bs and then graduated. Chill Wills and Slim Pickens, two of the most famous of the Texas sidekicks, were prominent in movies with John Wayne. Wills is John Wayne's chief sidekick in the movie about West Texas called *McLintock*, and it is Chill Wills who plays the conscience of Bick and Leslie Benedict in *Giant*. Never to be forgotten is Texas chauvinist Pickens who, as Major King Kong, rides the bomb down toward Russia in Texan Terry Southern's *Dr. Strangelove*.

The sidekick always has been with us in drama and persists unabated in present-day TV and movies. There are all sorts of variations on the type, but the 1930s and 1940s B-movie sidekick was carried over into television in such characters as De Kalb, Texas, native Dan Blocker as Hoss Cartwright on *Bonanza*. Blocker grew up in West Texas and attended Sul Ross State College before going into acting. He is buried back in East Texas in the town of De Kalb. Also memorable are Dennis Weaver as Chester, who joined Festus and Doc as Matt Dillon's sidekicks on *Gunsmoke*. Singer Ken Curtis, *Gunsmoke's* Festus, once played the lead in a western featuring Bob Wills and the Texas Playboys, the Hoosier Hotshots, and the Pied Pipers. Curtis, who was the famous director John Ford's son-in-law, appeared in many westerns as a singer and was a buffoonish, lovelorn Texan in *The Searchers*, directed by Ford and starring John Wayne as the hero. That film also featured one of John Wayne's most enduring sidekicks, Ward Bond, as a preacher who is also a Texas Ranger.

Most of the John Wayne/John Ford films included sidekicks in plenty. At one time or another Wayne employed Ward Bond, Bruce Cabot, Harry Carey, Harry Carey, Jr., Ken Curtis, Chill Wills, Ben Johnson, Warren Oates, Hank Worden, and Noah Berry, Jr., in sidekick roles—often there would be five or six of the

Duke's favorites in a single film. Noah Berry, Jr., went from juve-
nile to senior-citizen sidekick as James Garner's father on television's *The Rockford Files*.

Texas history and myth are filled with super sidekicks. Davy
Crockett and a host of others were sidekicking Sam Houston in
the dark days of the Alamo. Ma Ferguson, Pa's mouthpiece and
helpmeet, even rode astride the governor's saddle for Pa. John
Connally, who wanted to be president, could never escape his role
as Lyndon's boy. Liz Carpenter made a profession as Lady Bird's
sidekick. In retirement, she returned to Texas as sidekick/den
mother to all of Austin.

Do sidekicks in real life and on film lament along with Eliot's
Prufrock, "I am not Price Hamlet nor was meant to be/ Am an
attendant lord [a sidekick], fit to start a scene or swell a
progress"? Some argue that George W. Bush is really the sidekick
of one or more political figures. Some say he is subservient to Dick
Cheney, some say to Karl Rove, Bush's senior political adviser,
often called "King Karl." In the 2003 redistricting fight in Texas,
it could be argued that the entire Republican legislature was acting as sidekick to Congressman Tom DeLay.

PART III

Some

Part of Me

A Start in Life

14

I was fourteen in that late summer of 1945 when the world was starting a new life. "The War" had ended less than a month before, and the world had suddenly become different—light, sunny, expectant, and peaceful. If a new world was being reborn, why shouldn't I be born anew with it? I had prepared myself. By the late summer that saw the end of the war, I had read every word written by John R. Tunis and Ralph Henry Barbour. These two men wrote books about boys of the right sort, boys who started new lives by becoming star athletes at boarding schools called "Prep" by the lads or chaps or fellas who attended them. After prep school, these young stalwarts went off to "State" or "Tech" or "the Varsity." Boys at Prep were upright and honest and decent. They lived for good, clean sport. Schoolwork never seemed to rear its ugly head.

In the worlds of the Tunis/Barbour novels cowards were banished to outer darkness by the fellas, often with the aid of the "masters," men whose sole duties were to make boys manly and inculcate moral and spiritual and athletic values. In this world of my dreams, the masters were strong of jaw and clean of limb and cheered the boys to victory. The headmaster was stern but kind.

The coach, tough but fair. When a boy faltered, there was always a man to steer him on a new course and help him toughen himself for the playing fields of life. And we all knew that the "playing fields of Eton" had prepared six generations of young English boys to rule the British Empire. Though I was clumsy and awkward and without athletic prowess in that late summer that ended my old life, I truly believed that a term at Prep would make me like Jack Armstrong or Frank Bickley of Yale, make me fit for Empire. So luck or fate was on my side, and I was off to Prep.

To get there, I did not go by roadster or runabout or family sedan through the fall-tinged woods of New England as the boys in the Barbour and Tunis books did. Instead, I rode the Greyhound bus from Tuscaloosa, Alabama, to Birmingham. Then I took the train from Birmingham to the Southern Railway Station in Chattanooga, Tennessee. Arriving in Chattanooga, I walked across town to the Nashville, Chattanooga, and St. Louis Station and took the train to Cowan, Tennessee. At Cowan I took the jitney from the tiny railway station up the mountain through Sewanee to St. Andrew's School. It was a new world and a new beginning. I was ready to slough off the cheap Alabama boardinghouse where my mother and I had lived so we could be near my father, now in the fourth year of an eight-year stay in the veterans' hospital.

If I could shake the dust of Tuscaloosa off my feet and banish the smell of the paper mill at Holt from my nostrils, I could live my dream. I was ready to be surrounded by adoring younger boys and interesting older chaps. The boys' books were full of chaps. There were no guys outside Dead End Kids movies, and dudes in those days were men a little too well dressed. Adolph Menjou of the movies was a dude.

It must have been every boy's dream to be driven grandly up to Prep, be helped with his expensive leather Gladstone bags by handsome, stout fellas, and find himself welcomed into the bosom of a brand new fraternity of manly boys who, like the perfect youth in Kipling's "If," could "make one heap of all their winnings and risk it on one turn of pitch and toss / And lose, and start again at their beginnings and never breathe a word about their loss." It took a manly boy to live up to Rudyard Kipling, but we all tried. We planned to "meet with triumph and disaster and treat those two imposters just the same." But triumph was what we strove for.

When I got to the main building of St. Andrew's School for Boys, carrying a cheap tin footlocker and a pasteboard suitcase, the place was completely deserted. Not like the Prep of my dreams. Not a chap in sight. Not a lad, not a fella, not even a cad—and every school was expected to have one cad for leavening. The silence was oppressive and total. Disappointed and dispirited, I tiptoed about on the cool flagstone floors of the main building and read the signs on the doors: "Bursar," "Headmaster," "Prior." I knew what a headmaster was, but who in the John R. Tunis books had ever heard of a bursar? And was there a prior in Ralph Henry Barbour? No, not one! After peeking into a huge space labeled "Common Room" and banging the front door several times to attract attention, if any attention could be attracted, I put my hands in the pockets of my cheap new suit from J. C. Penney (I had at that time never heard of Brooks Brothers or J. Press of New Haven) and sat, "disconsolately," Tom Swift might have said, on the flagstone stairs leading upward into who-knewwhere. Dark recesses? An attic? A place for Mrs. Rochester to run mad? I sat and pondered. Boys pondered back then as we were edging into a new world. The war was over, and worry was no more. So we pondered. Not "weak and weary over many a quaint and curious volume of forgotten lore." We pondered over touchdowns, double plays, speared line drives, blond girls in runabouts.

As I was drifting into a Ralph Henry Barbour reverie, remembering the line drive "Brick" Bowman speared to defeat State in the bottom of the ninth, I heard a rustling behind me. I jumped to my feet and turned to see an aged man in a white dress slowly descending the staircase toward me. Not only was the ancient with white hair dressed in a flowing garment that touched the floor, he was wearing a red beanie on his head and had a black rope tied around his middle.

"My God," I blasphemed. "It's a monk."

But wait! Monks were only in the movies. In the Zorro movies monks had bald heads and wore brown drab uniforms. And were fat. So what was this monk—if indeed he was a monk—doing invading my new life, my dream life?

"Hello," he said, "I am Bishop Campbell. You must be the new boy."

I gaped.

"Well, are you the new boy? School began day before yesterday," he said. And suddenly he became a part of my new dream. Here was a kindly old gentleman and a bishop no less, and he was proving himself to be as concerned as the masters in all the boys' books I had lived on for years.

"Yessir, I . . . " And I foundered. All my opening remarks had been rehearsed for chaps and fellows. I had none for a bishop. Anyway, what exactly was a bishop? I was a Presbyterian, and Presbyterians had nothing closer to a bishop than Dr. Dale Le Count of the Sixth Avenue Presbyterian Church in Birmingham. And anyway I had never seen Dr. Le Count—only his name on the lighted board outside the grand Presbyterian church, the cathedral of all the Presbyterians as far as I knew, a Vatican for the "elect" of Alabama. In Leeds, a coal-mining and cement-plant town fifteen miles from Birmingham, all we had was Brother Broughdon. He wasn't a doctor like Dr. Dale Le Count. Or a bishop like the ancient man who stretched his hand out to me and asked my name. I had seen one of the Three Musketeers kiss a bishop's ring in a Technicolor movie, but I wasn't sure how to go about that. Did I drop to one knee, or did I sweep my plumed hat off my head and bow low over the ring? I didn't have a plumed hat. Or any kind of hat. So I just stood and gaped.

Then I remembered what my scoutmaster, Mr. Baker, had said. "Boys," he told us, "look a man in the eye and shake his hand in a firm and manly way." So I put out my hand and worried—well, pondered—whether I might belong on my knees on the flagstone floor. But Bishop Campbell took my hand, shook it, and said, "Welcome to Saint Andrew's. I will find Father Turkington, and he can take you down to the playing fields where the boys are now."

"Playing fields!" Now we were getting somewhere.

Out of nowhere, another man in a white dress with a black rope but no beanie came out of the door marked "Headmaster," and said, "You must be Lee."

"Yessir," I said, "I am Jim Lee." I almost slipped and said, "Jimmy." I had only been Jim Lee for about an hour. I had to kill the weak and ineffectual Jimmy Lee in one short and merciless stroke when I got to Cowan. The Jimmy Lee that had hung like a millstone around my neck for fourteen years was safely in the grave. I was a new man on a new plane on a renewed planet. And I required a manly name. Jimmy didn't work. Sissies and crooked movie accountants were named Jimmy. I was now just plain Jim. And I would remain so until the chaps gave me an appropriate nickname, maybe Brick or Rock or something befitting a new start in life.

Father Turkington took me out the front door, down the walkway past a three-story stone building covered in ivy, past a neat house with a garage which obviously belonged to one of the "masters" and his beautiful wife full of motherly concern. As we came out from behind the stone building, the classroom building, Father Turkington said, "There are the boys at play."

"At play!" Now we're really getting somewhere! Now we were talking a language I knew from Tunis and Barbour! Then I stood,

like "stout Cortez and all his men / Silent upon a peak in Darien."
Or, like Moses in the Scriptures, I gazed on the Promised Land.
Ranged before me were over a hundred boys in various stages of
athletic dress and undress. Some were playing football, some were
running around the track, and some were gawking at a fourteen-
year-old "new boy" in a chalk-striped, double-breasted J. C.
Penney suit with a bow tie. A bow tie! What had my mother been
thinking when she outfitted me for Prep? The boys began to
scream, "Frankie! Frankie!"

When I looked around to see where Frankie was, I saw that I
was Frankie. Sinatra was the rage that year. And Sinatra wore
bow ties. And I was Frankie. I could kiss "Brick" or "Rock" goodbye. Now what had I done? Why had I come off into the fast-
nesses of Tennessee only to be hooted at and called Frankie?
Nothing was changed from the sorry world I deserted. I was a
dead man in my new life. In the old one, Jimmy was awkward and
clumsy and non-athletic. He was back. The boy who fumbled his
way through the public schools of Alabama—first at Leeds, then
at two different seventh grades and one eighth in Birmingham.
Then six months at Woodlawn High School, the very school
where Harry Gilmer had made all-city, all-state, and all-southern
before going on to the University of Alabama to be an All-
American. Then to Tuscaloosa where stumbling Jimmy had finished out the ninth grade. With an F in Spanish, I might add.
What wasn't mediocre about Jimmy Lee was worse. He was no
scholar, no athlete, no chap, no fella.

And now in one short and merciless stroke, the new me was
killed the way I had killed Jimmy only two hours before. Frankie!
What could be worse? Was I back where I started in Tuscaloosa
not three months ago? Had I made a terrible blunder that hot
Tuscaloosa night at a filling station across the highway from the
Red Elephant Cafe? As I sat listening to my elders talk about war
and the atom bomb and peace and life its ownself, one of them
chanced to mention a boy from Tuscaloosa who had gone to a

boy's school in Tennessee. And they said this school only charged what a boy or his family could pay. I knew in an eye-blink that this school called St. Andrew's must be Prep! When I asked how a fella (see, I was already halfway there!) got to go to such a place, they said the boy from Tuscaloosa just wrote them a letter.

"Where is this school?" I asked. Or maybe I queried. Boys in the John R. Tunis books queried more often than they asked. And if I was going to write a letter to Prep, it had better be query.

One of the old ladies—she must have been in her late thirties—said, "I think Roy Jr., said it was in St. Andrew's, Tennessee."

In those days before zip codes, I knew all I needed to know. So I sat myself down and wrote a letter to St. Andrew's School at St. Andrews, Tennessee, and asked what you had to do to come to St. Andrews School—the apostrophe was still a mystery to me in 1945.

Miraculously, a letter came back to me in a week from the Reverend William R. D. Turkington, OHC. He told me to have my father or guardian write him and tell how much we could pay; he explained that all the boys worked and that tuition depended on what a family had. My father and mother and I, in conclave assembled, crafted a letter to the Reverend William R. D. Turkington, OHC—we puzzled long over what OHC might mean, but we couldn't come up with anything that fitted those initials. We could afford for me to go to this expensive school. We were flush right then. After going for three years on my jobs at the dry cleaners and the soda fountain and my mother's work as a sometime practical nurse, my father's $130-a-month pension from the government had started to come in. It was a king's ransom to us in 1945. With a flourish, my father wrote saying that we could pay $35 per month.

Time passed. I knew in reason that $35 wouldn't pay for a week, or even a day, at Prep. But hope sprang eternal in my new 1945-model breast. I tore the mail out of the mail carrier's hand

every day for ten days. Then my father got a letter up at the V.A.
Hospital saying that Jimmy Ward Lee could indeed matriculate at
St. Andrew's for $35 a month. I was given a list of furnishings to
buy—khaki uniforms, brown shoes, brown ties, underwear and
sheets and pillowcases, and all the bathroom truck needed by a
lad at a decent Prep.

So here I was, naked to my enemies, in a cheap suit and a bow
tie, before the hundred or so boys "at play." I was ruined. It got
worse as the good father and I walked back toward the main
building. Father Turkington said, "Do you smoke?"

Well, I thought, here we go again! "No, sir," I more or less
lied.

"Then why are you carrying that box of matches?"

Without thinking, I had taken the penny box of Blue Tips out
of my pocket and was nervously tossing it from hand to hand.

"Oh, I quit when I got to Cowan," I said.

And that was the truth. I had shucked Jimmy and quit smoking in a dirty little depot in a town of four hundred on the NC&
St.L line. And a fat lot of good the murder of Jimmy was going to
do me now. I was Forever Frankie. I was a liar with a penny box
of matches. Boy, was I making a new start!

But at least I learned that I could smoke. (This was back
when cigarettes were good for you if they didn't stunt your
growth—"not a cough in a car load," one of the companies
claimed. And didn't Jolting Joe and Ted Williams advertise the
benefits of smoking?)

"It's all right. We let the boys smoke here. If we don't, they
will sneak and burn down a building. So we have some smoking
areas."

And I had just thrown away a half-full package of Old Golds
in the toilet of the NC&St.L station in Cowan! There went a
dime down the drain! Anyway, if all else turned to ashes here, at
least I could smoke. And, who knows, maybe the handling of a

cigarette in a manly way would make up for the cries of "Frankie!" that still echoed in my ears as Father Turkington and I walked away from "the Field."

But "all's well that ends well," as Gabby Hayes said in a movie I once saw in Leeds. I did make a new start in life at St. Andrew's. I never achieved the grace and fluidity of Brick and Rock in the sports novels that I gave up in favor of Charles Dickens and Anthony Trollope and Mark Twain. I did letter in track—as the manager! But I did learn to read and study and listen in class. In the new world of learning I had many models. One was Father Flye, the finest history teacher I ever sat before. Father Flye lived to be an even hundred, which, I fear, is a commentary on clean living and right thinking. He neither smoked nor ate meat. And at the tender age of seventy, he ran wherever he went. I met him in New York City when he was ninety, and he still remembered the poems he knew by heart when he was my teacher. Oh, and I should mention that Bishop Campbell was hale and hearty at ninety-six when I saw him for the last time. Between Father Flye and Father Turkington and Father Spencer, who replaced Bishop Campbell as prior, and a cadre of other fine teachers, I gave up my contempt for learning and my dependence on swagger and athletic prowess and being a good fella. After a year, I forswore the comfort of Presbyterian predestination and took the harder and less certain path of High Church Episcopalianism. I say "harder" because "election" gets you off the hook. Well, for that matter, so does "reprobation" but in an altogether different way. With the Holy Cross fathers salvation was day-by-day and week-by-week and confession and communion and chapel every single day except Sunday and then at least twice. The monks of the Order of the Holy Cross were so "high church" that they made the Pope look like a Methodist. The fathers said that confession was good for the soul. Maybe, but Father Flye was serious about penance. So we all tried to line up at Father Wright's booth, where a couple of "Hail Marys" would do penance for our boyish sins. Going to church eight times a week finally gets to be a comfort and not a chore. And to hear Father Spencer and Father Turkington read the comforting words of the Book of Common Prayer and the King James Version did more than just instill an appreciation for the language of William Shakespeare and John Milton and Christopher Marlowe.

Alas, I was never called Brick or Rock. But we all had nicknames, and since I was from Alabama, and the 6' 8" governor of the state, His Excellency James E. Folsom, was called Big Jim. I got that as a nickname for awhile; then "Big Jim" became "Large James" and finally just "Large." At class reunions, I am still "Large" to others on the bad side of seventy who answer to "Lumpy" and "Moo Moo" and "Sloth." But there it is. Though the years have done serious damage to our faces, St. Andrew's is still with us. At one reunion, Lumpy had T-shirts made for us. Mine has my 1948 graduation picture screened on it, and under the picture it says, simply, "Large." Many might think Large is the shirt size. It is not. (I now take an XXL.) And if I haven't grown "in wisdom and favor with God," at least I have grown "in stature."

Everyone is due at least one new start in life. Mine began on September 4, 1945.

Boot Camp Days

15

In late summer my mind drifts back to what A. E. Housman calls "the land of lost content," back to a time when I was fifty-four years younger and fifty-seven pounds lighter, back to August of 1950 when I left my native home to go and make the world a better place for South Koreans. Hardly anyone remembers the Korean War nowadays. But I still remember it a little bit. I remember Charles Howell and Doc Carter and a gang of redneck boys entraining for California to go to boot camp. I joined Charles and Doc and a raggedy bunch of young slackers and stragglers at the Navy Recruiting Office in Birmingham, Alabama, to swear to uphold the Constitution of the United States and serve, as far as my limited capacities would let me, as a member of the regular U. S. Navy for a term of four years. Duly weighed and measured and sworn, we were marched in a body to the Moulton Hotel to be fed supper. After an uninspiring meal at this mid-level Birmingham hotel, we were marched, never in step and never in neat rows, to the Terminal Station to board a night train headed west to San Diego, a short five days away.

At the Moulton, our lone African-American recruit was fed in the kitchen or some other nether reach of the hotel. Once on the train, many of my co-racialists declared that they would neither eat nor sleep in the same accommodations with "that nigger." The peasant boys who had grown up on the sorghum farms of Sand Mountain and the recent graduates of the Boys' Industrial School (the Alabama reformatory) were loud in their denunciations of the whole African-American race and the perfidy of the U.S. Navy for subjecting us to this "black nigger." But as the grumbling grew, the train conductor called us all together and told us that on this train he was our commanding officer and anyone who refused to accept one Charles Howell of Mobile, Alabama, as an equal, would be put off the train at the nearest military installation and confined to a U.S. Marine Corps brig for the rest of his natural life.

The grumbling was muted, though in the privacies of the lavatories, some of the street urchins laid plans to mug young Charles Howell somewhere between Holly Springs and Memphis and throw him from the train. But fears of the marine brig soon stilled the planned insurrections. As we passed Jasper—birthplace of Tallulah Bankhead—the Pullman bunks were made down and the peasant boys and urbanite street thugs were bedded. All thoughts of doing in Charles Howell were forgotten as these seamen recruits manqué sank into the arms of Morpheus while the big eight-wheeler rolled farther down the line from the Heart of Dixie. By dawn we were in Little Rock, and by breakfast, in Texarkana. We were all marched into what was for us an elegant dining car, and three of us sat with Charles Howell as we devoured a better meal than some of us had ever had.

Charles Howell turned out to be better educated than most of the rednecks on the train, and before long he was seen teaching three boys from the Black Belt of Alabama the subtleties of a game called—say what you will!—"Spades." Before we had reached El Paso, Charles had become our mascot, and we duly christened him with the very politically, socially, and pigmentally incorrect name of "Snowball." These were the days before Thurgood Marshall argued and won the Brown *v.* Topeka (Kansas) Board of Education decision, before George Corley Wallace backed down before the U.S. Marshals in Tuscaloosa, and before Dwight Eisenhower sent the National Guard to Little Rock to allow black students to attend the Central High School. But it was not before Harry S. Truman integrated the armed forces of the United States. It turned out that Charles "Snowball" Howell was a smart, tolerant, and accomplished sailor. He was given the rank of recruit petty officer and was assigned to bear the guidon flag of our boot camp company once we learned to march in step and stay in neat lines. Sad to say, I suspect Charles was given the post of guidon bearer more because of his very dark skin than his innate good sense and intellect. I guess it looked good to have a company of towheaded Anglo-Saxon Protestants being led by someone as dark as the late Nat "King" Cole.

Once in San Diego, we were shorn of our locks and would have been stripped of our dignity if we had had any. The barbers were civilians, but not a one of them was a stylist and only two of them had ever been to barber college. They were paid by the close-cropped head. Gone were the "Hollywood haircuts" with ducktails. Gone were the "knotted and combined locks" plastered down with that red brilliantine hair oil so popular in a bygone era. Brilliantine, our chief petty officer said, "smells like a Panamanian whorehouse." But never having been to Panama, I . . . .

It got a lot worse. We were stripped buck nekkid and lined up in a room with some three hundred new "boots" to be stared at by one another and glanced at by some amazingly bored navy doctors. We all had to turn our heads and cough (the men may understand this better than the women), and then we were told to "bend over and grab our cheeks," but, as Polonius says, "a foolish figure and farewell it." A navy corpsman made three or four tries to find a vein in my left arm and then just punched the needle in from the side to draw some of my Alabama blood. I still have the mark where the needle went in, but the swelling and discoloration were gone within two weeks. And by then things were so horrible that I might have gone back to give more blood to get out of the incessant marching on asphalt "grinders." We were learning to march so that we could ride around on naval vessels of the U.S. Pacific Fleet. Once out of boot camp, I never marched another step, but by God I knew how.

After the fake physical, we were sent into a huge room to have people glance at us for a second to see what sizes we wore and then to throw clothes of other sizes at us. Six pairs of WAVE dungarees, six denim shirts, some dress blues and dress whites, some undress blues and undress whites, a pair of brogans (the best shoes I ever owned), a pair of plain black dress shoes, a pea coat, some white hats, six pairs of socks, six sets of skivvies, and some shaving and tooth-brushing equipment to be kept in what I thought was the effeminately named "ditty bag." And then the big canvas sea bag which would not hold all we owned—that is until we had been taught for about three weeks how to roll all these garments and tie them with bits of string before packing. (Note one: I hate to say this, but the U.S. Navy called these pieces of string "tie-ties." Note two: WAVE dungarees were WWII blue jeans that were cut in a pattern like regular pants and were large enough in the seat to accommodate what sailors thought was the standard female derriere. Old salts scuttled those pants as soon as possible in favor of "patch pocket tailor-mades" that could be bought at naval tailors on shore. Patch pockets were as tight as Britney Spears's fishnets. You can see these garments on the little sailor on the CrackerJack box. WAVE dungarees were wonderfully comfortable and were perfect for anyone with a hint of the callipygious.)

James Thurber ended the essay, "University Days," by saying, "I don't think about it much anymore." I don't think much about those days either. Except in the dog days of summer and when I actually celebrate the date of August 16, 1950, when I "swore etc. etc. etc." Then I remember Charles "Snowball" Howell of Mobile and Doc Carter, a chiropractor from Anniston who joined up for some unaccountable reason after taking his D.C. from the Palmer School of Chiropractic in Davenport, Iowa. Maybe, like the late radioman third class Rabbit Adney of Little Rock, he was told by a judge to join or go to jail. For whatever reason, Dr. Seaman Recruit Carter was with us on the train and in the early days of boot camp. Doc, who, by his own admission, could cure the common cold and most forms of cancer by simple "adjustments," was a godsend to those of us he liked. After we had pounded the grinders all day and were sore of back and head, Doc would lay us out on the barracks tables and give a quick jerk or two. Then the world seemed none so bad until we remembered that we were still in boot camp. Sad to say, Doc was not with us long. He was snatched away by a "press gang" from the U.S. Naval Training Center football team to adjust away their athletic aches. Before he left, he "adjusted" a sailor eager to get out of the Navy by tying his back in knots and sending him off to sickbay. He told the slacker to go to a chiropractor as soon as he got discharged. The chiropractor could untangle him and fix him as good as new. That young traitor is probably drawing disability payments to this day.

I don't think about it much anymore. But if they try to draft me to go off and fight the Al Qaeda, I am just like Jack Nicholson in *Five Easy Pieces*: I am out of here on the first red log truck headed for Canada.

The Rain in Korea is
Awful Cold and Wet

16

U p to now, I have tried to keep it quiet that I was involved in the Korean War. A World War II vet friend of mine always called it, "the war we tied." He was a member of "the Greatest Generation," and Tom Brokaw had written him up. I am not a warlike sort, but I come from a long line of killers. My father served in the First Division in the Argonne Forest in the Great War, or the War to End All Wars. My great-granddaddy Wyatt was in the 30th Alabama and died following Vicksburg. Another ancestor of mine was at Cerro Gordo in the Mexican War, and of course there was Lighthorse Harry Lee in the Revolution. He and Robert E. were cousins of my great-great-grandfather, Needham Lee, Sr., who founded the Alabama dynasty and then had to flee Shelby County to live among the Cherokees because he was guilty of counterfeiting. He may have been a criminal, but he had forty-four sons and grandsons who fought on the side of the Confederacy.

I was mixed up in a war so insignificant that even Pulitzer Prize-winning historian Joseph Ellis wouldn't have bothered to lie about serving in it. (Remember him? He used to brag to his students about how he fought hard in Vietnam only to have it all revealed as a lie.) Anyway, Korea wasn't a war. It was a police action—only fifty-four thousand Americans died and another hundred-sixty-four thousand got wounded. Vietnam and Desert Storm were fought on television and got all the publicity, but we pretty much conducted our police action in secret—and way off camera. Only a few of us remember the song with the lines, "The rain in Korea is awful cold and wet/And them rotation papers is mighty hard to get." Those fifty-four thousand dead escaped the rain finally. And are now forgot. We don't even have a wall that everybody who goes to Washington has to see.

I was not a hero. And I didn't get shot at but once or twice—once by one of our guys. It would have been wasted effort to tell my classes lies the way Joseph Ellis did. My students didn't know Korea existed, and most of them thought WWII was in 1776.

Well, fifty and more winters have passed, and I am ready with my lies. Oh, my, yes, we had our narrow escapes. We could have all died. One night an ensign who had come fresh from the U.S. Naval Academy was on watch when a Chinese junk was discovered on radar. Ensign Pulver—I think that was his name—woke up the two Korean liaison officers, broke out the guns, and readied the searchlight. The Chinese junk crew was told to surrender peacefully or be killed by American fire. The Korean officers warned them that we were going to turn on the searchlight and we had better see hands in the air Gene Autry style.

No reply.

"All right," Mr. Pulver said, "tell them to get ready."

The Korean officers said something noisome and incomprehensible, and we turned on the light.

The buoy we illuminated bobbed gently in the water, and a good time was had by all. All except the ensign, who proved what we common sailors had known about him all along.

Two nights later, same ensign, same Korean officers, same

rifles, same searchlight, same threats, same buoy. We all knew we had lost that round to the enemy buoy and went on our way to fight at a later day.

The very next night I had an early watch and slept through until morning. When I went on deck, I found five or six North Korean youths standing around a crude wooden boat and two battered oars.

"Ohmigod" I said, "we have been captured, and they didn't wake me up."

Wrong again. The Koreans had slipped up on our ship in the night and had banged on the fantail with the oars, begging to sur-render. Somebody finally told Pulver that we had company, and he slowed down enough to take the enemy aboard. We then dressed them in navy dungarees and blue shirts and let them wan-der around the ship for several days until we came upon a South Korean frigate. We transferred the prisoners and drifted on to future glory. I always suspected that the South Koreans slit the throats of these bold pirates and took the new uniforms.

But, hey, war is hell.

It was really hell for some old North Korean guy up near Yangyang Harbor. (I made up that name because I can't remem-ber the real harbor.) He was trying to make a crop up on a hillside while we were bombarding the town about half a mile below him. He seemed to be plowing with a mule, but it could have been a water buffalo. (They didn't teach animal husbandry in boot camp.) Anyway, he seemed to be a little unconcerned about the firing aimed in his general direction. He thought no better of our marksmen than I did. I knew we couldn't hit anything on purpose, but the old farmer might have lost a mule just from one of our strays. Our objective was a tall smokestack rising up out of the town of Yangyang. (Whatever.) Why we wanted to hit it was never clear—gunnery practice I suppose. So every morning about 8:00 we lay off Yangyang and fired our twenty allotted 5-inch rounds. Every morning we missed the smokestack, though I am sure we killed lots of women and children and dogs and cats. But we had not hit the smokestack when we were sent off to the Yellow Sea on the other side of Korea to lay waste to more Korean countryside. If we could hit it.

Once we rounded the bend of Korea and headed north up the Yellow Sea side we lowered the U.S. flag and raised the tasteful blue-and-white of the United Nations. Now we were policing for the whole civilized world. And we ran with Colombian destroyers, New Zealand frigates, Australian carriers, Canadian vessels of one sort or another, and the occasional Thai gunboat.

Our job up there was purely shore bombardment, for we had done so well on the other edge of Korea that we were a natural for the more serious Yellow Sea side. So we steamed slowly up and down the west coast of Korea firing off occasional shots at farmers and ranchers and rice paddy workers. Once, in a dense fog, our radar picked up the ever-present Chinese junk. Even though nobody in the navy ever saw a Chinese junk, we all knew that the waters were crammed with them. "Thick on the ground," one old country boy from North Carolina said.

Very quietly, without all that bonging that usually signals general quarters, we were whispered to our battle stations. We were ready to kill us some Commies. Blow them out of the water with our 5-inch guns and then wipe out the survivors with our 20 mm. machine guns.

I was on the bridge manning some headphones between the captain and the gunnery officer. The fire control radar began to twist and turn and someone whispered, "Lock On!"

"Stand by to fire," the captain said.

I told the gunnery officer on the headphone, "Stand by to fire."

"Standing by," the gunnery officer said back to me on the headphone.

Suddenly from up on the fire control radar atop the bridge, a reserve officer who had a full-time job at Sears Roebuck, said, "Wait! Wait! Wait!"

The fog had lifted enough to reveal the Chinese junk as a Canadian cruiser with nine or so 8-inch guns. All trained on us.

We stood down. And so did the Canadians. I was relieved, but in later years I wondered if the Canadians could shoot any better than we could. Maybe they could. I don't know, but I do know that in 1989 I bought a Canadian-made Ford Crown Victoria that ran like a Singer sewing machine, so maybe they did have some technical know-how. And I could be lying at the bottom of the Yellow Sea right now.

I wasn't much scared back in those halcyon days, but now I am terrified when I think how much of a mess our war was and how we had hundreds of quick-trained young officers whose incompetence could have gotten all of us killed. Maybe there is a reason nobody remembers Korea. We were inept, but I am sure all our present-day warriors know exactly what they are doing. So Bin Laden had better watch it.

Later in the war—the Po-lice Action—I was sent down to the South Pacific to help out with the H-bomb tests, and I am proud to say that only one H-bomb got away from us. No Americans were killed outright, but several Japanese fishermen on *The Fortunate Dragon* went to join their ancestors.

I am a coward, and I'd rather drive between Dallas and Austin on Labor Day Weekend than to tie the North Koreans again. Oh, I have one medal from that war: it is the U.S. Navy Good Conduct Medal.

Hydrogen Bomb Days

17

If Attorney General John Ashcroft reads this, as I am sure he will, I may find myself incarcerated in the Federal Correctional Institution in Fort Worth, Texas, keeping company with ex-governor Edwin Edwards of Louisiana. That is, if I am lucky. If I am unlucky, I may serve my time at the Portsmouth, New Hampshire, naval brig. Since the offense I am about to confess took place in the United States Navy, I am not sure whether I will be tried under the Uniform Code of Military Justice, sometimes called "the Rocks and Shoals," or just in a federal courthouse under the United States Criminal Code. What I am confessing is probably a serious federal crime. I am sure I have betrayed military secrets in talking about the hydrogen bomb. About fifty years ago, I signed a paper saying I would never talk or write or otherwise communicate with anyone about my atomic bomb and hydrogen bomb experiences. Now I am about to tell all.

Chances are that nobody reading this has ever seen an atomic bomb or hydrogen bomb go off. I have seen lots of them. Well, not exactly lots, but one atomic bomb and seven hydrogen bombs. All this activity was half a century ago on a series of atolls in the far Pacific Ocean. Now it is time to reveal atomic secrets and blow the lid off these nuclear weapons of mass destruction. Actually, I don't really know as much as every freshman student knows about atomic energy. In fact, I know less than anybody who has ever learned how to make a bomb on the Internet. But I was there and saw some stuff, and it is what I saw that is so deeply secret.

In 1951, my destroyer, the USS *Radford* DDE 446, was assigned to go to the Marshall Islands to participate in the bomb tests. For four months we patrolled around Eniwetok and Bikini atolls to see that no Russian sloops or Chinese junks or Peruvian frigates crept around these atolls where we were going to fire off some WMDs. We trained hard and listened to many lectures. We learned that it was dangerous to swim in the barracuda-infested waters, that exposure to the South Pacific sun might cause cancer, that tempers can flare in the hotter latitudes. Oh, and there was some slight danger from radiation and fallout dust. Nothing serious, but we were supposed to wash off the ship with salt water from the same seas that had just been nuked. At least we had no dangerous natives. They had all been spirited away. All we had were male soldiers and sailors and airmen and atomic energy workers and probably some Russian spies. The closest woman was six hundred miles away, so we didn't get to see all those venereal disease movies we saw in boot camp.

Some of the troops were dangerous. Once, on shore patrol, a thirty-four-year-old signalman named "Old Folks" Bream and I manned the docks at the end of liberty call on Eniwetok Island. As the drunks stumbled back or were carried by MPs and shore patrolmen, Old Folks and I stacked the drunks like cordwood while we waited for their launches to come and take them back to the ships anchored in the middle of the atoll. Just calm, common, nautical, passed-out drunks. As their launches pulled alongside the dock, Old Folks took their feet and I took their arms and we passed them down to the coxswain of the boat. Just normal sailor stuff. An air force general saw the drunks Old Folks and I were piling up on the docks and assumed a disaster. He reported to our captain that a riot had occurred on the docks, but when we were called in to explain, Old Folks said, in his whiskey-and-Lucky-Strikes voice, "Captain, I have seen blood running in the docks in Tsingtao, China. This wasn't nothing."

The captain, a serious drunk himself, said, "All right, men, don't let this happen again."

After the air force general had flown to the safety of Hickam Field in Hawaii, things became normal again. Everyone else on the island knew how liberty worked in a hot climate. How important cold beer was and the occasional gin and tonic.

Really hot climates are not conducive to walking in beauty. One day as I was about to take the watch as petty officer of the deck, I saw some stretcher bearers hauling a bloody sailor down the gangway, headed for the island hospital. The victim was a gunner's mate named Acevez, a bad-news pachuco from LA Acevez was covered with blood, and I stood in wonder as he was put aboard the ship's lifeboat and taken away. The guy I was to relieve on the watch danced from foot to foot as he unstrapped the .45 Colt automatic from his waist and passed it to me. I signed the log and instantly became PO of the watch. Dog Lathrop, the guy I relieved, said, "Acevez slapped old Smith around, and Smith put a knife in his back right at the backbone and then just walked around that bad-ass Messican."

Smith was a wormy little ship's serviceman seaman from Harlan County, Kentucky, who worked in the laundry. He weighed about 120 pounds and talked with a back-country accent. Only us southern boys knew what Harlan County meant. If you showed up in Harlan without a knife, they made you rent one. Harlan County was coal-mining country and Saturday-night-killing country. We knew better than to mess with a Kentucky redneck, but Acevez was a thug from LA, who was so tough his arms hung out from his body when he walked. He had tattoos on his fingers that spelled out something in Spanish that could probably be translated as "shock and awe." Or worse.

I never did find out why Acevez made the mistake of slapping Smith. Before Dog could tell me, the officer of the deck turned to me and said, "Go down to the fantail compartment and arrest Smith."

"Arrest Smith, sir?"

"Right. He put a knife in Acevez and cut him bad. He may not live."

"Sir, what am I supposed to do when I get Smith?"

"Arrest him and take him to the wardroom to be questioned."

My first thought was to throw myself over the side and swim for it. My second thought was to beg to be relieved as PO of the watch. My third was to throw up and make a dash for sickbay. My fourth thought was a question—what would Randolph Scott do?

Randy would have gone after Smith with his right arm crooked above his six-gun. I didn't have a six-gun. I had a 1911 model Colt .45 that I had never loaded or shot. I wasn't even sure how it worked. We had to wear them on watch, but we were not trusted to learn how to work them. If the Commies came, we were probably supposed to throw the gun at them and run.

I dragged my slow feet toward the stern of the ship. I was pretty sure Smith would knife me the way he had Acevez, but this was 1952 and I had my duty. As my mother used to say, "I didn't know whether to shit or go blind."

As I got to the hatch leading down into the compartment, I could see that it was dark. Great! I climbed down the ladder, still not knowing what I was going to do. I looked around and saw nobody. That cinched it: Smith was lurking in the darkness with his bloody knife ready to sever my jugular vein. (This was before carotid arteries.).

I left the gun where it was in the holster.

I said, "Uh, Smith, er, come on." I sounded like Andy Devine, the old high-voiced sidekick from the Saturday westerns.

"Smith?"

"Yeah, I'm coming."

I turned and climbed the ladder that led back on deck hoping Smith would not stab me until we got in the open air where I might be able to jump over the side before he cut me too badly.

Nothing happened, so I walked along in front of Smith all the way past the staring sailors, past the quaking officer of the deck, and into the wardroom. Smith and I sat down, not talking at all, waiting for some officer to come and do whatever he was going to do. The officer in question had spent a semester at the unaccredited Cumberland University Law School in Lebanon, Tennessee, and was our legal authority. He had seen a lot of Boston Blackie movies and fell to questioning Smith in third-degree fashion. I sat silent. All Smith had to say was, "That Messican slapped me because his uniform weren't arned to suit him, so what could I do. I cut the sumbitch." The officer asked over and over, and Smith said the same thing over and over.

Finally, the officer talked to the captain, and it was decided that I was to take Smith back to the sail locker and "brig him up."

Here is the short version. Smith was courtmartialed, but the case was thrown out. When a real lawyer looked into it, he found that Smith had not been told that he could remain silent. But we knew it was not over. Everybody said that when Acevez recovered from his wounds, he would come back and fix Smith once and for all. A month or so later, Acevez returned and the ship's crew gathered around to ask how he was going to handle Smith. Acevez said, "I have had all of Smith that I want."

So we went back to WMDs. Actually, I never got to see but one hydrogen bomb. Mostly, they locked us up and made us watch on radar if we were near a set. But on the final shot, we all got to go on deck one morning before daylight and sit facing away

from Bikini Atoll, a little over 180 miles away. We were told to put
our eyes in the crook of our elbows and close them tight. They
stressed that the blast would blind us if we looked. Then they
counted down from ten to zero. When the H-bomb went, I had
the impression I could see my bones through my arm and closed
eyes, but I know that is not true. I saw light. Serious light. After
a few minutes, we heard the noise and felt the blast rock the ship,
and we were told we could look. It was daylight. Not real daylight,
but H-bomb daylight, and stayed that way until the sun came up
minutes and minutes later. As it grew naturally light, the redness
of the bomb faded, and we watched the mushroom cloud climb
for what seemed like all the rest of the morning.

This was on my second trip to the test site. We went first in
1952, and then, when I had transferred to another destroyer, the
USS *Renshaw* DDE 499, we were sent back for the second round.
That was late 1953 into 1954. On the first trip, they fired off an
insignificant A-bomb on a little island not twenty miles from
where we were, but A-bombs are kid stuff. The H-bomb on that
test dug a hole on some island big enough to hold a seventeen-
story building. (I read that on the Internet, so I guess other people are breaking the silence.) All the test A-bomb did that time
was vaporize the tiny island in Eniwetok Atoll. It had been on our
radar, but after the blast, it was no longer there. On the second
trip down, the Atomic Energy Commission fired off seven or eight
H-bombs, if I remember right. The first one got away from them
and caused a lot of radiation. My ship had to go evacuate natives
off some little island. That bomb caused the Japanese fishing ship,
The Fortunate Dragon, to be radiated so badly that several of the
fishermen died.

The other bombs in the second series were big blasts, but the
AEC people must have had them under control, for nothing bad
ever happened. I don't know how the radiation and fallout dust

affected anyone else, but I don't have to sleep with a nightlight nowadays.

H-bombs are probably good for you. I am still here fifty years later. I am not the only one, for some group in Oregon is made up of Operation Ivy (the official name of the 1952 tests) survivors. All this stuff is on the Internet now, but I did sign a paper saying I would keep mum. O.K. This is off my chest. I am ready for La Tuna or the FCI in Fort Worth or whatever that prison is in Big Spring.

My Forty Years in a Quandary
and How They Grew

18

I came to Texas in 1958 to stay. From a boyhood in Alabama and Tennessee, a stint as a destroyer sailor in the U.S. Navy during the Korean War, and some time in graduate school in Alabama and Arkansas, I took at job as an instructor in English at North Texas State College in Denton. I came armed and dangerous with a wife, two sons, an almost Ph.D., and a 1951 Chevrolet Suburban purchased used from the Lee County Hospital in Opelika, Alabama. I loved literature and the chance to teach it, so I was put to teaching remedial composition. I longed for sessions in the faculty lounge where men in tweed sports coats with patches on the sleeves smoked pipes and would "come and go talking of Michelangelo." Instead I found men talking about salaries and real estate and sex and student misbehavior. The women sat apart talking about who knew what: Michelangelo, salary inequity, or estrogen.

This was an era when English teachers taught five classes, four of composition and one of sophomore literature. Long before advanced techniques arrived to make students instantly literate with little effort on anyone one's part, we slogged away with students who wrote a theme a week. At the end of the term, the students wrote a departmental essay, which was designed to demonstrate their shortcomings as writers and our ineffectiveness as instructors. Nobody wanted to appear soft, so when it came time to read and score themes written in other faculty members' classes, almost everybody in my department gave all the good themes between sixty and sixty-five. All totally failing themes were given forty-five (there was no need to be ugly and assign a twenty; after all, F is F). Themes that were average got a grade of about fifty-five. If your student made below fifty-five, you had to appeal the grade in order to pass the student. If you appealed, three more people read the theme and each gave it fifty-five. You could pass the student then, but you were suitably disgraced because you were shown to have no standards. If you could have had Russell Banks, Bertrand Russell, and Russell Baker in your classes, you would not have dared to give them higher than Bs. You didn't dare give anybody an A in those days because somebody would bring this to the attention of all your colleagues when the student got his obligatory sixty-five on the departmental. So if Bertie, Russell, and Russell had made Bs all along and got sixty-fives on their departmentals, you had to lower them to a C+ for the final grade. It was a perfect system. It fought hubris to an absolute standstill.

You were expected to fail twenty percent of your students. The one person in my department who passed everyone was so abused by the rest of the faculty that he went to Hillcrest Sanitarium for a round of shock treatments. He struggled on for awhile, but finally he gave the whole business up and took to painting pictures. The rest of us younger faculty lived lives of quiet desperation. One, in my second year, took an overdose of sleeping pills and died on his couch. I attribute his death to freshman composition, but then it almost killed me, so I may have a prejudice here.

There was no talk of "writing as process" and "The Bay Area Writing Project." Such world-saving pedagogies came along later and made American freshmen write like Russell, Russell, and Baker. Or so I have heard in my retirement. Computers did exist somewhere, but they were the size of Chrysler New Yorkers and Cadillac Fleetwoods and were not seen on college campuses. Nowadays I am told that writing labs are constructed so that students can surreptitiously play video games when the writing coaches are looking away. But all this progress was still far in the future. Video games were years away. It was all stub pencils and lined paper.

But we had a lot of perfect things in those days. God was in His Heaven and all was right with the world. (It was only later that God was in Her Heaven). Example: Here was an article of faith for all senior college faculty: all junior college transfers were louts who had gone to TCJC or Cooke County or Ranger or Cisco to "get their freshman English off" because there was no way they could pass at North Texas. Therefore, when a student in sophomore English or an advanced course wrote poorly or confused "lie" and "lay," it was clear that we were looking at one of the proudest products of Navarro or El Centro or Henderson County. After almost twenty years of believing this, we did a study. It turned out that students who "got their English off" at Cisco or Ranger or Howard County performed exactly as did those who had "got their English off" at North Texas, TCU, Texas Tech, the University of Texas, or the University of Arkansas at Pine Bluff, for that matter. It made no difference. And one of the dumbest graduate students I ever taught took his B.A. at Princeton. Hubris dies proudly once again.

In what I like to call "my day," men faculty wore coats and ties to class and scraped their faces of all hair before meeting eight o'clock classes. Beads and Roman sandals were not seen. The male students wore Gant shirts and chinos with little belts on the back straight from what one of my literate freshmen called "the Ivory League." The girls—this is pre-women days we're talking here— wore bouffant hairdos and panty girdles. The hairdos were in imitation of Annette Funicello in *Beach Blanket Bingo*, and most of their little heads would not have fitted into a Number Three washtub. And how do I know about the girdles? Well, the skirts were short and the crossed legs presented dozens of chubby thighs swathed in yards of white latex. Skinny thighs too, for those panty girdles were not so much for compressing fat as for following the fad of the day. And forget jeans and slacks: at North Texas State College in those days no woman student was ever seen in either garment unless at least two inches of snow layered the ground.

Our department was run by a director, who reported directly to the president. The dean of arts and sciences made out degree plans and had no connection with the faculty. I was a member of the faculty for thirteen years before I ever met him. And that was too soon. We had one vice president of undefined duties, a night watchman who punched one of those time clocks slung around the shoulders on a belt, and a rampaging dean of women who was high sheriff of female virtue and chastity. If raises were in the offing, men got first chance because "they had families." The few women faculty in those days were thought to have working husbands or were spinsters who had been taught to live frugally. The few women faculty we had were expected to teach the usual heavy load of composition plus grammar, methods of teaching in the public schools, and children's literature. Men did freshman composition too, but methods and kiddie lit were women's work. And it cut little ice whether the woman had degrees from Berkeley, Yale, or Harvard. She was known to be inferior to the man with his degrees from Oklahoma Body and Fender and the Alabama School of Mines at Marquetta. Probably also inferior even in stature, wisdom, and favor with God. Feminine hubris takes a beating here and elsewhere.

And on the matter of tenure and promotion, these were in the best of the good old days. In my day, in order to get tenure, you had to remain unindicted for major crimes for three long years. A DWI arrest didn't count against you. Hell, boys *will* take a drink. If you avoided crimes like rape, communist sympathizing, atheism, and felony murder, you had the word "temporary" (in parentheses) removed from your rank. There was no talk of tenure exactly, but we all knew what losing "temporary" meant and what it didn't mean. Two of our full professors got crossways with the president of NTSC and found the word "temporary" put back on their next contracts. They were given a message, and the temp status was removed only after the miscreants proved themselves pure of heart once again. One of the full professors in question ran off with a woman not his wife, and the president sent the director of the department to Michigan or some other northern state to drag him back. He returned, tail tucked between his legs, and behaved as a devoted husband until he left several years later to take a high-paying job in technical writing. After a stint at that, he joined the faculty of a large midwestern university. Little was heard of him for a long time, but then rumors drifted in that he was, to use that term of terrorism to faculty, "in administration." Fifteen or so years later, I was doing a summer institute at his university and casually asked someone if he had ever heard of Professor X. "Oh, yes," I was told, "he is the chancellor." I sought him out, and he took me to dinner, explained that he had been divorced for years, and was living with a female colleague on one of the branch campuses under his direction. When he was offered the chancellorship, he told the regents all about his non-traditional living arrangements and they said, "So?" Maybe hubris was making a comeback here and Bob Dylan was right when he said change was "blowin' in the wind."

Another full professor wrote an article comparing schools of education to dung heaps. And since the president was an old high school principal, the fans were filled with feces. The attacker of the educationists had temporary put back on his contract for a few years. Several years later, I saw the salary list and found I was making more as an assistant professor than he was as a full professor. And he had a distinguished record of publication and had been president of every professional and learned society in the state. Who was ahead on hubris points now?

We had a clearly defined system for scholarship: it was publish and perish; you presented a paper or wrote an article at your peril. If you did, the non-publishing members of the department would rake it over the coals for days and weeks and months. One pipe-smoking, chin-stroking full professor who came to NTSC in the 1930s and lived and died completely innocent of papers or publications, always said the same thing of others' works: "I thought that was pretty thin fare." We were all too polite, or cowardly, to suggest that he thicken up the broth of learning himself. He was one of three on the schedule committee, so cross him and you would find yourself teaching a full load of freshman English beginning at 8:00 A.M. on MWF and on TTS. Coupled with that, you would find some late afternoon classes to keep you on your toes all day. TTS? Yes, in those days schedules ran all six days of the week. This learned scholar always announced that he would someday retire and "do some writing." He died as innocent of publication as the day he was born. He took *The Atlantic Monthly* and probably didn't feel the need to otherwise establish his literary credentials. He was said to be a throbbing bore in his classes, but he was a man of certainties in the faculty lounge where it really counted.

The third member of the governing troika was equally unpublished, though he had once read a paper on the seriousness of *Peyton Place*. He was the world's foremost authority. Philosophy faculty members used to drop by the English department lounge to pose questions to him about Immanuel Kant or Paul Tillich or

St. Thomas Aquinas. He always spoke learnedly and at serious length. We nodded thoughtfully as he spoke and spoke and spoke, but we held our applause until the philosophers left. The visitors to our lounge suppressed their laughter until they were out of earshot. He could be as wrong about Kant as he could about Marcel Proust, but his dogmatism never deserted him about either. He had once been described as "a young man of promise," but that designation was made sometime in the late 1930s. By the 1950s he spoke forcefully against liberalism, irreligion, and godless Communism. He and his close pal, the department director, read *Human Events*, a right-wing flag-waver that may still seek the impeachment of Earl Warren. These two heavyweights left copies in the lounge for the benefit of the ignorant and misguided. The whippersnapper element was always afraid to throw the copies away, so by March, all the coffee tables were weighted with the wisdom of J. Edgar Hoover, Barry Goldwater, and Robert Welch, founder of the John Birch Society. The word was that the director had his subscription from the governor of the state of Texas, who just happened to be his first cousin. Talk about job security.

Promotion in those days was as clear as tenure. You didn't have to publish, of course. You had to stay out of jail and in favor with the administration of the department and the university. The department meant the director, and the university meant the president. At the proper time, if you had no felony arrests and if you had not been too blatantly a liberal Democrat, the director of the department hand-carried his recommended list of promotions to the president where it was scanned to insure against radicalism, homosexual tendencies, and anti-administration rhetoric. Advisements would be taken. Considerations would be made. Mistakes would be avoided. Radicals would be shunned. Passive voice would be used. And then, out of nowhere, promotions would come through. Or not. Once, the director sent forward the name of an associate professor and recommended that he be promoted. Not only was he promoted, but the dangerous radical whose name was just above his on the associate roster was also upgraded to full professor. The president's secretary had typed in his name by mistake. The "mistake" was a man much out of favor and was amazed to see his promotion come through. He rushed in to thank the director, who made an emergency visit to the president to protest. The president, however, acting on the dictum that a card laid is a card played, or the Greek theory that one god cannot undo the work of another, let the promotion stand. The mistaken promotee was never the wiser and went to his grave never knowing that he died a full professor instead of an associate professor because "mistakes were made."

We were never allowed to forget that we had signed a loyalty oath that forbade us to teach and advocate the overthrow of the government by force and violence. We were also forced to donate a specified amount to the Community Chest (now the United Way). This was not voluntary, for we had to take our checks to the bursar's window when we picked up our salary checks. And you didn't get your salary unless you paid up. We also had to join the Conference of College Teachers of English. The director wanted us to be the only institution in the state with a hundred-percent membership. As if all this government and academic stress was not enough, there was the religious. A new faculty member barely had time to unload his U-Haul of its meager load before someone came, pie in hand, to ask, "What church do you attend?" And that is not all; sometime in the sixties, the Texas legislature considered a bill that would require all teachers to affirm belief in a supreme being. The bill did not pass, but for many months the unchurched and ungodly were left to twist slowly in the wind.

We didn't exactly have Nazi "nights of long knives" in those days, nor did we have midnight firings, but we did lose a few faculty suddenly. One newly among us attempted to integrate

269

Denton's Campus Theatre. He organized mass demonstrations on the downtown showplace by having students go to the ticket window and say, "If I were black, would you sell me a ticket?" When the answer was no, the student would go to the end of the line prepared to ask again. It worked to the extent that the show could not go on that night. The next day, the director called the instructor in and fired him. All this was pretty clearly on the orders of the president/principal, for the director made no moves without the authority of the president. When the faculty member sued in federal court, the administrators went to Sherman and swore that the faculty member was fired not for integration tactics but because he and his wife had taken some students down to Lake Dallas and done some nekkid swimming. It was also alleged that he was not prompt in paying his debts. These things were true, but the administrators did not know them when they fired him; they were drummed up later.

All men are as mortal as Socrates of the famous syllogism. And all sometimes retire. When the principal/president retired, the faculty saw a chance to speak out for once. We demanded that the regents find someone from off campus and someone without a degree in education. I am sure they paid no attention to us, but nevertheless they chose a historian who had a degree from "up north" and had been provost of a Midwestern university where faculty governance was part of the program. Now the fat was in the fire.

Right away, the new president, not only a liberal but a Catholic, set about destroying the works of his predecessor. He decreed that we establish a faculty senate. Then the department directors were reduced to chairmen (not chairs, for that came later), and the dean of the College of Arts and Sciences suddenly had to supervise more than degree plans. Chairmen now reported to him instead of the president. It was somewhere in these years that I first met the dean. The chairman took me to see him because I was doing some minor administrative thing. The chairman said, "Dean, you know Jim Lee, don't you?" The dean said, "Oh, ah, yes, I, oh, ah, know him." He then called me Bill for the rest of the time I was in his office. That suited me, for one of the things drilled into my head in the U.S. Navy was to stay away from the authorities. I never met the dean again. He did not remain dean long. The new president was sabotaged by the old president's friends and left after a very few years. But his reforms were longer lasting. Faculty who had tasted freedom were never going back to the days of loyalty oaths, enforced charities, fears of sudden firings, and high-school administration.

It was not long before the new president came and swept some floors that needed cleaning. Soon many male faculty ceased to scrape the whiskers off their faces. The next thing you knew beads and Roman sandals were seen, and a lot of other stuff that Merle Haggard says does not go on in Muskogee, Oklahoma, USA. Under new deans and chairs and a cloud of vice presidents and associates and assistants we developed hiring policies and tenure reviews and requirements that faculty publish if they wanted promotions. That made it hard on all concerned. The old time-servers fought every step of the way. It was hard to deny promotion to young faculty for not publishing books and articles if you had never set pen to paper. Many tried. The director/chair and the aged "young man of promise" and the pipe-smoking, chin-stroking *Atlantic* intellectual fought hard but in the end proved mortal.

All these changes were taking place when faculty and students were marching in support of peace or Martin Luther King or Ralph Nader. Across the campus could be heard cries of "Better red than dead," "Dump the Hump," and "Hell, no, we won't go." Some went away to Canada or Sweden to avoid the draft that would take them to the jungles of Vietnam. Hippies were everywhere, all in the uniforms they wore to establish their individuality. Seeing the next generation decked out reminded me of the navy and its obligatory dress codes. The proper college student of this era wore long, straight hair, dirty blue jeans, tie-dyed T-shirts, sandals or no shoes at all, beads around the neck, and peace signs bedecking their ponchos or army field jackets. The looks on the faces of the old-timers would have curdled sweet milk when a cadre of hippies came through the classroom door—late, of course, and trailing clouds of marijuana smoke.

As the old faculty died or retired, we hired new faculty who were sure to bring us into line with the works at the great universities, which we were hoping to become. It was not long before we hired Bright Young Things who knew about Michel Foucault and Jacques Derrida and Noam Chomsky. As they grew in influence, Cleanth Brooks gave way to Geoffrey Hartmann, Arthur Quiller-Couch was replaced by Stanley Fish, transformational trees and stems superceded old-fashioned grammar. The world was turned upside down. Soon people who had read poems and plays and scintillating essays by Robert Louis Stevenson and E. B. White were derided for not knowing what the young people called "theory." The new theorists had little interest in literature and had not immersed themselves in what Matthew Arnold called "the best that has been thought and said." Many of them thought that Jane Austen was the author of *The Prince and the Showgirl.* If these changes were not startling enough, graduate students began to be infected and wanted oldsters to talk deconstruction and reader-response theory. The culture wars had come.

From being a young radical once, I found myself an old conservative—at least in matters academic. Since I found no beauty in theory and kept being dragged into arguments I could not win, I decided to hang up the old cap and gown and try, like the Navajos in Tony Hillerman's novels, to "walk in beauty. . . ."

■

Index